Billboard.

USA TOP 1000 SINGLES

The 1000 Biggest Hits from 1955-86

Compiled by Joel Whitburn

GUINNESS BOOKS

D1596301

Copyright ©1986 by Joel Whitburn,
Hal Leonard Books,
and Billboard Publications, Inc.

WARNING

All rights reserved, which includes the right to reproduce this book or portions thereof in any form whatsoever.

Library of Congress Cataloging-In-Publication Data

Whitburn, Joel.
  Billboard® Top 1000 Singles, 1955-1986

  Compiled from Billboard's pop singles charts, 1955-1986.
  1. Music, Popular (Songs, etc.)—United States—Discography.
  2. Music, Popular (Songs, etc.)—United States—Statistics.
    I. Billboard   II. Title.
ML156.4P6W454   1986   784.5'00973   86-20004
ISBN 0-88188-475-8

First printing October, 1986
Printed in the U.S.A.

The chart and popularity data used herein is reproduced by permission of Billboard Publications, Inc. Copyright 1955-1986, Billboard Publications, Inc.

Billboard® is a registered trademark of
Billboard Publications, Inc., used by permission.

The Hot 100® is a registered trademark of
Billboard Publications, Inc., used by permission.

Distributed in the United Kingdom by Guinness Books, 33 London Road,
  Enfield, Middlesex EN2 6DJ, England

ISBN 0-85112-491-7

"Guinness" is a registered trademark of Guinness Superlatives Ltd.

Manufactured in the United States of America

CONTENTS

Throughout this book you will find fascinating reproductions of original full page ads and reviews which appeared in Billboard at the time many of these Top 1000 singles were breaking onto the charts. Watch for an upcoming Record Research book showing hundreds more of these interesting and rarely seen ads along with the records original review comments.

AUTHOR'S NOTES

It is with a wonderful feeling of bliss that I welcome you to a fantastic trip down memory lane. From the summer of 1955 when *ROCK AROUND THE CLOCK* recorded by Bill Haley and His Comets burst through as the nation's first #1 rock hit, to the summer of 1986 when Simply Red was "Holding Back The Years", these are the 1000 most played and most purchased records of the rock era.

Here, indeed, are the ultimate greatest hits of the past 32 years...the music and sounds that bring back a moment as only a song can. Songs like *GREAT BALLS OF FIRE, BAD MOON RISING, MELLOW YELLOW* and *BLUEBERRY HILL* . . . artists like The Coasters, The Byrds, Buddy Knox and Buddy Holly . . . all part of 1000 sweet and bittersweet memories.

The number 1000 may seem like a huge number of titles, however, it represents slightly less than 1% of the total 45rpm records released during the past 32 years. When you're dealing with the top 1% of anything, it surely represents the very best you have to offer, and this is exactly what this book is all about. These are the top pop songs, honored for achieving the highest rankings on *BILLBOARD'S* national pop singles charts. These are the songs that climbed the chart ladder to its highest rungs.

As you browse through the list or whether you count down the Top 10, Top 100, or the entire list, do it slowly and lovingly. Remember, these are America's favorite songs from the past several exciting and stormy decades. These are the songs we listened to while wading through Watergate, Vietnam, seven presidential eras and many cultural changes; in addition, to laughing and crying through millions of weddings, births and graduations. These are the songs that gave us euphoria as high as the sky and sorrow as deep as the ocean . . . the songs that bring memories of heartbreak and of genuine love.

So, whether you're a fan of Styx or Steppenwolf, or whether your favorite song is *BARBARA ANN* or *DANIEL,* you're sure to find your favorite artists and songs among these listed herein. And whether you own all 1000 of these hits or just 10 of them, it's fascinating to see exactly where their slot in music history lies. Did *THE CISCO KID* ride over *LIL' RED RIDING HOOD* . . . was *MR. CUSTER* wiped out by *THE LEADER OF THE PACK* . . . did *TRAVELIN' MAN* make it past *KANSAS CITY?* For these answers and hundreds more, simply turn the pages . . . "memories are made of these".

JOEL WHITBURN

THE RANKING SYSTEM

The basic concept for ranking 30 years of hits is a logical and simple one based on the principle that the highest position at which a record peaks is the single most important factor during its chart life. Climbing and inching its way to the upper echelons of the chart is a battle each hit record wages in the never ending race for chart superiority. And when the dust has settled and each record has ended its chart run, the record's peak position is the primary statistic used in the rankings for this book. All records that peaked at position #1 and #2 plus a few that peaked at #3 were needed to fill out this Top 1000 ranking. In a nutshell, records that peaked at #2 will never be ranked over records that peaked at #1, #3 records will never be ranked over those peaking at #2.

Following is the chronology used in ranking the Top 1000 hits:

1) Peak position

    a) All records peaking at #1 are listed first, followed by records peaking at #2, etc.

    b) Ties among each highest position grouping are broken in the following order:

2) Total weeks record held its peak position

3) Total weeks charted in Top 10

4) Total weeks charted in Top 40

5) Total weeks charted

If there are still ties, a computerized inverse point system is used to calculate a point total for each record based on its weekly chart positions. Each week a record appears on the charts it is given points based on its chart position for that week (#1=100 points, #2=99 points, etc.). These points are added together to create a raw point total for each record, which is used to break any remaining ties.

The *BILLBOARD* pop charts were used exclusively in compiling this data. For the years 1955-1958, the following *Billboard* pop charts were researched, with each record's highest position taken from whichever chart it attained a higher ranking: "Top 100", "Best Sellers", "Most Played by Jockeys" and "Most Played in Juke Boxes". From 1958 to the present, the sole all-encompassing pop chart used was *Billboard's* "Hot 100 Singles".

THE RANKING

This section lists, in rank order, the Top 1000 hits from 1955-1986. The peak position and the total weeks at the peak position are shown in a shaded box above the corresponding titles. The shaded box is shown at the top of each new page whether or not there is a change in peak position/peak weeks.

Columnar headings show the following data:

YR: Year record reached its peak position
CHR: Total weeks charted
T 40: Total weeks charted in the Top 40
T 10: Total weeks charted in the Top 10
RNK: Top 1000 ranking (highlighted in dark type)

I Have

I Want

YR	WEEKS			RNK	Title . . . Artist
	CHR	T 40	T 10		
					Peak Pos 1 **Peak Wks 11**
56	28	24	21	1	☐ Don't Be Cruel/Hound Dog . . . Elvis Presley
					Peak Pos 1 **Peak Wks 10**
56	26	22	17	2	☐ Singing The Blues . . . Guy Mitchell
81	26	21	15	3	☐ Physical . . . Olivia Newton-John
77	25	21	14	4	☐ You Light Up My Life . . . Debby Boone
					Peak Pos 1 **Peak Wks 9**
59	26	22	16	5	☐ Mack The Knife . . . Bobby Darin
57	30	22	15	6	☐ All Shook Up . . . Elvis Presley
81	26	20	14	7	☐ Bette Davis Eyes . . . Kim Carnes
68	19	19	14	8	☐ Hey Jude . . . The Beatles
81	27	19	13	9	☐ Endless Love . . . Diana Ross & Lionel Richie
60	21	17	12	10	☐ The Theme From "A Summer Place" . . . Percy Faith
					Peak Pos 1 **Peak Wks 8**
55	38	25	19	11	☐ Rock Around The Clock . . . Bill Haley & His Comets
56	37	22	16	12	☐ The Wayward Wind . . . Gogi Grant
55	22	19	16	13	☐ Sixteen Tons . . . Tennessee Ernie Ford
56	27	22	15	14	☐ Heartbreak Hotel . . . Elvis Presley
83	22	20	13	15	☐ Every Breath You Take . . . The Police
78	20	18	13	16	☐ Night Fever . . . Bee Gees
76	23	17	11	17	☐ Tonight's The Night (Gonna Be Alright) . . . Rod Stewart
					Peak Pos 1 **Peak Wks 7**
57	34	24	17	18	☐ Love Letters In The Sand . . . Pat Boone
57	27	19	15	19	☐ Jailhouse Rock . . . Elvis Presley
57	25	18	14	20	☐ (Let Me Be Your) Teddy Bear . . . Elvis Presley
78	25	19	12	21	☐ Shadow Dancing . . . Andy Gibb
58	21	18	12	22	☐ At The Hop . . . Danny & The Juniors
61	23	17	12	23	☐ Tossin' And Turnin' . . . Bobby Lewis
82	20	16	12	24	☐ I Love Rock 'N Roll . . . Joan Jett & The Blackhearts
82	19	15	12	25	☐ Ebony And Ivory . . . Paul McCartney & Stevie Wonder
64	15	14	12	26	☐ I Want To Hold Your Hand . . . The Beatles
66	15	13	12	27	☐ I'm A Believer . . . The Monkees
83	24	17	11	28	☐ Billie Jean . . . Michael Jackson
68	15	15	11	29	☐ I Heard It Through The Grapevine . . . Marvin Gaye
					Peak Pos 1 **Peak Wks 6**
55	21	21	17	30	☐ Love Is A Many-Splendored Thing . . . Four Aces
56	25	20	16	31	☐ Rock And Roll Waltz . . . Kay Starr
55	19	19	16	32	☐ The Yellow Rose Of Texas . . . Mitch Miller
56	24	20	15	33	☐ The Poor People Of Paris . . . Les Baxter
78	25	19	15	34	☐ Le Freak . . . Chic
56	24	19	15	35	☐ Memories Are Made Of This . . . Dean Martin
82	25	18	15	36	☐ Eye Of The Tiger . . . Survivor

YR	WEEKS CHR	T 40	T 10	RNK	Title . . . Artist

		Peak Pos **1**	Peak Wks **6**		
83	25	20	14	37	☐ **Flashdance...What A Feeling** . . . Irene Cara
57	26	19	14	38	☐ **April Love** . . . Pat Boone
80	25	19	13	39	☐ **Lady** . . . Kenny Rogers
83	22	18	13	40	☐ **Say Say Say** . . . Paul McCartney & Michael Jackson
59	21	18	13	41	☐ **The Battle Of New Orleans** . . . Johnny Horton
57	21	17	13	42	☐ **Young Love** . . . Tab Hunter
82	25	20	12	43	☐ **Centerfold** . . . The J. Geils Band
80	25	19	12	44	☐ **Call Me** . . . Blondie
58	22	19	12	45	☐ **It's All In The Game** . . . Tommy Edwards
79	22	16	12	46	☐ **My Sharona** . . . The Knack
69	17	16	11	47	☐ **Aquarius/Let The Sunshine In** . . . The 5th Dimension
72	18	15	11	48	☐ **The First Time Ever I Saw Your Face** . . . Roberta Flack
72	18	15	11	49	☐ **Alone Again (Naturally)** . . . Gilbert O'Sullivan
71	17	15	11	50	☐ **Joy To The World** . . . Three Dog Night
60	16	14	11	51	☐ **Are You Lonesome To-night?** . . . Elvis Presley
58	14	14	10	52	☐ **The Purple People Eater** . . . Sheb Wooley
70	14	13	10	53	☐ **Bridge Over Troubled Water** . . . Simon & Garfunkel
84	19	14	9	54	☐ **Like A Virgin** . . . Madonna
69	13	12	9	55	☐ **In The Year 2525** . . . Zager & Evans

		Peak Pos **1**	Peak Wks **5**		
57	31	23	16	56	☐ **Tammy** . . . Debbie Reynolds
56	23	19	15	57	☐ **Love Me Tender** . . . Elvis Presley
56	23	20	14	58	☐ **My Prayer** . . . The Platters
80	22	19	14	59	☐ **(Just Like) Starting Over** . . . John Lennon
77	23	17	12	60	☐ **Best Of My Love** . . . Emotions
58	19	16	12	61	☐ **All I Have To Do Is Dream** . . . The Everly Brothers
84	21	16	11	62	☐ **When Doves Cry** . . . Prince
60	20	16	11	63	☐ **It's Now Or Never** . . . Elvis Presley
58	19	16	11	64	☐ **Tequila** . . . The Champs
70	16	16	11	65	☐ **I'll Be There** . . . The Jackson 5
76	19	15	11	66	☐ **Silly Love Songs** . . . Wings
71	17	15	11	67	☐ **Maggie May** . . . Rod Stewart
62	18	14	11	68	☐ **I Can't Stop Loving You** . . . Ray Charles
58	20	16	10	69	☐ **Don't** . . . Elvis Presley
84	21	15	10	70	☐ **Jump** . . . Van Halen
79	20	15	10	71	☐ **Bad Girls** . . . Donna Summer
68	18	15	10	72	☐ **Love Is Blue** . . . Paul Mauriat
71	17	15	10	73	☐ **It's Too Late** . . . Carole King
59	17	14	10	74	☐ **Venus** . . . Frankie Avalon
62	16	14	10	75	☐ **Big Girls Don't Cry** . . . The 4 Seasons
58	16	13	10	76	☐ **Nel Blu Dipinto Di Blu (Volare)** . . . Domenico Modugno
61	16	13	10	77	☐ **Big Bad John** . . . Jimmy Dean
63	15	13	10	78	☐ **Sugar Shack** . . . Jimmy Gilmer & The Fireballs

YR	WEEKS CHR	WEEKS T 40	WEEKS T 10	RNK	Title . . . Artist
					Peak Pos **1** Peak Wks **5**
68	15	13	10	79	☐ **Honey** . . . Bobby Goldsboro
67	17	15	9	80	☐ **To Sir With Love** . . . Lulu
60	17	13	9	81	☐ **Cathy's Clown** . . . The Everly Brothers
73	16	13	9	82	☐ **Killing Me Softly With His Song** . . . Roberta Flack
68	14	13	9	83	☐ **People Got To Be Free** . . . The Rascals
71	15	12	9	84	☐ **One Bad Apple** . . . The Osmonds
69	12	12	9	85	☐ **Get Back** . . . The Beatles
66	13	11	9	86	☐ **The Ballad Of The Green Berets** . . . SSgt Barry Sadler
62	14	12	7	87	☐ **Sherry** . . . The 4 Seasons
64	10	9	6	88	☐ **Can't Buy Me Love** . . . The Beatles
					Peak Pos **1** Peak Wks **4**
55	26	26	18	89	☐ **Autumn Leaves** . . . Roger Williams
56	29	24	17	90	☐ **Lisbon Antigua** . . . Nelson Riddle
77	31	23	16	91	☐ **I Just Want To Be Your Everything** . . . Andy Gibb
56	23	19	14	92	☐ **I Almost Lost My Mind** . . . Pat Boone
80	29	17	14	93	☐ **Upside Down** . . . Diana Ross
57	28	23	13	94	☐ **Honeycomb** . . . Jimmie Rodgers
78	27	22	13	95	☐ **Stayin' Alive** . . . Bee Gees
70	22	19	13	96	☐ **Raindrops Keep Fallin' On My Head** . . . B.J. Thomas
83	24	17	13	97	☐ **All Night Long (All Night)** . . . Lionel Richie
82	23	17	13	98	☐ **Maneater** . . . Daryl Hall & John Oates
80	25	19	12	99	☐ **Another Brick In The Wall (Part II)** . . . Pink Floyd
58	23	19	12	100	☐ **Sugartime** . . . The McGuire Sisters
69	22	18	12	101	☐ **Sugar, Sugar** . . . The Archies
79	21	18	12	102	☐ **Da Ya Think I'm Sexy?** . . . Rod Stewart
78	23	17	12	103	☐ **Kiss You All Over** . . . Exile
80	22	17	12	104	☐ **Crazy Little Thing Called Love** . . . Queen
57	26	20	11	105	☐ **Wake Up Little Susie** . . . The Everly Brothers
83	29	18	11	106	☐ **Total Eclipse Of The Heart** . . . Bonnie Tyler
73	23	17	11	107	☐ **Tie A Yellow Ribbon Round The Ole Oak Tree** . . . Dawn featuring Tony Orlando
72	19	17	11	108	☐ **American Pie – Parts I & II** . . . Don McLean
70	17	15	11	109	☐ **(They Long To Be) Close To You** . . . Carpenters
68	16	14	11	110	☐ **(Sittin' On) The Dock Of The Bay** . . . Otis Redding
69	15	14	11	111	☐ **Honky Tonk Women** . . . The Rolling Stones
83	25	19	10	112	☐ **Down Under** . . . Men At Work
86	23	17	10	113	☐ **That's What Friends Are For** . . . Dionne Warwick & Friends
82	22	17	10	114	☐ **Jack & Diane** . . . John Cougar
79	23	15	10	115	☐ **Reunited** . . . Peaches & Herb
59	21	15	10	116	☐ **Stagger Lee** . . . Lloyd Price
59	17	14	10	117	☐ **The Three Bells** . . . The Browns
59	15	14	10	118	☐ **Lonely Boy** . . . Paul Anka

YR	WEEKS CHR	T 40	T 10	RNK	Title ... Artist
					Peak Pos **1** Peak Wks **4**
71	15	14	10	119	☐ **How Can You Mend A Broken Heart** ... The Bee Gees
60	16	13	10	120	☐ **Stuck On You** ... Elvis Presley
62	15	13	10	121	☐ **Roses Are Red (My Love)** ... Bobby Vinton
70	14	13	10	122	☐ **My Sweet Lord** ... George Harrison
67	12	12	10	123	☐ **Daydream Believer** ... The Monkees
80	24	19	9	124	☐ **Rock With You** ... Michael Jackson
80	23	16	9	125	☐ **Magic** ... Olivia Newton-John
85	20	16	9	126	☐ **Say You, Say Me** ... Lionel Richie
80	23	15	9	127	☐ **Funkytown** ... Lipps, Inc.
73	18	15	9	128	☐ **My Love** ... Paul McCartney & Wings
69	19	14	9	129	☐ **Everyday People** ... Sly & The Family Stone
72	19	14	9	130	☐ **Without You** ... Nilsson
58	19	14	9	131	☐ **He's Got The Whole World (In His Hands)** ... Laurie London
69	15	13	9	132	☐ **Dizzy** ... Tommy Roe
67	14	13	9	133	☐ **Windy** ... The Association
67	20	12	9	134	☐ **Ode To Billie Joe** ... Bobbie Gentry
61	17	12	9	135	☐ **Runaway** ... Del Shannon
63	15	12	9	136	☐ **He's So Fine** ... The Chiffons
65	14	12	9	137	☐ **(I Can't Get No) Satisfaction** ... The Rolling Stones
63	13	12	9	138	☐ **Dominique** ... The Singing Nun
64	13	12	9	139	☐ **There! I've Said It Again** ... Bobby Vinton
67	13	11	9	140	☐ **Somethin' Stupid** ... Nancy Sinatra & Frank Sinatra
67	13	11	9	141	☐ **Groovin'** ... The Young Rascals
76	20	15	8	142	☐ **Don't Go Breaking My Heart** ... Elton John & Kiki Dee
72	20	14	8	143	☐ **I Can See Clearly Now** ... Johnny Nash
76	19	13	8	144	☐ **Disco Lady** ... Johnnie Taylor
67	16	13	8	145	☐ **The Letter** ... The Box Tops
85	18	12	8	146	☐ **We Are The World** ... USA for Africa
59	16	12	8	147	☐ **Come Softly To Me** ... Fleetwoods
68	14	12	8	148	☐ **This Guy's In Love With You** ... Herb Alpert
64	13	12	8	149	☐ **Baby Love** ... The Supremes
75	23	16	6	150	☐ **Love Will Keep Us Together** ... The Captain & Tennille
58	28	13	6	151	☐ **The Chipmunk Song** ... The Chipmunks
65	11	9	6	152	☐ **Yesterday** ... The Beatles
					Peak Pos **1** Peak Wks **3**
60	39	33	25	153	☐ **The Twist** ... Chubby Checker
56	26	22	18	154	☐ **The Green Door** ... Jim Lowe
77	33	26	17	155	☐ **How Deep Is Your Love** ... Bee Gees
56	27	22	15	156	☐ **Moonglow and Theme From "Picnic"** ... Morris Stoloff
80	31	21	15	157	☐ **Another One Bites The Dust** ... Queen
79	21	17	14	158	☐ **Hot Stuff** ... Donna Summer

YR	WEEKS CHR	T 40	T 10	RNK	Title ... Artist
					Peak Pos **1** Peak Wks **3**
77	25	18	13	159	☐ **Love Theme From "A Star Is Born" (Evergreen)** ... Barbra Streisand
79	27	17	13	160	☐ **I Will Survive** ... Gloria Gaynor
57	26	17	13	161	☐ **You Send Me** ... Sam Cooke
82	28	21	12	162	☐ **Don't You Want Me** ... The Human League
58	19	18	12	163	☐ **Witch Doctor** ... David Seville
81	24	17	12	164	☐ **Arthur's Theme (Best That You Can Do)** ... Christopher Cross
78	23	17	12	165	☐ **Boogie Oogie Oogie** ... A Taste Of Honey
80	24	19	11	166	☐ **Woman In Love** ... Barbra Streisand
60	23	18	11	167	☐ **I'm Sorry** ... Brenda Lee
58	23	18	11	168	☐ **To Know Him, Is To Love Him** ... The Teddy Bears
84	23	16	11	169	☐ **Footloose** ... Kenny Loggins
80	21	16	11	170	☐ **Coming Up (Live at Glasgow)** ... Paul McCartney & Wings
70	19	16	11	171	☐ **I Think I Love You** ... The Partridge Family
71	18	16	11	172	☐ **Knock Three Times** ... Dawn
62	18	14	11	173	☐ **Peppermint Twist - Part I** ... Joey Dee & The Starliters
73	17	14	11	174	☐ **You're So Vain** ... Carly Simon
84	28	18	10	175	☐ **What's Love Got To Do With It** ... Tina Turner
83	25	18	10	176	☐ **Beat It** ... Michael Jackson
76	25	18	10	177	☐ **Play That Funky Music** ... Wild Cherry
78	32	16	10	178	☐ **Baby Come Back** ... Player
84	24	16	10	179	☐ **Against All Odds (Take A Look At Me Now)** ... Phil Collins
79	21	16	10	180	☐ **Escape (The Pina Colada Song)** ... Rupert Holmes
59	19	16	10	181	☐ **Smoke Gets In Your Eyes** ... The Platters
84	26	15	10	182	☐ **I Just Called To Say I Love You** ... Stevie Wonder
61	17	15	10	183	☐ **Wonderland By Night** ... Bert Kaempfert
60	27	14	10	184	☐ **Running Bear** ... Johnny Preston
84	21	14	10	185	☐ **Ghostbusters** ... Ray Parker Jr.
57	20	14	10	186	☐ **Butterfly** ... Andy Williams
71	18	14	10	187	☐ **Brand New Key** ... Melanie
66	15	13	10	188	☐ **Winchester Cathedral** ... The New Vaudeville Band
72	14	12	10	189	☐ **A Horse With No Name** ... America
74	23	17	9	190	☐ **The Way We Were** ... Barbra Streisand
85	21	17	9	191	☐ **Careless Whisper** ... Wham! featuring George Michael
84	22	16	9	192	☐ **Karma Chameleon** ... Culture Club
78	20	15	9	193	☐ **MacArthur Park** ... Donna Summer
67	23	14	9	194	☐ **Light My Fire** ... Doors
60	18	14	9	195	☐ **Save The Last Dance For Me** ... The Drifters
73	17	14	9	196	☐ **Crocodile Rock** ... Elton John
57	17	14	9	197	☐ **Too Much** ... Elvis Presley

Another Smash By

THE PLATTERS

WHO SKYROCKETED TO FAME
WITH THEIR GREAT HIT
OF "ONLY YOU"

"THE GREAT PRETENDER"

A TRULY GREAT RECORD

COUPLED WITH

"I'M JUST A DANCING PARTNER"

MERCURY 70753

THE PLATTERS
The Great Pretender (Pera, BMI)—Mercury 70753—This great act, currently riding way up on the r.&b. and pop charts both with "Only You," has a hunk of great follow-up material here. It's a strong song with definite two-market potential again. The flip is a three-beater, "I'm Just a Dancing Partner" (Admont, ASCAP). It's different, and this, too, has a good chance.

The Billboard Music Popularity Charts   POPULAR RECORDS

• Best Sellers in Stores

For survey week ending June 29

RECORDS are ranked in order of their current national selling importance at the retail level, as determined by The Billboard's weekly survey of the top volume dealers in every important market area. When significant action is reported on both sides of a record, points are combined to determine position on the chart. In such a case, both sides are listed in bold type, the leading side on top.

	This Week	Last Week	Weeks on Chart
1. ROCK AROUND THE CLOCK (ASCAP)—B. Haley. Thirteen Women (BMI)—Dec 29124		2	9
2. CHERRY PINK AND APPLE BLOSSOM WHITE (ASCAP)—P. Prado. Marie Elena Rumba (ASCAP)—Vic 20-5965		1	19
3. BLOSSOM FELL (ASCAP)— Nat (King) Cole. IF I MAY (BMI)—Cap 3095		3	10
4. UNCHAINED MELODY (ASCAP)— L. Baxter. Medic (ASCAP)—Cap 3055		4	14
5. LEARNIN' THE BLUES (ASCAP)— F. Sinatra. If I Had Three Wishes (ASCAP)—Cap 3102		5	9
6. HONEY BABE (ASCAP)—A. Mooney. No Regrets (ASCAP)—M-G-M 11900		6	12
7. SOMETHING'S GOTTA GIVE (ASCAP)—McGuire Sisters. Rhythm 'n' Blues (BMI)—Coral 61423		8	6
8. HARD TO GET (ASCAP)— G. MacKenzie. Boston Fancy (BMI)—"X" 0137		11	6
9. UNCHAINED MELODY (ASCAP)— A. Hibbler. Daybreak (ASCAP)—Dec 29441		7	14
10. SOMETHING'S GOTTA GIVE (ASCAP)—S. Davis Jr. LOVE ME OR LEAVE ME (ASCAP) Dec 29484		12	7
11. DANCE WITH ME, HENRY (BMI)— G. Gibbs. Every Road Must Have a Turning (BMI)— Mercury 70572		9	16
12. IT'S A SIN TO TELL A LIE (ASCAP)—S. Smith & The Redheads. My Baby Just Cares for Me (ASCAP)—Epic 9093		10	15
13. UNCHAINED MELODY (ASCAP)— R. Hamilton. From Here to Eternity (ASCAP)—Epic 9102		13	12
14. SWEET AND GENTLE (BMI)— A. Dale. You Still Mean the Same to Me (ASCAP)— Coral 61435		17	2
15. BALLAD OF DAVY CROCKETT (BMI)—B. Hayes. Farewell (BMI)—Cadence 1256		14	20
16. THAT OLD BLACK MAGIC (ASCAP)—S. Davis Jr. Man With a Dream (ASCAP)—Dec 29541		24	3
17. HEART (ASCAP)—E. Fisher. Near to You (ASCAP)—Vic 20-6097		15	8
18. MAN IN THE RAINCOAT (BMI)— P. Wright. Please Have Mercy (BMI)—Unique 303		22	3
19. AIN'T IT A SHAME (BMI)—P. Boone. Tennessee Saturday Night (BMI)—Dot 15377		—	1
20. STORY UNTOLD (BMI)—Crew Cuts. Carmen's Boogie (BMI)—Mercury 70634		24	3
21. ALABAMA JUBILEE (ASCAP)— Ferko String Band. Sing a Little Melody (BMI)—Media 1010		18	4
22. HOUSE OF BLUE LIGHTS (ASCAP)—C. Miller. Can't Help Wonderin' (ASCAP)—Mercury 70627		20	4
23. HEY, MR. BANJO (ASCAP)— Sunnysiders. Zoom, Zoom, Zoom (ASCAP)—Kapp 113		23	8
24. SEVENTEEN (BMI)—B. Bennett. Little Old You-All (BMI)—King 1470		—	1
25. BALLAD OF DAVY CROCKETT (BMI)—Tennessee Ernie Ford. Farewell (BMI)—Cap 3058		21	17
25. BREEZE AND I (BMI)—C. Valente. Jalousie (ASCAP)—Dec 29467		—	13

• This Week's Best Buys

According to sales reports in key markets, the following recent releases are recommended for extra profits:

SEVENTEEN (Lois, BMI)—Boyd Bennett—King 1470

A sleeper that emerged this week as one of the country's hottest new disks. Now No. 24 on the national retail chart, the record also placed on the Pittsburgh, Cincinnati and Cleveland territorial listings with excellent sales ratings in many other cities to its credit. Flip is "Little Ole You-All" (Lois, BMI).

THE POPCORN SONG (Central, BMI)—Cliffie Stone—Capitol 3131

This novelty has also been a left-field surprise in many areas, appealing to customers in both the pop and hillbilly markets. Currently the top record in Kansas City, "Popcorn Song," is also a good seller in New York, Buffalo, Pittsburgh, Milwaukee, Richmond, Nashville, Durham, Atlanta, St. Louis and Baltimore. Flip is "Barracuda."

THE BANJO'S BACK IN TOWN (World, ASCAP)—Teresa Brewer—Coral 61448

In the past 10 days this disk has taken off with almost all territories catching the spark at once. Sales are good to strong and growing rapidly in Boston, Providence, Philadelphia, Baltimore, Buffalo, Pittsburgh, Cleveland, Chicago, Milwaukee, St. Louis, Durham, Nashville and Atlanta. Flip is "How to Be Very, Very Popular." A previous Billboard "Spotlight" pick.

EXPERIENCE UNNECESSARY (Pincus, ASCAP)—Sarah Vaughan—Mercury 70646

While this has not been one of the thrush's fastest moving disks, it is now beginning to show a fine spread of good sales reports and is shaping up as a record with chart potential. Best areas for Miss Vaughan so far have been Philadelphia, Buffalo, Baltimore, Providence, Pittsburgh, Cincinnati, Chicago, Milwaukee, St. Louis, Detroit and Nashville. Flip is "Slowly With Feeling" (Planetary, ASCAP). A previous Billboard "Spotlight" pick.

• Most Played in Juke Boxes

For survey week ending June 29

RECORDS are ranked in order of the greatest number of plays in juke boxes throuout the country, as determined by The Billboard's weekly survey of the nation's juke box operators. When significant play is reported on both sides of a record, points are combined to determine position on the chart. In such a case, both sides are listed in bold type, the leading side on top.

	This Week	Last Week	Weeks on Chart
1. CHERRY PINK AND APPLE BLOSSOM WHITE (ASCAP)— P. Prado. Marie Elena Rumba (ASCAP)—Vic 20-5965		1	14
2. BLOSSOM FELL (ASCAP)—Nat (King) Cole. If I May (BMI)—Cap 3095		3	7
3. DANCE WITH ME HENRY (BMI)— G. Gibbs. Every Road Must Have a Turning (BMI)— Mercury 70572		2	15
4. UNCHAINED MELODY (ASCAP)— L. Baxter. Medic (ASCAP)—Cap 3055		4	10
5. ROCK AROUND THE CLOCK (ASCAP)—B. Haley. Thirteen Women (BMI)—Dec 29124		6	4
6. LEARNIN' THE BLUES (ASCAP)— F. Sinatra. If I Had Three Wishes (ASCAP)—Cap 3102		7	4
7. UNCHAINED MELODY (ASCAP)— A. Hibbler. Daybreak (ASCAP)—Dec 29441		4	11
8. HONEY BABE (ASCAP)—A. Mooney. No Regrets (ASCAP)—M-G-M 11900		8	8
9. SOMETHING'S GOTTA GIVE (ASCAP)—McGuire Sisters. Rhythm 'n' Blues (BMI)—Coral 61423		9	5
10. UNCHAINED MELODY (ASCAP)— R. Hamilton. From Here to Eternity (ASCAP)—Epic 9102		10	10
11. HARD TO GET (ASCAP)— G. MacKenzie. Boston Fancy (BMI)—"X" 0137		—	1
12. IT'S A SIN TO TELL A LIE (ASCAP)— S. Smith & th Redheads. My Baby Just Cares for Me—Epic 9093		11	6
13. HEART (ASCAP)—E. Fisher. Near to You (ASCAP)—Vic 20-6097		14	6
14. BALLAD OF DAVY CROCKETT (BMI)—B. Hayes. Farewell (BMI)—Cadence 1256		12	18
15. BALLAD OF DAVY CROCKETT (BMI)—Tennessee Ernie. Farewell (BMI)—Cap 3058		13	13
16. SWEET AND GENTLE (BMI)— A. Dale. You Still Mean the Same to Me (ASCAP)— Coral 61435		—	1
17. WHATEVER LOLA WANTS (ASCAP)—S. Vaughan. Oh Yeah (ASCAP)—Mercury 70595		15	3
18. HEY, MR. BANJO (ASCAP)— Sunnysiders. Zoom, Zoom, Zoom (ASCAP)—Kapp 113		16	7
18. CHEE CHEE OO CHEE— P. Como & J. P. Morgan. Two Lost Souls (BMI)—Vic 20-6137		19	2
18. SOMETHING'S GOTTA GIVE (ASCAP)—S. Davis Jr. Love Me or Leave Me (ASCAP)—Dec 29484		—	1

• Most Played by Jockeys

For survey week ending June 29

SIDES are ranked in order of the greatest number of plays on disk jockey radio shows throuout the country. Results are based on The Billboard's weekly survey among the nation's disk jockeys. The reverse side of each record is also listed.

	This Week	Last Week	Weeks on Chart
1. LEARNING THE BLUES—F. Sinatra. If I Had Three Wishes (ASCAP)—Cap 3102		2	10
2. UNCHAINED MELODY—L. Baxter. Medic (ASCAP)—Cap 3055		3	14
3. ROCK AROUND THE CLOCK— B. Haley. Thirteen Women (ASCAP)—Dec 29124		4	7
4. BLOSSOM FELL—Nat (King) Cole. If I May (ASCAP)—Cap 3095		5	9
5. CHERRY PINK AND APPLE BLOSSOM WHITE—P. Prado. Marie Elena Rumba (ASCAP)—Vic 20-5965		1	13
6. SOMETHING'S GOTTA GIVE— McGuire Sisters. Rhythm 'n' Blues (ASCAP)—Coral 61423		7	6
7. UNCHAINED MELODY—A. Hibbler. Daybreak (ASCAP)—Dec 29441		6	12
8. HEART—E. Fisher. Near to You (ASCAP)—Vic 20-6097		8	9
9. UNCHAINED MELODY—R. Hamilton. From Here to Eternity (ASCAP)—Epic 9102		11	7
10. SWEET AND GENTLE—A. Dale. You Still Mean the Same to Me— Coral 61435		—	1
11. HONEY BABE—A. Mooney. No Regrets (ASCAP)—M-G-M 11900		10	5
12. CHEE CHEE OO CHEE— P. Como & J. P. Morgan. Two Lost Souls (BMI)—Vic 20-6137		13	5
13. DANCE WITH ME HENRY—G. Gibbs. Every Road Must Have a Turning (BMI)— Mercury 70572		9	14
14. IF I MAY—Nat (King) Cole. Blossom Fell (ASCAP)—Cap 3095		12	6
15. THAT OLD BLACK MAGIC (ASCAP) —S. Davis Jr. Man With a Dream (ASCAP)—Dec 29541		—	1
16. HARD TO GET—G. MacKenzie. Boston Fancy (ASCAP)—"X" 0137		17	2
17. HEART—Four Aces. Sluefoot (ASCAP)—Dec 29476		16	6
18. HUMMINGBIRD SONG (ASCAP) —L. Paul & Mary Ford. Goodbye My Love (ASCAP)—Cap 3165		—	1
19. LOVE ME OR LEAVE ME—L. Horne. I Love You (ASCAP)—Vic 20-6073		—	1
20. SWEET AND GENTLE—G. Gibbs. Blueberries (BMI)—Mercury 70647		—	1

YR	WEEKS CHR	T 40	T 10	RNK	Title . . . Artist
					Peak Pos **1** Peak Wks **3**
72	18	13	9	198	☐ **Baby Don't Get Hooked On Me** . . . Mac Davis
71	15	13	9	199	☐ **Go Away Little Girl** . . . Donny Osmond
71	14	13	9	200	☐ **Family Affair** . . . Sly & The Family Stone
70	14	13	9	201	☐ **Ain't No Mountain High Enough** . . . Diana Ross
67	15	12	9	202	☐ **Happy Together** . . . The Turtles
63	15	12	9	203	☐ **Hey Paula** . . . Paul & Paula
63	14	12	9	204	☐ **My Boyfriend's Back** . . . The Angels
81	23	17	8	205	☐ **Kiss On My List** . . . Daryl Hall & John Oates
74	21	15	8	206	☐ **Seasons In The Sun** . . . Terry Jacks
84	24	14	8	207	☐ **Wake Me Up Before You Go-Go** . . . Wham!
85	18	14	8	208	☐ **Can't Fight This Feeling** . . . REO Speedwagon
61	16	14	8	209	☐ **Pony Time** . . . Chubby Checker
72	16	14	8	210	☐ **Me And Mrs. Jones** . . . Billy Paul
64	15	14	8	211	☐ **Oh, Pretty Woman** . . . Roy Orbison
70	15	14	8	212	☐ **American Woman** . . . The Guess Who
69	15	14	8	213	☐ **Wedding Bell Blues** . . . The 5th Dimension
85	22	13	8	214	☐ **Money For Nothing** . . . Dire Straits
77	17	13	8	215	☐ **Sir Duke** . . . Stevie Wonder
62	16	13	8	216	☐ **Telstar** . . . The Tornadoes
70	15	13	8	217	☐ **War** . . . Edwin Starr
61	15	13	8	218	☐ **The Lion Sleeps Tonight** . . . The Tokens
62	14	13	8	219	☐ **Soldier Boy** . . . The Shirelles
74	17	12	8	220	☐ **The Streak** . . . Ray Stevens
63	15	12	8	221	☐ **Blue Velvet** . . . Bobby Vinton
62	15	12	8	222	☐ **Hey! Baby** . . . Bruce Channel
63	14	12	8	223	☐ **Sukiyaki** . . . Kyu Sakamoto
62	15	11	8	224	☐ **Duke Of Earl** . . . Gene Chandler
65	14	11	8	225	☐ **Turn! Turn! Turn!** . . . The Byrds
61	14	11	8	226	☐ **Blue Moon** . . . The Marcels
63	14	11	8	227	☐ **I Will Follow Him** . . . Little Peggy March
66	13	11	8	228	☐ **(You're My) Soul And Inspiration** . . . The Righteous Brothers
66	12	10	8	229	☐ **Monday, Monday** . . . The Mama's & The Papa's
67	11	10	8	230	☐ **Hello Goodbye** . . . The Beatles
64	11	10	8	231	☐ **The House Of The Rising Sun** . . . The Animals
72	21	16	7	232	☐ **The Candy Man** . . . Sammy Davis, Jr.
82	23	15	7	233	☐ **Up Where We Belong** . . . Joe Cocker & Jennifer Warnes
86	23	15	7	234	☐ **On My Own** . . . Patti LaBelle & Michael McDonald
72	19	14	7	235	☐ **Lean On Me** . . . Bill Withers
86	18	14	7	236	☐ **Greatest Love Of All** . . . Whitney Houston
85	19	13	7	237	☐ **Shout** . . . Tears For Fears
75	17	13	7	238	☐ **Fly, Robin, Fly** . . . Silver Convention
86	17	13	7	239	☐ **Rock Me Amadeus** . . . Falco

YR	WEEKS			RNK	Title . . . Artist
	CHR	T 40	T 10		
					Peak Pos **1** Peak Wks **3**
75	15	12	7	240	☐ **Island Girl** . . . Elton John
63	15	12	7	241	☐ **Fingertips - Pt 2** . . . Little Stevie Wonder
68	13	12	7	242	☐ **Mrs. Robinson** . . . Simon & Garfunkel
63	13	12	7	243	☐ **Walk Like A Man** . . . The 4 Seasons
61	15	11	7	244	☐ **Take Good Care Of My Baby** . . . Bobby Vee
64	13	11	7	245	☐ **Chapel Of Love** . . . The Dixie Cups
66	12	11	7	246	☐ **We Can Work It Out** . . . The Beatles
65	11	11	7	247	☐ **Mrs. Brown You've Got A Lovely Daughter** . . . Herman's Hermits
64	11	11	7	248	☐ **I Feel Fine** . . . The Beatles
65	14	10	7	249	☐ **I Got You Babe** . . . Sonny & Cher
66	11	10	7	250	☐ **Summer In The City** . . . The Lovin' Spoonful
76	27	15	6	251	☐ **December, 1963 (Oh, What a Night)** . . . The Four Seasons
76	17	13	6	252	☐ **50 Ways To Leave Your Lover** . . . Paul Simon
66	14	12	6	253	☐ **Cherish** . . . The Association
65	13	12	6	254	☐ **Help!** . . . The Beatles
74	15	11	6	255	☐ **(You're) Having My Baby** . . . Paul Anka
75	14	10	6	256	☐ **He Don't Love You (Like I Love You)** . . . Tony Orlando & Dawn
75	14	12	5	257	☐ **Bad Blood** . . . Neil Sedaka
					Peak Pos **1** Peak Wks **2**
55	21	21	18	258	☐ **Learnin' The Blues** . . . Frank Sinatra
55	20	20	15	259	☐ **Ain't That A Shame** . . . Pat Boone
57	29	19	14	260	☐ **Round And Round** . . . Perry Como
82	25	19	14	261	☐ **Abracadabra** . . . The Steve Miller Band
56	24	19	14	262	☐ **The Great Pretender** . . . The Platters
73	19	17	13	263	☐ **Let's Get It On** . . . Marvin Gaye
81	32	22	12	264	☐ **Jessie's Girl** . . . Rick Springfield
83	25	18	12	265	☐ **Islands In The Stream** . . . Kenny Rogers & Dolly Parton
82	24	18	12	266	☐ **Hard To Say I'm Sorry** . . . Chicago
78	29	22	11	267	☐ **(Love Is) Thicker Than Water** . . . Andy Gibb
80	21	19	11	268	☐ **It's Still Rock And Roll To Me** . . . Billy Joel
78	20	16	11	269	☐ **Three Times A Lady** . . . Commodores
79	21	15	11	270	☐ **Ring My Bell** . . . Anita Ward
69	17	15	11	271	☐ **I Can't Get Next To You** . . . The Temptations
68	16	15	11	272	☐ **Love Child** . . . Diana Ross & The Supremes
69	16	15	11	273	☐ **Crimson And Clover** . . . Tommy James & The Shondells
58	15	15	11	274	☐ **Poor Little Fool** . . . Ricky Nelson
79	19	14	11	275	☐ **Babe** . . . Styx
64	15	14	11	276	☐ **She Loves You** . . . The Beatles
70	14	13	11	277	☐ **Let It Be** . . . The Beatles

| YR | WEEKS | | | RNK | Title . . . Artist |
	CHR	T 40	T 10		

YR	CHR	T 40	T 10	RNK	Title . . . Artist
84	24	17	10	278	☐ **Hello** . . . Lionel Richie
84	23	17	10	279	☐ **Owner Of A Lonely Heart** . . . Yes
58	21	17	10	280	☐ **It's Only Make Believe** . . . Conway Twitty
77	22	16	10	281	☐ **Torn Between Two Lovers** . . . Mary MacGregor
59	20	16	10	282	☐ **Heartaches By The Number** . . . Guy Mitchell
73	19	16	10	283	☐ **Keep On Truckin' (Part 1)** . . . Eddie Kendricks
78	17	15	10	284	☐ **You Don't Bring Me Flowers** . . . Barbra Streisand & Neil Diamond
60	18	14	10	285	☐ **Teen Angel** . . . Mark Dinning
60	17	14	10	286	☐ **My Heart Has A Mind Of Its Own** . . . Connie Francis
70	16	14	10	287	☐ **The Tears Of A Clown** . . . Smokey Robinson & The Miracles
82	18	13	10	288	☐ **Truly** . . . Lionel Richie
65	14	13	10	289	☐ **I Can't Help Myself** . . . Four Tops
83	32	18	9	290	☐ **Baby, Come To Me** . . . Patti Austin & James Ingram
81	28	18	9	291	☐ **I Love A Rainy Night** . . . Eddie Rabbitt
81	26	18	9	292	☐ **9 To 5** . . . Dolly Parton
75	23	18	9	293	☐ **Rhinestone Cowboy** . . . Glen Campbell
76	26	17	9	294	☐ **Kiss And Say Goodbye** . . . Manhattans
81	23	17	9	295	☐ **Private Eyes** . . . Daryl Hall & John Oates
75	21	17	9	296	☐ **Philadelphia Freedom** . . . The Elton John Band
76	21	17	9	297	☐ **If You Leave Me Now** . . . Chicago
79	21	17	9	298	☐ **Too Much Heaven** . . . Bee Gees
84	23	16	9	299	☐ **Out Of Touch** . . . Daryl Hall & John Oates
83	22	16	9	300	☐ **Maniac** . . . Michael Sembello
60	22	16	9	301	☐ **El Paso** . . . Marty Robbins
73	19	16	9	302	☐ **Midnight Train To Georgia** . . . Gladys Knight & The Pips
79	25	15	9	303	☐ **Rise** . . . Herb Alpert
85	22	15	9	304	☐ **Broken Wings** . . . Mr. Mister
84	20	14	9	305	☐ **Time After Time** . . . Cyndi Lauper
84	19	14	9	306	☐ **Let's Hear It For The Boy** . . . Deniece Williams
84	19	14	9	307	☐ **Let's Go Crazy** . . . Prince & the Revolution
71	16	14	9	308	☐ **Gypsys, Tramps & Thieves** . . . Cher
79	20	13	9	309	☐ **Tragedy** . . . Bee Gees
76	18	13	9	310	☐ **Love Hangover** . . . Diana Ross
59	18	13	9	311	☐ **Sleep Walk** . . . Santo & Johnny
61	17	13	9	312	☐ **Calcutta** . . . Lawrence Welk
65	16	13	9	313	☐ **You've Lost That Lovin' Feelin'** . . . The Righteous Brothers
75	16	13	9	314	☐ **That's The Way (I Like It)** . . . KC & The Sunshine Band
64	15	13	9	315	☐ **My Guy** . . . Mary Wells
64	15	13	9	316	☐ **I Get Around** . . . The Beach Boys

YR	WEEKS			RNK	Title ... Artist
	CHR	T 40	T 10		

| | | | | | Peak Pos **1** · Peak Wks **2** |

YR	CHR	T 40	T 10	RNK	Title ... Artist
71	15	13	9	317	☐ **Just My Imagination (Running Away With Me)** ... The Temptations
65	15	13	9	318	☐ **Downtown** ... Petula Clark
62	15	13	9	319	☐ **Johnny Angel** ... Shelley Fabares
70	15	13	9	320	☐ **Mama Told Me (Not To Come)** ... Three Dog Night
68	15	13	9	321	☐ **Tighten Up** ... Archie Bell & The Drells
79	15	13	9	322	☐ **No More Tears (Enough Is Enough)** ... Barbra Streisand/Donna Summer
64	14	13	9	323	☐ **Come See About Me** ... The Supremes
64	14	13	9	324	☐ **Where Did Our Love Go** ... The Supremes
63	17	12	9	325	☐ **Go Away Little Girl** ... Steve Lawrence
61	14	12	9	326	☐ **Runaround Sue** ... Dion
70	13	12	9	327	☐ **ABC** ... The Jackson 5
70	13	12	9	328	☐ **The Love You Save** ... The Jackson 5
71	13	12	9	329	☐ **Theme From Shaft** ... Isaac Hayes
64	13	12	9	330	☐ **Do Wah Diddy Diddy** ... Manfred Mann
61	17	11	9	331	☐ **Michael** ... The Highwaymen
65	12	11	9	332	☐ **This Diamond Ring** ... Gary Lewis & The Playboys
68	12	11	9	333	☐ **Hello, I Love You** ... Doors
62	37	24	8	334	☐ **Monster Mash** ... Bobby "Boris" Pickett & The Crypt-Kickers
73	22	16	8	335	☐ **Bad, Bad Leroy Brown** ... Jim Croce
85	21	16	8	336	☐ **I Want To Know What Love Is** ... Foreigner
73	20	16	8	337	☐ **Top Of The World** ... Carpenters
60	18	16	8	338	☐ **Everybody's Somebody's Fool** ... Connie Francis
78	22	15	8	339	☐ **Grease** ... Frankie Valli
84	21	15	8	340	☐ **The Reflex** ... Duran Duran
85	19	15	8	341	☐ **The Power Of Love** ... Huey Lewis & The News
73	18	15	8	342	☐ **Brother Louie** ... Stories
61	16	15	8	343	☐ **Travelin' Man** ... Ricky Nelson
85	24	14	8	344	☐ **Everybody Wants To Rule The World** ... Tears For Fears
73	22	14	8	345	☐ **Will It Go Round In Circles** ... Billy Preston
73	20	14	8	346	☐ **Half-Breed** ... Cher
81	20	14	8	347	☐ **Rapture** ... Blondie
76	20	14	8	348	☐ **Afternoon Delight** ... Starland Vocal Band
57	17	14	8	349	☐ **Butterfly** ... Charlie Gracie
69	16	13	8	350	☐ **Na Na Hey Hey Kiss Him Goodbye** ... Steam
68	16	13	8	351	☐ **Judy In Disguise (With Glasses)** ... John Fred & His Playboy Band
58	15	13	8	352	☐ **Get A Job** ... The Silhouettes
78	18	12	8	353	☐ **With A Little Luck** ... Wings
74	18	12	8	354	☐ **Kung Fu Fighting** ... Carl Douglas
75	17	12	8	355	☐ **Jive Talkin'** ... Bee Gees

| YR | WEEKS | | | RNK | Title . . . Artist |
	CHR	T 40	T 10		
					Peak Pos **1** Peak Wks **2**
59	16	12	8	356	☐ **Kansas City** . . . Wilbert Harrison
71	15	12	8	357	☐ **Me And Bobby McGee** . . . Janis Joplin
61	15	12	8	358	☐ **Quarter To Three** . . . U.S. Bonds
69	14	12	8	359	☐ **Love Theme From Romeo & Juliet** . . . Henry Mancini
64	13	12	8	360	☐ **A Hard Day's Night** . . . The Beatles
71	12	12	8	361	☐ **Brown Sugar** . . . The Rolling Stones
61	13	11	8	362	☐ **Hit The Road Jack** . . . Ray Charles
66	13	11	8	363	☐ **You Can't Hurry Love** . . . The Supremes
61	12	11	8	364	☐ **Surrender** . . . Elvis Presley
65	12	10	8	365	☐ **Stop! In The Name Of Love** . . . The Supremes
66	11	9	8	366	☐ **Wild Thing** . . . The Troggs
81	30	21	7	367	☐ **Celebration** . . . Kool & The Gang
84	26	15	7	368	☐ **Caribbean Queen (No More Love On The Run)** . . . Billy Ocean
85	24	15	7	369	☐ **We Built This City** . . . Starship
61	19	15	7	370	☐ **Will You Love Me Tomorrow** . . . The Shirelles
85	22	14	7	371	☐ **St. Elmo's Fire (Man In Motion)** . . . John Parr
73	20	14	7	372	☐ **The Night The Lights Went Out In Georgia** . . . Vicki Lawrence
86	20	13	7	373	☐ **Kyrie** . . . Mr. Mister
86	18	13	7	374	☐ **Kiss** . . . Prince & The Revolution
74	19	12	7	375	☐ **Billy, Don't Be A Hero** . . . Bo Donaldson & The Heywoods
62	18	12	7	376	☐ **He's A Rebel** . . . The Crystals
73	15	12	7	377	☐ **Time In A Bottle** . . . Jim Croce
63	15	12	7	378	☐ **I'm Leaving It Up To You** . . . Dale & Grace
62	14	12	7	379	☐ **Breaking Up Is Hard To Do** . . . Neil Sedaka
70	13	12	7	380	☐ **Thank You (Falettinme Be Mice Elf Agin)** . . . Sly & The Family Stone
74	17	11	7	381	☐ **Annie's Song** . . . John Denver
65	14	11	7	382	☐ **Help Me, Rhonda** . . . The Beach Boys
62	13	11	7	383	☐ **Good Luck Charm** . . . Elvis Presley
63	13	11	7	384	☐ **Surf City** . . . Jan & Dean
63	13	11	7	385	☐ **It's My Party** . . . Lesley Gore
63	13	11	7	386	☐ **Walk Right In** . . . The Rooftop Singers
64	12	11	7	387	☐ **Rag Doll** . . . The 4 Seasons
67	12	11	7	388	☐ **Respect** . . . Aretha Franklin
59	14	10	7	389	☐ **A Big Hunk O' Love** . . . Elvis Presley
63	13	10	7	390	☐ **Easier Said Than Done** . . . The Essex
67	13	10	7	391	☐ **Kind Of A Drag** . . . The Buckinghams
68	12	10	7	392	☐ **Grazing In The Grass** . . . Hugh Masekela
66	11	10	7	393	☐ **Paint It, Black** . . . The Rolling Stones
73	22	17	6	394	☐ **The Most Beautiful Girl** . . . Charlie Rich
86	23	16	6	395	☐ **How Will I Know** . . . Whitney Houston

YR	WEEKS			RNK	Title ... Artist
	CHR	T 40	T 10		

						Peak Pos 1	Peak Wks 2

YR	CHR	T 40	T 10	RNK	Title ... Artist
81	21	15	6	396	☐ **Morning Train (Nine To Five)** ... Sheena Easton
75	21	14	6	397	☐ **Fame** ... David Bowie
74	20	14	6	398	☐ **The Loco-Motion** ... Grand Funk
85	20	14	6	399	☐ **Everything She Wants** ... Wham!
77	20	14	6	400	☐ **Rich Girl** ... Daryl Hall & John Oates
85	19	14	6	401	☐ **Heaven** ... Bryan Adams
74	18	14	6	402	☐ **TSOP (The Sound Of Philadelphia)** ... MFSB featuring The Three Degrees
58	16	14	6	403	☐ **Hard Headed Woman** ... Elvis Presley
77	20	13	6	404	☐ **Star Wars Theme/Cantina Band** ... Meco
85	17	13	6	405	☐ **A View To A Kill** ... Duran Duran
70	15	13	6	406	☐ **Everything Is Beautiful** ... Ray Stevens
85	18	12	6	407	☐ **One More Night** ... Phil Collins
74	18	12	6	408	☐ **I Can Help** ... Billy Swan
72	17	12	6	409	☐ **My Ding-A-Ling** ... Chuck Berry
66	15	12	6	410	☐ **Reach Out I'll Be There** ... Four Tops
73	15	11	6	411	☐ **The Morning After** ... Maureen McGovern
62	14	11	6	412	☐ **Sheila** ... Tommy Roe
63	14	11	6	413	☐ **If You Wanna Be Happy** ... Jimmy Soul
65	12	11	6	414	☐ **Get Off Of My Cloud** ... The Rolling Stones
75	14	10	6	415	☐ **Lucy In The Sky With Diamonds** ... Elton John
66	13	10	6	416	☐ **When A Man Loves A Woman** ... Percy Sledge
66	13	10	6	417	☐ **My Love** ... Petula Clark
66	12	10	6	418	☐ **You Keep Me Hangin' On** ... The Supremes
66	12	10	6	419	☐ **Hanky Panky** ... Tommy James & The Shondells
70	10	10	6	420	☐ **The Long And Winding Road** ... The Beatles
65	10	10	6	421	☐ **I Hear A Symphony** ... The Supremes
65	11	8	6	422	☐ **I'm Telling You Now** ... Freddie & The Dreamers
66	14	12	5	423	☐ **The Sounds Of Silence** ... Simon & Garfunkel
74	23	10	5	424	☐ **I Honestly Love You** ... Olivia Newton-John
74	17	10	5	425	☐ **Rock Your Baby** ... George McCrae
66	10	10	5	426	☐ **Paperback Writer** ... The Beatles
65	10	9	5	427	☐ **Eight Days A Week** ... The Beatles

					Peak Pos 1	Peak Wks 1

YR	CHR	T 40	T 10	RNK	Title ... Artist
58	21	17	15	428	☐ **Patricia** ... Perez Prado
80	27	22	14	429	☐ **Do That To Me One More Time** ... The Captain & Tennille
56	23	20	14	430	☐ **Hot Diggity (Dog Ziggity Boom)** ... Perry Como
57	28	22	13	431	☐ **Chances Are** ... Johnny Mathis
56	24	19	13	432	☐ **I Want You, I Need You, I Love You** ... Elvis Presley
64	22	19	13	433	☐ **Hello, Dolly!** ... Louis Armstrong & The All Stars
57	21	17	13	434	☐ **Young Love** ... Sonny James
79	20	15	13	435	☐ **Still** ... Commodores
57	29	18	12	436	☐ **Diana** ... Paul Anka

A RED HOT STAR IS BORN ON RCA VICTOR RECORDS !

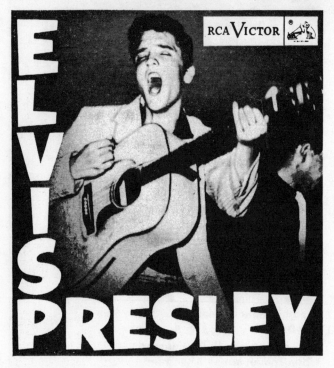

RCA VICTOR

ELVIS PRESLEY

Long Play (LPM-1254) **$3⁹⁸**

45 EP's (EPA-747) **$1.49**   (EPB-1254) **$2.98**

Recorded in Brilliant "New Orthophonic" High Fidelity

- Featured in ads in well-known record publications like *Hi-Fi Music at Home, Schwann's, This Month's Records, 45er* and *Long Player!*
- Ad Mats available in three convenient sizes!
- Colorful, attractive Streamer for walls, windows, listening booths!
- Special Promotion with DJ's!
- Stock up and Cash in . . . Elvis Presley means BIG SALES!

You'll also want this great new single by Elvis Presley . . . on its way to a million!

HEARTBREAK HOTEL / I WAS THE ONE
20/47-6420

Nationally Advertised Prices — optional

the dealer's choice   RCA VICTOR

ELVIS PRESLEY
Heartbreak Hotel (Tree, BMI)
I Was the One (Jungnickel, ASCAP—Victor 6420—
Presley's first Victor disk might easily break in both
markets. "Heartbreak Hotel" is a strong blues item
wrapped up in his usual powerful style and a great beat.
" I Was the One" is about as close to r.&b. as you can
get without horns, and has more pop appeal. Presley
is riding high right now with network TV appearances,
and this disk should benefit from all the special plugging.

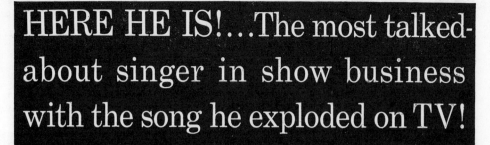

HERE HE IS!...The most talked-about singer in show business with the song he exploded on TV!

HOUND DOG

DON'T BE CRUEL
20/47-6604

"New Orthophonic" High Fidelity recording   **the dealer's choice**   RCA VICTOR

ELVIS PRESLEY....RCA Victor 6604.........................HOUND DOG
DON'T BE CRUEL..............(Presley & Shalimar, BMI)
Presley hypoed the "Hound Dog" side on a recent Steve Allen
TV airing which gave a solid, early kickoff. It's a highly charged
rhythm opus in Presley's characteristic style and should enjoy
heavy commercial acceptance. "Don't Be Cruel" is in a more
subdued, frankly poppish vein, and demonstrates that the singer
is a versatile stylist.
(Presley & Lion, BMI)

| YR | WEEKS | | | RNK | Title . . . Artist |
	CHR	T 40	T 10		

					Peak Pos **1**	Peak Wks **1**

YR	CHR	T 40	T 10	RNK	Title . . . Artist
58	21	18	12	437	☐ **Tom Dooley** . . . The Kingston Trio
82	21	17	12	438	☐ **I Can't Go For That (No Can Do)** . . . Daryl Hall & John Oates
58	23	16	12	439	☐ **Catch A Falling Star** . . . Perry Como
58	17	14	12	440	☐ **Twilight Time** . . . The Platters
57	22	19	11	441	☐ **Don't Forbid Me** . . . Pat Boone
80	26	18	11	442	☐ **Please Don't Go** . . . K.C. & The Sunshine Band
76	21	16	11	443	☐ **(Shake, Shake, Shake) Shake Your Booty** . . . KC & The Sunshine Band
58	19	16	11	444	☐ **Little Star** . . . The Elegants
62	21	15	11	445	☐ **Stranger On The Shore** . . . Mr. Acker Bilk
58	18	15	11	446	☐ **Bird Dog** . . . The Everly Brothers
59	20	12	11	447	☐ **Mr. Blue** . . . The Fleetwoods
76	28	22	10	448	☐ **A Fifth Of Beethoven** . . . Walter Murphy & The Big Apple Band
82	27	18	10	449	☐ **Mickey** . . . Toni Basil
81	26	17	10	450	☐ **The Tide Is High** . . . Blondie
76	25	16	10	451	☐ **Disco Duck (Part 1)** . . . Rick Dees & His Cast Of Idiots
78	22	16	10	452	☐ **If I Can't Have You** . . . Yvonne Elliman
76	20	16	10	453	☐ **I Write The Songs** . . . Barry Manilow
57	23	15	10	454	☐ **Party Doll** . . . Buddy Knox & The Rhythm Orchids
69	17	15	10	455	☐ **Leaving On A Jet Plane** . . . Peter, Paul & Mary
83	20	14	10	456	☐ **Let's Dance** . . . David Bowie
75	17	14	10	457	☐ **One Of These Nights** . . . Eagles
72	16	14	10	458	☐ **Brandy (You're A Fine Girl)** . . . Looking Glass
76	16	14	10	459	☐ **Love Rollercoaster** . . . Ohio Players
70	17	13	10	460	☐ **Make It With You** . . . Bread
81	28	20	9	461	☐ **Keep On Loving You** . . . REO Speedwagon
79	24	20	9	462	☐ **Pop Muzik** . . . M
79	27	19	9	463	☐ **Sad Eyes** . . . Robert John
78	31	18	9	464	☐ **Hot Child In The City** . . . Nick Gilder
82	27	17	9	465	☐ **Who Can It Be Now?** . . . Men At Work
83	26	17	9	466	☐ **Sweet Dreams (Are Made of This)** . . . Eurythmics
78	24	16	9	467	☐ **You're The One That I Want** . . . John Travolta & Olivia Newton-John
84	24	16	9	468	☐ **Missing You** . . . John Waite
57	22	16	9	469	☐ **That'll Be The Day** . . . The Crickets
85	21	16	9	470	☐ **Separate Lives** . . . Phil Collins & Marilyn Martin
78	20	16	9	471	☐ **Miss You** . . . The Rolling Stones
70	19	16	9	472	☐ **I Want You Back** . . . The Jackson 5
74	18	16	9	473	☐ **Bennie And The Jets** . . . Elton John
69	16	16	9	474	☐ **Come Together/Something** . . . The Beatles
82	28	15	9	475	☐ **Chariots Of Fire - Titles** . . . Vangelis

| YR | WEEKS | | | RNK | Title . . . Artist |
	CHR	T 40	T 10		

					Peak Pos **1** Peak Wks **1**
71	22	15	9	476	☐ **Indian Reservation (The Lament Of The Cherokee Reservation Indian)** . . . Raiders
77	18	15	9	477	☐ **Got To Give It Up – Pt. 1** . . . Marvin Gaye
69	16	15	9	478	☐ **Someday We'll Be Together** . . . Diana Ross & The Supremes
72	16	15	9	479	☐ **Let's Stay Together** . . . Al Green
58	16	15	9	480	☐ **Yakety Yak** . . . The Coasters
77	23	14	9	481	☐ **Car Wash** . . . Rose Royce
85	21	14	9	482	☐ **Crazy For You** . . . Madonna
79	20	14	9	483	☐ **What A Fool Believes** . . . Doobie Brothers
79	19	14	9	484	☐ **Good Times** . . . Chic
67	16	14	9	485	☐ **Incense And Peppermints** . . . Strawberry Alarm Clock
64	15	14	9	486	☐ **Mr. Lonely** . . . Bobby Vinton
75	18	13	9	487	☐ **I'm Sorry** . . . John Denver
62	17	13	9	488	☐ **The Stripper** . . . David Rose
79	15	13	9	489	☐ **Heartache Tonight** . . . Eagles
70	14	13	9	490	☐ **Venus** . . . The Shocking Blue
59	16	12	9	491	☐ **Why** . . . Frankie Avalon
66	15	12	9	492	☐ **96 Tears** . . . ? (Question Mark) & The Mysterians
66	15	12	9	493	☐ **Last Train To Clarksville** . . . The Monkees
68	13	12	9	494	☐ **Harper Valley P.T.A.** . . . Jeannie C. Riley
77	26	18	8	495	☐ **You Don't Have To Be A Star (To Be In My Show)** . . . Marilyn McCoo & Billy Davis, Jr.
78	26	17	8	496	☐ **You Needed Me** . . . Anne Murray
77	24	17	8	497	☐ **Don't Leave Me This Way** . . . Thelma Houston
73	21	16	8	498	☐ **Touch Me In The Morning** . . . Diana Ross
74	20	16	8	499	☐ **The Joker** . . . Steve Miller Band
85	23	15	8	500	☐ **Everytime You Go Away** . . . Paul Young
77	22	15	8	501	☐ **Dancing Queen** . . . Abba
75	21	15	8	502	☐ **Before The Next Teardrop Falls** . . . Freddy Fender
77	21	15	8	503	☐ **Southern Nights** . . . Glen Campbell
77	20	15	8	504	☐ **Blinded By The Light** . . . Manfred Mann's Earth Band
77	19	15	8	505	☐ **Hotel California** . . . Eagles
74	19	15	8	506	☐ **Then Came You** . . . Dionne Warwicke & Spinners
77	17	15	8	507	☐ **I Wish** . . . Stevie Wonder
75	23	14	8	508	☐ **My Eyes Adored You** . . . Frankie Valli
85	22	14	8	509	☐ **Don't You (Forget About Me)** . . . Simple Minds
72	22	14	8	510	☐ **I Am Woman** . . . Helen Reddy
81	21	14	8	511	☐ **Stars on 45 [Medley]** . . . Stars on 45
85	21	14	8	512	☐ **Part-Time Lover** . . . Stevie Wonder
73	20	14	8	513	☐ **Delta Dawn** . . . Helen Reddy
81	19	14	8	514	☐ **The One That You Love** . . . Air Supply
72	15	14	8	515	☐ **I'll Take You There** . . . The Staple Singers
77	20	13	8	516	☐ **Gonna Fly Now (Theme From "Rocky")** . . . Bill Conti

YR	WEEKS			RNK	Title . . . Artist
	CHR	T 40	T 10		
					Peak Pos **1** \ Peak Wks **1**
75	18	13	8	517	☐ **Lovin' You** . . . Minnie Riperton
64	15	13	8	518	☐ **Everybody Loves Somebody** . . . Dean Martin
60	15	13	8	519	☐ **Itsy Bitsy Teenie Weenie Yellow Polkadot Bikini** . . . Brian Hyland
72	14	13	8	520	☐ **Heart Of Gold** . . . Neil Young
61	14	12	8	521	☐ **Mother-In-Law** . . . Ernie K-Doe
71	14	12	8	522	☐ **You've Got A Friend** . . . James Taylor
78	18	11	8	523	☐ **Too Much, Too Little, Too Late** . . . Johnny Mathis/Deniece Williams
60	15	11	8	524	☐ **Alley-Oop** . . . Hollywood Argyles
65	13	11	8	525	☐ **My Girl** . . . The Temptations
64	12	11	8	526	☐ **A World Without Love** . . . Peter & Gordon
62	13	10	8	527	☐ **Don't Break The Heart That Loves You** . . . Connie Francis
77	25	17	7	528	☐ **Undercover Angel** . . . Alan O'Day
77	21	17	7	529	☐ **You Make Me Feel Like Dancing** . . . Leo Sayer
74	22	16	7	530	☐ **Love's Theme** . . . Love Unlimited Orchestra
74	22	16	7	531	☐ **Show And Tell** . . . Al Wilson
85	27	15	7	532	☐ **Take On Me** . . . A-Ha
61	23	15	7	533	☐ **Please Mr. Postman** . . . The Marvelettes
85	22	15	7	534	☐ **Saving All My Love For You** . . . Whitney Houston
76	21	15	7	535	☐ **Boogie Fever** . . . Sylvers
75	20	15	7	536	☐ **Laughter In The Rain** . . . Neil Sedaka
83	18	15	7	537	☐ **Tell Her About It** . . . Billy Joel
86	22	14	7	538	☐ **Addicted To Love** . . . Robert Palmer
79	21	14	7	539	☐ **Heart Of Glass** . . . Blondie
86	20	14	7	540	☐ **West End Girls** . . . Pet Shop Boys
77	20	14	7	541	☐ **When I Need You** . . . Leo Sayer
86	20	14	7	542	☐ **There'll Be Sad Songs (To Make You Cry)** . . . Billy Ocean
73	20	14	7	543	☐ **Frankenstein** . . . The Edgar Winter Group
74	19	14	7	544	☐ **You Haven't Done Nothin** . . . Stevie Wonder
74	18	14	7	545	☐ **Nothing From Nothing** . . . Billy Preston
75	18	14	7	546	☐ **(Hey Won't You Play) Another Somebody Done Somebody Wrong Song** . . . B.J. Thomas
59	17	14	7	547	☐ **The Happy Organ** . . . Dave "Baby" Cortez
74	17	14	7	548	☐ **Hooked On A Feeling** . . . Blue Swede
70	15	14	7	549	☐ **Cracklin' Rosie** . . . Neil Diamond
72	15	14	7	550	☐ **Oh Girl** . . . Chi-Lites
85	22	13	7	551	☐ **Miami Vice Theme** . . . Jan Hammer
80	21	13	7	552	☐ **Sailing** . . . Christopher Cross
86	20	13	7	553	☐ **Sara** . . . Starship
77	19	13	7	554	☐ **Don't Give Up On Us** . . . David Soul
77	19	13	7	555	☐ **Dreams** . . . Fleetwood Mac

YR	WEEKS CHR	T 40	T 10	RNK	Title . . . Artist
					Peak Pos 1 Peak Wks 1
74	18	13	7	556	☐ **Sunshine On My Shoulders** . . . John Denver
74	18	13	7	557	☐ **Band On The Run** . . . Paul McCartney & Wings
75	18	13	7	558	☐ **Lady Marmalade** . . . LaBelle
73	17	13	7	559	☐ **You Are The Sunshine Of My Life** . . . Stevie Wonder
75	17	13	7	560	☐ **Pick Up The Pieces** . . . AWB (Average White Band)
76	17	13	7	561	☐ **Theme From Mahogany (Do You Know Where You're Going To)** . . . Diana Ross
73	16	13	7	562	☐ **Angie** . . . The Rolling Stones
77	15	13	7	563	☐ **New Kid In Town** . . . Eagles
77	22	12	7	564	☐ **Da Doo Ron Ron** . . . Shaun Cassidy
76	20	12	7	565	☐ **You Should Be Dancing** . . . Bee Gees
76	19	12	7	566	☐ **Let Your Love Flow** . . . Bellamy Brothers
75	19	12	7	567	☐ **The Hustle** . . . Van McCoy & The Soul City Symphony
75	17	12	7	568	☐ **Black Water** . . . The Doobie Brothers
62	16	12	7	569	☐ **The Loco-Motion** . . . Little Eva
61	16	12	7	570	☐ **Wooden Heart** . . . Joe Dowell
74	15	12	7	571	☐ **You're Sixteen** . . . Ringo Starr
75	15	12	7	572	☐ **Let's Do It Again** . . . The Staple Singers
66	15	12	7	573	☐ **Poor Side Of Town** . . . Johnny Rivers
63	15	12	7	574	☐ **So Much In Love** . . . The Tymes
63	15	12	7	575	☐ **Deep Purple** . . . Nino Tempo & April Stevens
66	14	12	7	576	☐ **These Boots Are Made For Walkin'** . . . Nancy Sinatra
66	14	12	7	577	☐ **Good Vibrations** . . . The Beach Boys
66	14	12	7	578	☐ **Good Lovin'** . . . The Young Rascals
71	13	12	7	579	☐ **Uncle Albert/Admiral Halsey** . . . Paul & Linda McCartney
68	13	12	7	580	☐ **Green Tambourine** . . . The Lemon Pipers
74	18	11	7	581	☐ **Sundown** . . . Gordon Lightfoot
72	16	11	7	582	☐ **Ben** . . . Michael Jackson
75	16	11	7	583	☐ **Have You Never Been Mellow** . . . Olivia Newton-John
76	16	11	7	584	☐ **Convoy** . . . C.W. McCall
66	15	11	7	585	☐ **Strangers In The Night** . . . Frank Sinatra
76	14	11	7	586	☐ **Welcome Back** . . . John Sebastian
75	14	11	7	587	☐ **Listen To What The Man Said** . . . Wings
73	14	11	7	588	☐ **Give Me Love (Give Me Peace On Earth)** . . . George Harrison
65	14	11	7	589	☐ **Hang On Sloopy** . . . The McCoys
60	13	10	7	590	☐ **Mr. Custer** . . . Larry Verne
66	13	10	7	591	☐ **Sunshine Superman** . . . Donovan
65	13	10	7	592	☐ **Mr. Tambourine Man** . . . The Byrds
64	12	10	7	593	☐ **Ringo** . . . Lorne Greene
67	11	10	7	594	☐ **Love Is Here And Now You're Gone** . . . The Supremes
65	11	10	7	595	☐ **Eve Of Destruction** . . . Barry McGuire

YR	WEEKS CHR	T 40	T 10	RNK	Title . . . Artist

| | | | | | Peak Pos **1** Peak Wks **1** |

YR	CHR	T 40	T 10	RNK	Title . . . Artist
67	12	9	7	596	☐ **Ruby Tuesday** . . . The Rolling Stones
67	11	9	7	597	☐ **All You Need Is Love** . . . The Beatles
76	28	19	6	598	☐ **Love Machine (Part 1)** . . . The Miracles
77	23	16	6	599	☐ **I'm Your Boogie Man** . . . KC & The Sunshine Band
83	21	16	6	600	☐ **Africa** . . . Toto
83	23	14	6	601	☐ **Come On Eileen** . . . Dexys Midnight Runners
86	23	14	6	602	☐ **Holding Back The Years** . . . Simply Red
79	20	14	6	603	☐ **Knock On Wood** . . . Amii Stewart
75	19	14	6	604	☐ **Best Of My Love** . . . The Eagles
85	17	14	6	605	☐ **Sussudio** . . . Phil Collins
85	21	13	6	606	☐ **Oh Sheila** . . . Ready For The World
86	20	13	6	607	☐ **These Dreams** . . . Heart
74	18	13	6	608	☐ **Rock Me Gently** . . . Andy Kim
86	18	13	6	609	☐ **Live To Tell** . . . Madonna
74	17	13	6	610	☐ **Angie Baby** . . . Helen Reddy
73	17	13	6	611	☐ **We're An American Band** . . . Grand Funk
71	16	13	6	612	☐ **Want Ads** . . . The Honey Cone
73	16	13	6	613	☐ **Superstition** . . . Stevie Wonder
74	16	13	6	614	☐ **Feel Like Makin' Love** . . . Roberta Flack
60	15	13	6	615	☐ **I Want To Be Wanted** . . . Brenda Lee
69	15	13	6	616	☐ **Suspicious Minds** . . . Elvis Presley
73	14	13	6	617	☐ **Love Train** . . . O'Jays
76	24	12	6	618	☐ **Theme From S.W.A.T.** . . . Rhythm Heritage
79	21	12	6	619	☐ **Don't Stop 'Til You Get Enough** . . . Michael Jackson
74	19	12	6	620	☐ **Cat's In The Cradle** . . . Harry Chapin
76	17	12	6	621	☐ **Saturday Night** . . . Bay City Rollers
75	17	12	6	622	☐ **Fallin' In Love** . . . Hamilton, Joe Frank & Reynolds
73	16	12	6	623	☐ **Photograph** . . . Ringo Starr
74	16	12	6	624	☐ **Dark Lady** . . . Cher
72	16	12	6	625	☐ **Papa Was A Rollin' Stone** . . . The Temptations
61	15	12	6	626	☐ **Moody River** . . . Pat Boone
72	13	12	6	627	☐ **Song Sung Blue** . . . Neil Diamond
74	17	11	6	628	☐ **The Night Chicago Died** . . . Paper Lace
64	14	11	6	629	☐ **Love Me Do** . . . The Beatles
65	12	11	6	630	☐ **Over And Over** . . . The Dave Clark Five
66	15	10	6	631	☐ **Lightnin' Strikes** . . . Lou Christie
63	13	10	6	632	☐ **Our Day Will Come** . . . Ruby & The Romantics
67	11	10	6	633	☐ **The Happening** . . . The Supremes
65	11	9	6	634	☐ **Ticket To Ride** . . . The Beatles
65	10	8	6	635	☐ **I'm Henry VIII, I Am** . . . Herman's Hermits
75	19	15	5	636	☐ **Thank God I'm A Country Boy** . . . John Denver
75	20	14	5	637	☐ **Shining Star** . . . Earth, Wind & Fire
76	18	14	5	638	☐ **Rock'n Me** . . . Steve Miller
60	18	14	5	639	☐ **Stay** . . . Maurice Williams & The Zodiacs

YR	WEEKS			RNK	Title . . . Artist
	CHR	T 40	T 10		
					Peak Pos **1** / Peak Wks **1**
77	19	13	5	640	☐ **Looks Like We Made It** . . . Barry Manilow
79	19	13	5	641	☐ **Love You Inside Out** . . . Bee Gees
74	17	12	5	642	☐ **You Ain't Seen Nothing Yet** . . . Bachman-Turner Overdrive
75	17	12	5	643	☐ **Please Mr. Postman** . . . Carpenters
75	16	12	5	644	☐ **Mandy** . . . Barry Manilow
74	18	10	5	645	☐ **Rock The Boat** . . . The Hues Corporation
75	16	10	5	646	☐ **You're No Good** . . . Linda Ronstadt
74	14	10	5	647	☐ **I Shot The Sheriff** . . . Eric Clapton
60	13	10	5	648	☐ **Georgia On My Mind** . . . Ray Charles
64	12	10	5	649	☐ **Leader Of The Pack** . . . The Shangri-Las
65	11	10	5	650	☐ **Game Of Love** . . . Wayne Fontana & The Mindbenders
65	11	10	5	651	☐ **Back In My Arms Again** . . . The Supremes
72	11	9	5	652	☐ **Black & White** . . . Three Dog Night
67	10	9	5	653	☐ **Penny Lane** . . . The Beatles
61	17	15	4	654	☐ **Running Scared** . . . Roy Orbison
75	17	12	4	655	☐ **Fire** . . . Ohio Players
75	16	12	4	656	☐ **Sister Golden Hair** . . . America
75	15	9	4	657	☐ **Get Down Tonight** . . . K.C. & The Sunshine Band
74	12	9	4	658	☐ **Can't Get Enough Of Your Love, Babe** . . . Barry White
74	15	11	3	659	☐ **Whatever Gets You Thru The Night** . . . John Lennon with The Plastic Ono Nuclear Band
					Peak Pos **2** / Peak Wks **10**
81	23	19	15	660	☐ **Waiting For A Girl Like You** . . . Foreigner
					Peak Pos **2** / Peak Wks **8**
57	26	21	10	661	☐ **Little Darlin'** . . . The Diamonds
					Peak Pos **2** / Peak Wks **6**
55	25	25	19	662	☐ **Moments To Remember** . . . The Four Lads
82	18	14	10	663	☐ **Open Arms** . . . Journey
78	20	15	9	664	☐ **Baker Street** . . . Gerry Rafferty
63	18	13	9	665	☐ **Louie Louie** . . . The Kingsmen
					Peak Pos **2** / Peak Wks **5**
82	23	18	11	666	☐ **Rosanna** . . . Toto
62	16	14	10	667	☐ **Return To Sender** . . . Elvis Presley
80	23	15	9	668	☐ **More Than I Can Say** . . . Leo Sayer
83	22	15	8	669	☐ **Electric Avenue** . . . Eddy Grant
					Peak Pos **2** / Peak Wks **4**
57	38	26	18	670	☐ **So Rare** . . . Jimmy Dorsey
82	28	22	16	671	☐ **Hurt So Good** . . . John Cougar
57	27	22	15	672	☐ **Bye Bye Love** . . . The Everly Brothers
56	24	19	12	673	☐ **No, Not Much!** . . . The Four Lads

THEY'RE ALL RUNNING TO COVER
—BUT YOU
CAN'T TOP THE ORIGINAL!

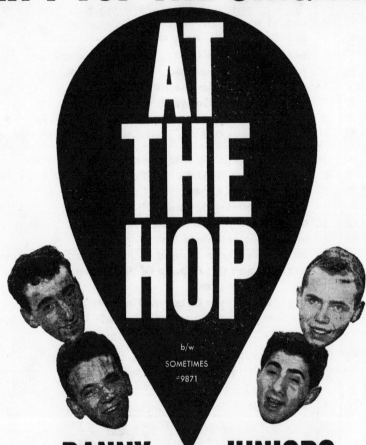

AT THE HOP

b/w
SOMETIMES
#9871

DANNY AND THE JUNIORS

ABC-PARAMOUNT
FULL COLOR FIDELITY

(Distributed in Canada by Sparton of Canada, Ltd.)

DANNY & THE JUNIORS....ABC-Paramount 9871...............AT THE HOP
Singular, BMI
Platter was purchased from Singular Records. The medium-paced rockabilly blues is a very danceable item with a strong vocal by the group that can attract plenty of teen coin. Flip, "Sometimes," is a ballad with rhythm backing that is also well-treated. Singular, BMI.

THE ORIGINAL!

....*has it's own* SATELITE

THE BALL OF FIRE

Jerry Lee Lewis

Singing His Fabulous New — SUN RELEASE

"GREAT BALLS OF FIRE"

(From the Warner Bros. picture "Jamboree")

and YOU WIN AGAIN

Sun 281

D.J.'s—Thanks for Your Spins. The copies of my new record are on their way to you now.

GREAT BALLS OF FIRE!

Here's The Next Sensation Of The Musical World!

JERRY LEE LEWIS....Sun 281......................GREAT BALL OF FIRE
BRS, BMI
YOU WIN AGAIN ....Acuff-Rose, BMI
Lewis pours his all into "Fire," a rockabilly tune which he performs in the flick, "Jamboree." Side appears a strong bet to match the success of "Whole Lotta Shakin' Goin' On." Flip is an appealing styling of Hank William's old hit that should also be a winner. Both sides figure in all markets.

YR	WEEKS			RNK	Title . . . Artist
	CHR	T 40	T 10		
					Peak Pos **2** Peak Wks **4**
56	21	17	11	674	☐ **Blue Suede Shoes** . . . Carl Perkins
82	21	16	11	675	☐ **Don't Talk To Strangers** . . . Rick Springfield
80	27	17	10	676	☐ **All Out Of Love** . . . Air Supply
60	20	15	10	677	☐ **Last Date** . . . Floyd Cramer
83	18	15	10	678	☐ **Say It Isn't So** . . . Daryl Hall & John Oates
80	21	17	9	679	☐ **Ride Like The Wind** . . . Christopher Cross
84	21	15	9	680	☐ **Dancing In The Dark** . . . Bruce Springsteen
60	20	15	9	681	☐ **Greenfields** . . . The Brothers Four
70	17	14	9	682	☐ **We've Only Just Begun** . . . Carpenters
58	21	13	9	683	☐ **Great Balls Of Fire** . . . Jerry Lee Lewis
83	21	19	8	684	☐ **Shame On The Moon** . . . Bob Seger & The Silver Bullet Band
84	18	14	8	685	☐ **The Wild Boys** . . . Duran Duran
66	12	11	8	686	☐ **Snoopy Vs. The Red Baron** . . . The Royal Guardsmen
63	15	12	7	687	☐ **Can't Get Used To Losing You** . . . Andy Williams
68	13	11	7	688	☐ **(Theme From) Valley Of The Dolls** . . . Dionne Warwick
64	11	9	7	689	☐ **Twist And Shout** . . . The Beatles
73	14	11	6	690	☐ **Dueling Banjos** . . . Eric Weissberg & Steve Mandell (from "Deliverance")
					Peak Pos **2** Peak Wks **3**
56	39	22	16	691	☐ **Honky Tonk (Parts 1 & 2)** . . . Bill Doggett
57	27	21	16	692	☐ **Blueberry Hill** . . . Fats Domino
56	27	22	15	693	☐ **Whatever Will Be, Will Be (Que Sera, Sera)** . . . Doris Day
55	18	17	14	694	☐ **I Hear You Knocking** . . . Gale Storm
79	26	20	12	695	☐ **Y.M.C.A.** . . . Village People
60	23	20	12	696	☐ **He'll Have To Go** . . . Jim Reeves
81	20	17	12	697	☐ **Woman** . . . John Lennon
81	24	19	11	698	☐ **Start Me Up** . . . The Rolling Stones
81	24	16	11	699	☐ **Slow Hand** . . . Pointer Sisters
81	24	16	11	700	☐ **Just The Two Of Us** . . . Grover Washington, Jr./Bill Withers
59	18	14	11	701	☐ **Put Your Head On My Shoulder** . . . Paul Anka
82	36	22	10	702	☐ **Gloria** . . . Laura Branigan
77	26	18	10	703	☐ **Don't It Make My Brown Eyes Blue** . . . Crystal Gayle
81	20	17	10	704	☐ **Love On The Rocks** . . . Neil Diamond
81	25	16	10	705	☐ **Being With You** . . . Smokey Robinson
59	19	14	10	706	☐ **Personality** . . . Lloyd Price
83	18	14	10	707	☐ **The Girl Is Mine** . . . Michael Jackson/Paul McCartney
83	25	18	9	708	☐ **Do You Really Want To Hurt Me** . . . Culture Club
83	25	17	9	709	☐ **Making Love Out Of Nothing At All** . . . Air Supply
76	21	17	9	710	☐ **The Rubberband Man** . . . Spinners

YR	WEEKS			RNK	Title . . . Artist
	CHR	T 40	T 10		
					Peak Pos **2** Peak Wks **3**
76	21	15	9	711	☐ **Get Up And Boogie (That's Right)** . . . Silver Convention
82	19	15	9	712	☐ **We Got The Beat** . . . Go-Go's
85	22	14	9	713	☐ **Party All The Time** . . . Eddie Murphy
67	17	14	9	714	☐ **I Heard It Through The Grapevine** . . . Gladys Knight & The Pips
69	15	12	9	715	☐ **Crystal Blue Persuasion** . . . Tommy James & The Shondells
77	25	15	8	716	☐ **Nobody Does It Better** . . . Carly Simon
76	20	14	8	717	☐ **Dream Weaver** . . . Gary Wright
58	20	14	8	718	☐ **26 Miles (Santa Catalina)** . . . The Four Preps
84	19	14	8	719	☐ **Somebody's Watching Me** . . . Rockwell
58	18	14	8	720	☐ **Stood Up** . . . Ricky Nelson
68	15	13	8	721	☐ **Young Girl** . . . The Union Gap featuring Gary Puckett
71	15	13	8	722	☐ **What's Going On** . . . Marvin Gaye
61	16	12	8	723	☐ **The Boll Weevil Song** . . . Brook Benton
59	15	12	8	724	☐ **Charlie Brown** . . . The Coasters
67	15	11	8	725	☐ **Soul Man** . . . Sam & Dave
66	12	10	8	726	☐ **Mellow Yellow** . . . Donovan
85	25	15	7	727	☐ **Cherish** . . . Kool & The Gang
77	20	14	7	728	☐ **Keep It Comin' Love** . . . KC & The Sunshine Band
73	17	14	7	729	☐ **Goodbye Yellow Brick Road** . . . Elton John
68	14	12	7	730	☐ **Those Were The Days** . . . Mary Hopkin
69	14	12	7	731	☐ **Proud Mary** . . . Creedence Clearwater Revival
73	14	12	7	732	☐ **Live And Let Die** . . . Wings
69	13	12	7	733	☐ **Spinning Wheel** . . . Blood, Sweat & Tears
58	16	11	7	734	☐ **Sweet Little Sixteen** . . . Chuck Berry
69	12	11	7	735	☐ **A Boy Named Sue** . . . Johnny Cash
71	12	11	7	736	☐ **Never Can Say Goodbye** . . . The Jackson 5
61	17	10	7	737	☐ **I Like It Like That, Part 1** . . . Chris Kenner
76	19	14	6	738	☐ **All By Myself** . . . Eric Carmen
77	20	13	6	739	☐ **I'm In You** . . . Peter Frampton
68	14	12	6	740	☐ **The Horse** . . . Cliff Nobles & Co.
68	13	12	6	741	☐ **Born To Be Wild** . . . Steppenwolf
81	16	11	6	742	☐ **All Those Years Ago** . . . George Harrison
65	15	11	6	743	☐ **A Lover's Concerto** . . . The Toys
63	13	11	6	744	☐ **Ruby Baby** . . . Dion
69	13	11	6	745	☐ **You've Made Me So Very Happy** . . . Blood, Sweat & Tears
63	13	10	6	746	☐ **Be My Baby** . . . The Ronettes
66	10	9	6	747	☐ **19th Nervous Breakdown** . . . Rolling Stones
67	10	9	6	748	☐ **Dedicated To The One I Love** . . . The Mamas & The Papas
63	10	8	6	749	☐ **Hello Mudduh, Hello Fadduh! (A Letter From Camp)** . . . Allan Sherman

YR	WEEKS CHR	WEEKS T 40	WEEKS T 10	RNK	Title . . . Artist
					Peak Pos **2** · Peak Wks **3**
78	20	13	5	750	☐ **Short People** . . . Randy Newman
75	17	11	5	751	☐ **I'm Not In Love** . . . 10cc
64	13	10	5	752	☐ **You Don't Own Me** . . . Lesley Gore
					Peak Pos **2** · Peak Wks **2**
56	31	23	14	753	☐ **Canadian Sunset** . . . Hugo Winterhalter/Eddie Heywood
56	27	22	12	754	☐ **Allegheny Moon** . . . Patti Page
62	23	17	12	755	☐ **Limbo Rock** . . . Chubby Checker
81	27	19	10	756	☐ **Queen Of Hearts** . . . Juice Newton
58	21	19	10	757	☐ **Rock-in Robin** . . . Bobby Day
81	26	18	10	758	☐ **Theme From "Greatest American Hero" (Believe It or Not)** . . . Joey Scarbury
59	23	18	10	759	☐ **Donna** . . . Ritchie Valens
76	24	17	10	760	☐ **I'd Really Love To See You Tonight** . . . England Dan & John Ford Coley
72	21	16	10	761	☐ **I Gotcha** . . . Joe Tex
70	19	15	10	762	☐ **One Less Bell To Answer** . . . The 5th Dimension
57	19	14	10	763	☐ **Love Me** . . . Elvis Presley
77	27	17	9	764	☐ **Boogie Nights** . . . Heatwave
74	22	16	9	765	☐ **Dancing Machine** . . . The Jackson 5
62	18	15	9	766	☐ **Mashed Potato Time** . . . Dee Dee Sharp
79	21	14	9	767	☐ **Dim All The Lights** . . . Donna Summer
65	18	14	9	768	☐ **Wooly Bully** . . . Sam The Sham & The Pharaohs
61	16	14	9	769	☐ **Bristol Stomp** . . . The Dovells
83	18	13	9	770	☐ **Time (Clock Of The Heart)** . . . Culture Club
79	17	13	9	771	☐ **After The Love Has Gone** . . . Earth, Wind & Fire
67	16	13	9	772	☐ **Little Bit O'Soul** . . . The Music Explosion
80	25	16	8	773	☐ **Working My Way Back To You/Forgive Me, Girl** . . . Spinners
79	23	16	8	774	☐ **Fire** . . . Pointer Sisters
73	23	15	8	775	☐ **Playground In My Mind** . . . Clint Holmes
76	20	15	8	776	☐ **Right Back Where We Started From** . . . Maxine Nightingale
84	25	14	8	777	☐ **Girls Just Want To Have Fun** . . . Cyndi Lauper
74	25	14	8	778	☐ **You Make Me Feel Brand New** . . . The Stylistics
59	21	14	8	779	☐ **16 Candles** . . . The Crests
78	20	14	8	780	☐ **The Closer I Get To You** . . . Roberta Flack with Donny Hathaway
76	21	13	8	781	☐ **You'll Never Find Another Love Like Mine** . . . Lou Rawls
60	16	13	8	782	☐ **Chain Gang** . . . Sam Cooke
71	16	13	8	783	☐ **Mr. Big Stuff** . . . Jean Knight
62	16	13	8	784	☐ **Ramblin' Rose** . . . Nat King Cole
69	15	13	8	785	☐ **Hair** . . . The Cowsills
72	15	13	8	786	☐ **Long Cool Woman (In A Black Dress)** . . . The Hollies

YR	WEEKS			RNK	Title ... Artist
	CHR	T 40	T 10		
					Peak Pos **2** Peak Wks **2**
67	16	12	8	787	☐ **The Rain, The Park & Other Things** ... The Cowsills
67	16	12	8	788	☐ **Georgy Girl** ... The Seekers
71	13	12	8	789	☐ **Superstar** ... Carpenters
69	13	12	8	790	☐ **I'm Gonna Make You Love Me** ... Diana Ross & The Supremes & The Temptations
72	14	11	8	791	☐ **Too Late To Turn Back Now** ... Cornelius Brothers & Sister Rose
67	14	11	8	792	☐ **Never My Love** ... The Association
68	14	11	8	793	☐ **For Once In My Life** ... Stevie Wonder
72	13	11	8	794	☐ **Rockin' Robin** ... Michael Jackson
76	27	18	7	795	☐ **Love Is Alive** ... Gary Wright
85	23	16	7	796	☐ **Easy Lover** ... Philip Bailey with Phil Collins
80	23	16	7	797	☐ **Yes, I'm Ready** ... Teri DeSario with K.C.
76	18	14	7	798	☐ **Love To Love You Baby** ... Donna Summer
74	18	14	7	799	☐ **Do It ('Til You're Satisfied)** ... B.T. Express
59	18	14	7	800	☐ **My Happiness** ... Connie Francis
72	18	14	7	801	☐ **Nights In White Satin** ... The Moody Blues
72	16	14	7	802	☐ **Clair** ... Gilbert O'Sullivan
80	22	13	7	803	☐ **Longer** ... Dan Fogelberg
85	21	13	7	804	☐ **You Belong To The City** ... Glenn Frey
69	16	13	7	805	☐ **Hot Fun In The Summertime** ... Sly & The Family Stone
75	15	13	7	806	☐ **When Will I Be Loved** ... Linda Ronstadt
67	15	12	7	807	☐ **I Was Made To Love Her** ... Stevie Wonder
75	15	12	7	808	☐ **You're The First, The Last, My Everything** ... Barry White
58	15	12	7	809	☐ **Lollipop** ... The Chordettes
69	14	12	7	810	☐ **Jean** ... Oliver
79	19	11	7	811	☐ **We Are Family** ... Sister Sledge
59	18	11	7	812	☐ **Sorry (I Ran All the Way Home)** ... Impalas
84	16	11	7	813	☐ **Purple Rain** ... Prince & the Revolution
64	14	11	7	814	☐ **Dancing In The Street** ... Martha & The Vandellas
60	14	11	7	815	☐ **Puppy Love** ... Paul Anka
73	14	11	7	816	☐ **Kodachrome** ... Paul Simon
66	14	11	7	817	☐ **Lil' Red Riding Hood** ... Sam The Sham & The Pharaohs
71	12	11	7	818	☐ **Rainy Days And Mondays** ... Carpenters
64	12	11	7	819	☐ **Bread And Butter** ... The Newbeats
68	12	11	7	820	☐ **Chain Of Fools** ... Aretha Franklin
66	12	10	7	821	☐ **Daydream** ... The Lovin' Spoonful
67	11	10	7	822	☐ **Reflections** ... Diana Ross & The Supremes
86	22	16	6	823	☐ **Burning Heart** ... Survivor
77	20	15	6	824	☐ **Fly Like An Eagle** ... Steve Miller
59	18	14	6	825	☐ **Sea Of Love** ... Phil Phillips

YR	WEEKS CHR	WEEKS T 40	WEEKS T 10	RNK	Title . . . Artist
					Peak Pos **2** Peak Wks **2**
76	21	13	6	826	☐ **The Wreck Of The Edmund Fitzgerald** . . . Gordon Lightfoot
74	18	13	6	827	☐ **Boogie Down** . . . Eddie Kendricks
85	22	12	6	828	☐ **All I Need** . . . Jack Wagner
78	20	12	6	829	☐ **Double Vision** . . . Foreigner
85	17	12	6	830	☐ **Material Girl** . . . Madonna
57	17	12	6	831	☐ **Teen-Age Crush** . . . Tommy Sands
73	16	12	6	832	☐ **Neither One Of Us (Wants To Be The First To Say Goodbye)** . . . Gladys Knight & The Pips
68	15	12	6	833	☐ **Cry Like A Baby** . . . The Box Tops
73	15	12	6	834	☐ **The Cisco Kid** . . . War
65	15	11	6	835	☐ **Can't You Hear My Heartbeat** . . . Herman's Hermits
66	15	11	6	836	☐ **Sunny** . . . Bobby Hebb
62	14	11	6	837	☐ **The Wah Watusi** . . . The Orlons
68	14	11	6	838	☐ **Classical Gas** . . . Mason Williams
75	14	11	6	839	☐ **Lyin' Eyes** . . . The Eagles
68	13	11	6	840	☐ **Lady Willpower** . . . Gary Puckett & The Union Gap
71	12	11	6	841	☐ **Spanish Harlem** . . . Aretha Franklin
72	12	11	6	842	☐ **Hurting Each Other** . . . Carpenters
69	13	10	6	843	☐ **Love (Can Make You Happy)** . . . Mercy
64	12	10	6	844	☐ **Memphis** . . . Johnny Rivers
63	12	10	6	845	☐ **Sally, Go 'Round The Roses** . . . The Jaynetts
66	11	9	6	846	☐ **Did You Ever Have To Make Up Your Mind?** . . . The Lovin' Spoonful
61	17	13	5	847	☐ **Apache** . . . Jorgen Ingmann & His Guitar
70	17	13	5	848	☐ **Which Way You Goin' Billy?** . . . The Poppy Family featuring Susan Jacks
77	16	11	5	849	☐ **Float On** . . . The Floaters
72	14	10	5	850	☐ **I'd Love You To Want Me** . . . Lobo
66	13	10	5	851	☐ **A Groovy Kind Of Love** . . . The Mindbenders
72	12	10	5	852	☐ **Use Me** . . . Bill Withers
74	15	9	5	853	☐ **Don't Let The Sun Go Down On Me** . . . Elton John
65	12	9	5	854	☐ **Like A Rolling Stone** . . . Bob Dylan
65	11	9	5	855	☐ **Treat Her Right** . . . Roy Head & The Traits
65	11	9	5	856	☐ **Count Me In** . . . Gary Lewis & The Playboys
70	10	9	5	857	☐ **Travelin' Band** . . . Creedence Clearwater Revival
71	10	9	5	858	☐ **Mama's Pearl** . . . The Jackson 5
66	11	9	4	859	☐ **Barbara Ann** . . . The Beach Boys
61	15	10	3	860	☐ **The Mountain's High** . . . Dick & DeeDee
					Peak Pos **2** Peak Wks **1**
56	28	23	18	861	☐ **Just Walking In The Rain** . . . Johnnie Ray
55	20	20	12	862	☐ **A Blossom Fell** . . . Nat "King" Cole
56	24	18	12	863	☐ **Ivory Tower** . . . Cathy Carr
61	21	18	11	864	☐ **Exodus** . . . Ferrante & Teicher

YR	WEEKS			RNK	Title . . . Artist
	CHR	T 40	T 10		
					Peak Pos **2** Peak Wks **1**
58	30	17	11	865	☐ **All The Way** . . . Frank Sinatra
57	26	21	10	866	☐ **A White Sport Coat (And A Pink Carnation)** . . . Marty Robbins
59	17	13	10	867	☐ **Dream Lover** . . . Bobby Darin
60	18	15	9	868	☐ **Handy Man** . . . Jimmy Jones
57	20	14	9	869	☐ **Raunchy** . . . Bill Justis
60	18	14	9	870	☐ **Walk--Don't Run** . . . The Ventures
58	15	13	9	871	☐ **Wear My Ring Around Your Neck** . . . Elvis Presley
60	21	15	8	872	☐ **Only The Lonely (Know How I Feel)** . . . Roy Orbison
57	19	15	8	873	☐ **A Teenager's Romance** . . . Ricky Nelson
59	18	15	8	874	☐ **Don't You Know** . . . Della Reese
71	23	14	8	875	☐ **Take Me Home, Country Roads** . . . John Denver with Fat City
67	16	14	8	876	☐ **Can't Take My Eyes Off You** . . . Frankie Valli
60	16	13	8	877	☐ **Wild One** . . . Bobby Rydell
64	20	12	8	878	☐ **Last Kiss** . . . J. Frank Wilson & The Cavaliers
68	17	12	8	879	☐ **Little Green Apples** . . . O.C. Smith
61	16	12	8	880	☐ **Raindrops** . . . Dee Clark
64	15	12	8	881	☐ **She's Not There** . . . The Zombies
71	14	12	8	882	☐ **She's A Lady** . . . Tom Jones
62	14	12	8	883	☐ **Can't Help Falling In Love** . . . Elvis Presley
67	14	11	8	884	☐ **Tell It Like It Is** . . . Aaron Neville
69	13	11	8	885	☐ **Green River** . . . Creedence Clearwater Revival
63	30	20	7	886	☐ **Wipe Out** . . . The Surfaris
77	27	17	7	887	☐ **(Your Love Has Lifted Me) Higher And Higher** . . . Rita Coolidge
83	22	14	7	888	☐ **Jeopardy** . . . Greg Kihn
68	22	14	7	889	☐ **The Good, The Bad And The Ugly** . . . Hugo Montenegro
73	16	14	7	890	☐ **Loves Me Like A Rock** . . . Paul Simon & The Dixie Hummingbirds
62	18	13	7	891	☐ **The Wanderer** . . . Dion
69	15	13	7	892	☐ **Take A Letter Maria** . . . R.B. Greaves
60	15	12	7	893	☐ **Poetry In Motion** . . . Johnny Tillotson
73	15	12	7	894	☐ **Daniel** . . . Elton John
63	15	12	7	895	☐ **Blowin' In The Wind** . . . Peter, Paul & Mary
69	14	12	7	896	☐ **It's Your Thing** . . . The Isley Brothers
62	14	12	7	897	☐ **Midnight In Moscow** . . . Kenny Ball & his Jazzmen
71	14	12	7	898	☐ **Put Your Hand In The Hand** . . . Ocean
63	14	12	7	899	☐ **Washington Square** . . . The Village Stompers
70	13	12	7	900	☐ **Lookin' Out My Back Door** . . . Creedence Clearwater Revival
69	13	12	7	901	☐ **And When I Die** . . . Blood, Sweat & Tears
67	15	11	7	902	☐ **Sweet Soul Music** . . . Arthur Conley

From his new
Aven Productions movie,
an M-G-M release...

JAIL HOUSE ROCK
TREAT ME NICE
47/20-7035

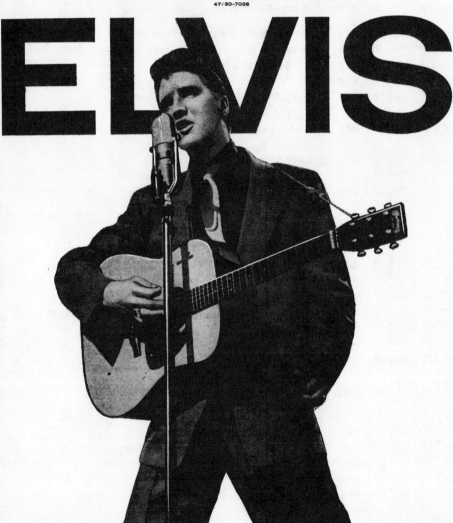

ELVIS

Watch for these NBC-TV network shows: PERRY COMO, GEORGE GOBEL, EDDIE FISHER, PRICE IS RIGHT, TIC TAC DOUGH. They'll all be sponsored by...  RCA VICTOR

ELVIS PRESLEY....RCA Victor 7035....................JAILHOUSE ROCK
                                                      (Presley, BMI)
TREAT ME NICE ....(Presley, BMI)
Another sock platter by the phenomenal artist. "Rock" is a vigorous rocker and is the title tune from Presley's forthcoming flick. Flip is an equally strong side somewhat like "Don't Be Cruel." Both should score.

THE TOP 100

For survey week ending December 5

A list of the Top 100 RECORD SIDES in the nation according to a COMBINED TABULATION of Dealer, Disk Jockey and Juke Box Operator replies to The Billboard's weekly popular record Best Seller and Most Played surveys. Its purpose is to provide Disk Jockeys with additional programming material and to give trade exposure to NEWER records just beginning to show action in the field.

Pos.	Song, Artist, Label	Last Week
1.	SINGING THE BLUES—G. Mitchell, Columbia	1
2.	LOVE ME TENDER—E. Presley, Victor	2
3.	GREEN DOOR—J. Lowe, Dot	3
4.	JUST WALKING IN THE RAIN—J. Ray, Columbia	4
5.	BLUEBERRY HILL—F. Domino, Imperial	6
6.	TRUE LOVE—B. Crosby-G. Kelly, Capitol	5
7.	HEY, JEALOUS LOVER—F. Sinatra, Capitol	7
8.	ROSE AND A BABY RUTH—G. Hamilton IV, ABC Paramount	10
9.	LOVE ME—E. Presley, Victor	17
10.	CINDY, OH, CINDY—E. Fisher, Victor	12
10.	HONKY TONK—B. Doggett, King	11
12.	GARDEN OF EDEN—J. Valino, Vik	14
13.	FRIENDLY PERSUASION—P. Boone, Dot	9
14.	DON'T BE CRUEL—E. Presley, Victor	8
14.	MAMA FROM THE TRAIN—P. Page, Mercury	13
16.	CINDY, OH, CINDY—V. Martin, Glory	15
17.	NIGHT LIGHTS—Nat (King) Cole, Capitol	16
18.	GONNA GET ALONG WITHOUT YA NOW—Patience & Prudence, Liberty	30
19.	TWO DIFFERENT WORLDS—D. Rondo, Jubilee	23
20.	CONFIDENTIAL—S. Knight, Dot	27
20.	MOONLIGHT GAMBLER—F. Laine, Columbia	31
22.	CANADIAN SUNSET—E. Heywood & H. Winterhalter, Victor	18
23.	ROCK-A-BYE YOUR BABY—J. Lewis, Decca	29
23.	SLOW WALK—S. Austin, Mercury	19
25.	MUTUAL ADMIRATION SOCIETY—T. Brewer, Coral	21
26.	SINCE I MET YOU, BABY—I. J. Hunter, Atlantic	23
27.	I WALK THE LINE—J. Cash, Sun	16
28.	YOU'LL NEVER, NEVER KNOW—Platters, Mercury	25
29.	BLUEBERRY HILL—L. Armstrong, Decca	25
30.	PETTICOATS OF PORTUGAL—D. Jacobs, Coral	20
31.	AUCTIONEER—L. Van Dyke–Dot	44
32.	TONIGHT YOU BELONG TO ME—Patience & Prudence, Liberty	33
33.	SINGING THE BLUES—M. Robbins, Columbia	26
34.	PRISCILLA—E. Cooley, Roost	—
35.	HOUND DOG—E. Presley, Victor	27
35.	LAY DOWN YOUR ARMS—Chordettes, Cadence	32
37.	SLOW WALK—B. Doggett, King	72
38.	CITY OF ANGELS—Highlights, Bally	36
39.	I DREAMED—B. Johnson, Bally	49
40.	JAMAICA FAREWELL—H. Belafonte, Victor	34
41.	TWO DIFFERENT WORLDS—R. Williams & J. Morgan, Kapp	52
42.	STAR YOU WISHED UPON LAST NIGHT—G. Mac Kenzie, Vik	42
43.	ANY WAY YOU WANT ME—E. Presley, Victor	42
44.	LOVE ME TENDER—H. Rene, Victor	64
45.	ON LONDON BRIDGE—J. Stafford, Columbia	55
46.	JUST IN TIME—T. Bennett, Columbia	55

47.	IN THE STILL OF THE NIGHT—Satins, Ember	49
47.	MUTUAL ADMIRATION SOCIETY—E. Arnold-J. P. Morgan, Victor	51
49.	WHEN MY BLUE MOON TURNS TO GOLD AGAIN—E. Presley Victor	61
50.	TRUE LOVE—J. Powell, Verve	61
51.	I SAW ESAU—Ames Brothers, Victor	68
52.	TRA LA LA—G. Gibbs, Mercury	83
52.	FIRST BORN—Tennessee Ernie, Capitol	66
54.	TONIGHT YOU BELONG TO ME—Lennon Sisters-L. Welk, Coral	39
55.	RUDY'S ROCK—B. Haley, Decca	36
55.	I MISS YOU SO—C. Connor, Atlantic	86
57.	SINCE I MET YOU, BABY—M. Carson, Columbia	—
57.	MONEY TREE—M. Whiting, Capitol	63
59.	CHINCHERINCHEE—P. Como, Victor	—
60.	OUT OF SIGHT, OUT OF MIND—Five Keys, Capitol	48
60.	IT ISN'T RIGHT—Platters, Mercury	40
62.	GOODNIGHT, MY LOVE—McGuire Sisters, Coral	66
63.	WHATEVER WILL BE, WILL BE—Doris Day, Columbia	46
63.	AUTUMN WALTZ—T. Bennett, Columbia	58
65.	WISDOM OF A FOOL—Five Keys, Capitol	—
66.	FADED SUMMER LOVE—G. Shaw, Decca	57
67.	FOOL—S. Clark, Dot	74
68.	SOMEONE TO LOVE—Four Aces, Decca	47
68.	CANADIAN SUNSET—A. Williams, Cadence	36
70.	WRITTEN ON THE WIND—Four Aces, Decca	—
71.	BABY DOLL—A. Williams, Cadence	54
71.	FRIENDLY PERSUASION—Four Aces, Decca	—
73.	CRAZY WITH LOVE—T. Brewer, Coral	88
74.	ALLEGHENY MOON—P. Page, Mercury	80
74.	CHEAT—S. Clark, Dot	98
76.	MY PRAYER—Platters, Mercury	—
77.	ARMEN'S THEME—J. Reisman, Victor	88
78.	I FEEL GOOD—Shirley & Lee, Aladdin	—
79.	TO THE ENDS OF THE EARTH—Nat (King) Cole, Capitol	58
80.	AIN'T GOT NO HOME—C. Henry, Argo	—
81.	SOFT SUMMER BREEZE—E. Heywood, Mercury	80
82.	ARMEN'S THEME—D. Seville, Liberty	—
83.	PETTICOATS OF PORTUGAL—B. Vaughn, Dot	—
84.	MONEY TREE—Patience & Prudence, Liberty	78
85.	LET THE GOOD TIMES ROLL—Shirley & Lee, Aladdin	88
86.	GIVE ME—E. Rodgers, Columbia	—
87.	I WOULDN'T KNOW WHERE TO BEGIN—E. Arnold, Victor	77
87.	MIRACLE OF LOVE—G. Gibson, ABC-Paramount	86
89.	MOONLIGHT LOVE—P. Como, Victor	84
90.	CRAZY WITH LOVE—G. Mitchell, Columbia	56
90.	IT HAPPENED AGAIN—S. Vaughan, Mercury	—
92.	SEE SAW—D. Cornell, Coral	70
93.	SADIE'S SHAWL—B. Sharples, London	91
94.	TRA LA LA—L. Baker, Atlantic	—
94.	JULIE—Doris Day, Columbia	68
96.	STILL—Fontane Sisters, Dot	—
96.	AFTER THE LIGHTS GO DOWN LOW—A. Hibbler, Decca	75
96.	CHAINS OF LOVE—P. Boone, Dot	73
99.	YOU DON'T KNOW ME—J. Vale, Columbia	—
100.	GIANT—L. Baxter, Capitol	76

CAUTION TO DEALERS AND JUKE BOX OPERATORS

The Billboard's Top 100 is NOT designed to provide tested information for buying purposes. This function is most reliably served by other regular weekly features: Best Sellers in Stores, Most Played in Juke Boxes, Coming Up Strong and Best Buys.

YR	WEEKS			RNK	Title . . . Artist
	CHR	T 40	T 10		
					Peak Pos **2** Peak Wks **1**
58	15	11	7	903	☐ **Problems** . . . The Everly Brothers
68	13	11	7	904	☐ **Fire** . . . The Crazy World Of Arthur Brown
65	15	10	7	905	☐ **1-2-3** . . . Len Barry
84	24	16	6	906	☐ **Joanna** . . . Kool & The Gang
85	21	15	6	907	☐ **Loverboy** . . . Billy Ocean
59	19	14	6	908	☐ **There Goes My Baby** . . . The Drifters
85	17	14	6	909	☐ **Raspberry Beret** . . . Prince & the Revolution
72	17	14	6	910	☐ **Outa-Space** . . . Billy Preston
85	24	13	6	911	☐ **The Heat Is On** . . . Glenn Frey
84	23	13	6	912	☐ **99 Luftballons** . . . Nena
74	18	13	6	913	☐ **When Will I See You Again** . . . The Three Degrees
63	17	13	6	914	☐ **The End Of The World** . . . Skeeter Davis
61	16	13	6	915	☐ **Shop Around** . . . The Miracles
73	16	13	6	916	☐ **Ramblin Man** . . . The Allman Brothers Band
61	15	13	6	917	☐ **Run To Him** . . . Bobby Vee
85	18	12	6	918	☐ **We Don't Need Another Hero (Thunderdome)** . . . Tina Turner
72	15	12	6	919	☐ **Burning Love** . . . Elvis Presley
69	14	12	6	920	☐ **Bad Moon Rising** . . . Creedence Clearwater Revival
70	14	12	6	921	☐ **Hey There Lonely Girl** . . . Eddie Holman
73	14	12	6	922	☐ **Yesterday Once More** . . . Carpenters
63	14	11	6	923	☐ **Puff The Magic Dragon** . . . Peter, Paul & Mary
70	13	11	6	924	☐ **The Rapper** . . . The Jaggerz
66	13	11	6	925	☐ **Red Rubber Ball** . . . The Cyrkle
73	12	10	6	926	☐ **Also Sprach Zarathustra (2001)** . . . Deodato
67	10	10	6	927	☐ **A Little Bit Me, A Little Bit You** . . . The Monkees
66	11	9	6	928	☐ **Bang Bang (My Baby Shot Me Down)** . . . Cher
66	9	8	6	929	☐ **Yellow Submarine** . . . The Beatles
86	23	14	5	930	☐ **When The Going Gets Tough, The Tough Get Going** . . . Billy Ocean
86	20	14	5	931	☐ **Manic Monday** . . . Bangles
61	16	14	5	932	☐ **Crying** . . . Roy Orbison
59	16	13	5	933	☐ **The All American Boy** . . . Bill Parsons
86	17	11	5	934	☐ **R.O.C.K. In The U.S.A. (A Salute To 60's Rock)** . . . John Cougar Mellencamp
59	15	11	5	935	☐ **(Now and Then There's) A Fool Such As I** . . . Elvis Presley
68	13	10	5	936	☐ **MacArthur Park** . . . Richard Harris
70	12	10	5	937	☐ **Vehicle** . . . The Ides Of March
64	12	9	5	938	☐ **My Boy Lollipop** . . . Millie Small
62	11	9	5	939	☐ **You Don't Know Me** . . . Ray Charles
64	11	9	5	940	☐ **Do You Want To Know A Secret** . . . The Beatles
65	11	9	5	941	☐ **Save Your Heart For Me** . . . Gary Lewis & The Playboys

YR	WEEKS			RNK	Title . . . Artist
	CHR	T 40	T 10		

					Peak Pos **2** · Peak Wks **1**
66	10	9	5	942	☐ **Rainy Day Women #12 & 35** . . . Bob Dylan
74	16	12	4	943	☐ **Jazzman** . . . Carole King
62	14	11	4	944	☐ **Only Love Can Break A Heart** . . . Gene Pitney
61	14	11	4	945	☐ **Daddy's Home** . . . Shep & The Limelites
69	12	10	4	946	☐ **Traces** . . . Classics IV featuring Dennis Yost

					Peak Pos **3** · Peak Wks **6**
81	21	15	10	947	☐ **Stop Draggin' My Heart Around** . . . Stevie Nicks with Tom Petty & The Heartbreakers

					Peak Pos **3** · Peak Wks **5**
83	22	16	10	948	☐ **Uptown Girl** . . . Billy Joel
81	24	16	9	949	☐ **Let's Groove** . . . Earth, Wind & Fire

					Peak Pos **3** · Peak Wks **4**
80	21	17	11	950	☐ **Little Jeannie** . . . Elton John
81	19	15	10	951	☐ **The Best Of Times** . . . Styx
57	23	18	9	952	☐ **I'm Gonna Sit Right Down And Write Myself A Letter** . . . Billy Williams
76	23	16	8	953	☐ **Love So Right** . . . Bee Gees
77	23	16	8	954	☐ **Blue Bayou** . . . Linda Ronstadt
76	22	16	8	955	☐ **Misty Blue** . . . Dorthy Moore
80	19	15	8	956	☐ **Coward Of The County** . . . Kenny Rogers
62	16	13	8	957	☐ **Bobby's Girl** . . . Marcie Blane
83	24	16	7	958	☐ **The Safety Dance** . . . Men Without Hats
82	21	13	7	959	☐ **Heart Attack** . . . Olivia Newton-John
79	17	13	7	960	☐ **The Main Event/Fight** . . . Barbra Streisand
76	16	11	7	961	☐ **Let 'Em In** . . . Wings
80	23	17	6	962	☐ **Lost In Love** . . . Air Supply
66	12	11	5	963	☐ **She's Just My Style** . . . Gary Lewis & The Playboys

					Peak Pos **3** · Peak Wks **3**
56	20	18	11	964	☐ **Standing On The Corner** . . . Four Lads
78	23	17	11	965	☐ **Lay Down Sally** . . . Eric Clapton
78	19	16	10	966	☐ **Can't Smile Without You** . . . Barry Manilow
79	19	16	10	967	☐ **My Life** . . . Billy Joel
83	21	15	10	968	☐ **Sexual Healing** . . . Marvin Gaye
83	19	14	10	969	☐ **Dirty Laundry** . . . Don Henley
84	26	17	9	970	☐ **I Feel For You** . . . Chaka Khan
83	23	16	9	971	☐ **Hungry Like The Wolf** . . . Duran Duran
57	22	16	9	972	☐ **Peggy Sue** . . . Buddy Holly
57	26	15	9	973	☐ **School Day** . . . Chuck Berry
70	15	13	9	974	☐ **Ball Of Confusion (That's What The World Is Today)** . . . The Temptations
82	25	17	8	975	☐ **Eye In The Sky** . . . The Alan Parsons Project
83	21	17	8	976	☐ **She Works Hard For The Money** . . . Donna Summer
80	25	16	8	977	☐ **The Rose** . . . Bette Midler

| YR | WEEKS | | | RNK | Title . . . Artist |
	CHR	T 40	T 10		
					Peak Pos **3** Peak Wks **3**
81	24	16	8	978	☐ **Sukiyaki** . . . A Taste Of Honey
76	21	15	8	979	☐ **You Sexy Thing** . . . Hot Chocolate
58	17	15	8	980	☐ **Secretly** . . . Jimmie Rodgers
58	21	14	8	981	☐ **Topsy II** . . . Cozy Cole
80	19	14	8	982	☐ **Biggest Part Of Me** . . . Ambrosia
84	18	14	8	983	☐ **She Bop** . . . Cyndi Lauper
70	16	14	8	984	☐ **Fire And Rain** . . . James Taylor
70	15	14	8	985	☐ **Spirit In The Sky** . . . Norman Greenbaum
76	19	13	8	986	☐ **Lonely Night (Angel Face)** . . . Captain & Tennille
72	17	13	8	987	☐ **The Lion Sleeps Tonight** . . . Robert John
69	15	13	8	988	☐ **Build Me Up Buttercup** . . . The Foundations
70	13	12	8	989	☐ **Instant Karma (We All Shine On)** . . . John Ono Lennon
71	13	12	8	990	☐ **Yo-Yo** . . . The Osmonds
59	24	16	7	991	☐ **My Heart Is An Open Book** . . . Carl Dobkins, Jr.
84	26	15	7	992	☐ **Talking In Your Sleep** . . . The Romantics
73	23	15	7	993	☐ **Little Willy** . . . The Sweet
78	21	14	7	994	☐ **How Much I Feel** . . . Ambrosia
84	19	14	7	995	☐ **Drive** . . . The Cars
67	16	13	7	996	☐ **Come Back When You Grow Up** . . . Bobby Vee
76	17	12	7	997	☐ **I'll Be Good To You** . . . The Brothers Johnson
68	16	12	7	998	☐ **Stoned Soul Picnic** . . . The 5th Dimension
68	15	12	7	999	☐ **Spooky** . . . Classics IV
60	15	10	7	1000	☐ **Good Timin'** . . . Jimmy Jones

THE YEARS

This section lists, in rank order, the Top 40 hits year by year. The ranking is based on the Top 1000 ranking system.

You will note, in order to round out the Top 40 records of each year, several hundred additional hits are listed which do not appear in the Top 1000.

Columnar headings show the following data:

PK DATE: Date record reached its peak position
PK POS: Highest charted position record attained
RNK: Top 40 ranking

THE TOP 40 HITS
1955

PK DATE	PK POS	RANK	TITLE	ARTIST
7/09	1	1.	Rock Around The Clock	Bill Haley & His Comets
11/26	1	2.	Sixteen Tons	Tennessee Ernie Ford
10/08	1	3.	Love Is A Many-Splendored Thing	Four Aces
9/03	1	4.	The Yellow Rose Of Texas	Mitch Miller
10/29	1	5.	Autumn Leaves	Roger Williams
7/09	1	6.	Learnin' The Blues	Frank Sinatra
9/17	1	7.	Ain't That A Shame	Pat Boone
10/29	2	8.	Moments To Remember	Four Lads
12/10	2	9.	I Hear You Knocking	Gale Storm
7/09	2	10.	A Blossom Fell	Nat "King" Cole
11/26	3	11.	The Shifting, Whispering Sands	Rusty Draper
10/08	3	12.	Seventeen	Fontane Sisters
9/17	3	13.	The Yellow Rose Of Texas	Johnny Desmond
8/13	4	14.	Hard To Get	Gisele MacKenzie
12/31	4	15.	He	Al Hibbler
10/22	5	16.	The Shifting Whispering Sands (Parts 1 & 2)	Billy Vaughn
11/05	5	17.	Only You (And You Alone)	Platters
11/26	5	18.	Love And Marriage	Frank Sinatra
10/15	5	19.	Tina Marie	Perry Como
7/23	5	20.	Something's Gotta Give	McGuire Sisters
9/10	5	21.	Maybellene	Chuck Berry
9/24	5	22.	Wake The Town And Tell The People	Les Baxter
9/03	5	23.	Seventeen	Boyd Bennett & his Rockets
9/17	6	24.	The Longest Walk	Jaye P. Morgan
10/29	6	25.	Black Denim Trousers	Cheers
11/05	6	26.	You Are My Love	Joni James
12/31	6	27.	Nuttin' For Christmas	Barry Gordon with Art Mooney & his Orchestra
8/13	7	28.	It's A Sin To Tell A Lie	Somethin' Smith & The Redheads
11/19	7	29.	At My Front Door (Crazy Little Mama)	Pat Boone
10/22	7	30.	The Bible Tells Me So	Don Cornell
8/27	7	31.	Hummingbird	Les Paul & Mary Ford
12/31	7	32.	White Christmas	Bing Crosby
12/31	8	33.	Only You (And You Alone)	Hilltoppers
7/16	8	34.	If I May	Nat "King" Cole & The Four Knights
7/16	9	35.	Something's Gotta Give	Sammy Davis, Jr.
8/27	9	36.	The House Of Blue Lights	Chuck Miller
12/17	9	37.	Cry Me A River	Julie London
12/31	9	38.	Burn That Candle	Bill Haley & His Comets
10/29	9	39.	Suddenly There's A Valley	Gogi Grant
7/09	10	40.	Sweet And Gentle	Alan Dale

Note: The above ranking begins with the nation's first #1 rock hit "Rock Around The Clock" from the summer of 1955, and does not include the earlier hits from 1955.

THE TOP 40 HITS
1956

PK DATE	PK POS	RANK	TITLE	ARTIST
8/18	1	1.	Don't Be Cruel/Hound Dog	Elvis Presley
12/08	1	2.	Singing The Blues	Guy Mitchell
6/16	1	3.	The Wayward Wind	Gogi Grant
4/21	1	4.	Heartbreak Hotel	Elvis Presley
2/18	1	5.	Rock And Roll Waltz	Kay Starr
3/17	1	6.	The Poor People Of Paris	Les Baxter
1/07	1	7.	Memories Are Made Of This	Dean Martin
11/03	1	8.	Love Me Tender	Elvis Presley
8/04	1	9.	My Prayer	Platters
2/25	1	10.	Lisbon Antigua	Nelson Riddle
7/28	1	11.	I Almost Lost My Mind	Pat Boone
11/03	1	12.	The Green Door	Jim Lowe
6/02	1	13.	Moonglow And Theme From "Picnic"	Morris Stoloff
2/18	1	14.	The Great Pretender	Platters
5/05	1	15.	Hot Diggity (Dog Ziggity Boom)	Perry Como
7/28	1	16.	I Want You, I Need You, I Love You	Elvis Presley
3/17	2	17.	No, Not Much!	Four Lads
5/19	2	18.	Blue Suede Shoes	Carl Perkins
10/06	2	19.	Honky Tonk (Parts 1 & 2)	Bill Doggett
8/18	2	20.	Whatever Will Be, Will Be (Que Sera, Sera)	Doris Day
10/13	2	21.	Canadian Sunset	Hugo Winterhalter/ Eddie Heywood
8/18	2	22.	Allegheny Moon	Patti Page
10/27	2	23.	Just Walking In The Rain	Johnnie Ray
6/16	2	24.	Ivory Tower	Cathy Carr
6/16	3	25.	Standing On The Corner	Four Lads
7/14	3	26.	I'm In Love Again	Fats Domino
11/10	3	27.	True Love	Bing Crosby & Grace Kelly
8/25	3	28.	The Flying Saucer (Parts 1 & 2)	Buchanan & Goodman
7/07	4	29.	On The Street Where You Live	Vic Damone
5/19	4	30.	(You've Got) The Magic Touch	Platters
4/07	4	31.	I'll Be Home	Pat Boone
1/07	4	32.	Band Of Gold	Don Cherry
10/06	4	33.	Tonight You Belong To Me	Patience & Prudence
6/02	4	34.	Moonglow And Theme From "Picnic"	George Cates
7/21	4	35.	More	Perry Como
5/12	5	36.	A Tear Fell	Teresa Brewer
7/14	5	37.	Born To Be With You	Chordettes
10/20	5	38.	Friendly Persuasion (Thee I Love)	Pat Boone
1/14	5	39.	Memories Are Made Of This	Gale Storm
2/11	6	40.	See You Later, Alligator	Bill Haley & His Comets

THE TOP 40 HITS
1957

PK DATE	PK POS	RANK	TITLE	ARTIST
4/13	1	1.	All Shook Up	Elvis Presley
6/03	1	2.	Love Letters In The Sand	Pat Boone
10/21	1	3.	Jailhouse Rock	Elvis Presley
7/08	1	4.	(Let Me Be Your) Teddy Bear	Elvis Presley
12/16	1	5.	April Love	Pat Boone
2/16	1	6.	Young Love	Tab Hunter
8/19	1	7.	Tammy	Debbie Reynolds
9/23	1	8.	Honeycomb	Jimmie Rodgers
10/14	1	9.	Wake Up Little Susie	Everly Brothers
12/02	1	10.	You Send Me	Sam Cooke
3/30	1	11.	Butterfly	Andy Williams
2/09	1	12.	Too Much	Elvis Presley
4/06	1	13.	Round And Round	Perry Como
4/06	1	14.	Butterfly	Charlie Gracie
10/21	1	15.	Chances Are	Johnny Mathis
2/09	1	16.	Young Love	Sonny James
9/09	1	17.	Diana	Paul Anka
2/09	1	18.	Don't Forbid Me	Pat Boone
3/30	1	19.	Party Doll	Buddy Knox with The Rhythm Orchids
9/23	1	20.	That'll Be The Day	Crickets
4/06	2	21.	Little Darlin'	Diamonds
6/17	2	22.	So Rare	Jimmy Dorsey
6/17	2	23.	Bye Bye Love	Everly Brothers
1/19	2	24.	Blueberry Hill	Fats Domino
1/05	2	25.	Love Me	Elvis Presley
3/16	2	26.	Teen-Age Crush	Tommy Sands
6/03	2	27.	A White Sport Coat (And A Pink Carnation)	Marty Robbins
12/16	2	28.	Raunchy	Bill Justis
6/10	2	29.	A Teenager's Romance	Ricky Nelson
8/05	3	30.	I'm Gonna Sit Right Down And Write Myself A Letter	Billy Williams
12/30	3	31.	Peggy Sue	Buddy Holly
5/13	3	32.	School Day	Chuck Berry
9/09	3	33.	Whole Lot Of Shakin' Going On	Jerry Lee Lewis
11/04	3	34.	Silhouettes	Rays
7/29	3	35.	Searchin'	Coasters
7/29	3	36.	Old Cape Cod	Patti Page
2/09	3	37.	Moonlight Gambler	Frankie Laine
1/12	3	38.	Hey! Jealous Lover	Frank Sinatra
12/16	3	39.	Kisses Sweeter Than Wine	Jimmie Rodgers
4/06	3	40.	Marianne	Hilltoppers

THE TOP 40 HITS
1958

PK DATE	PK POS	RANK	TITLE	ARTIST
1/06	1	1.	At The Hop	Danny & The Juniors
9/29	1	2.	It's All In The Game	Tommy Edwards
6/09	1	3.	The Purple People Eater	Sheb Wooley
5/12	1	4.	All I Have To Do Is Dream	Everly Brothers
3/17	1	5.	Tequila	Champs
2/10	1	6.	Don't	Elvis Presley
8/18	1	7.	Nel Blu Dipinto Di Blu (Volare)	Domenico Modugno
2/17	1	8.	Sugartime	McGuire Sisters
4/14	1	9.	He's Got The Whole World (In His Hands)	Laurie London
12/22	1	10.	The Chipmunk Song	Chipmunks
4/28	1	11.	Witch Doctor	David Seville
12/01	1	12.	To Know Him, Is To Love Him	Teddy Bears
8/04	1	13.	Poor Little Fool	Ricky Nelson
11/10	1	14.	It's Only Make Believe	Conway Twitty
2/24	1	15.	Get A Job	Silhouettes
7/21	1	16.	Hard Headed Woman	Elvis Presley
7/28	1	17.	Patricia	Perez Prado
11/17	1	18.	Tom Dooley	Kingston Trio
3/24	1	19.	Catch A Falling Star	Perry Como
4/21	1	20.	Twilight Time	Platters
8/25	1	21.	Little Star	Elegants
8/25	1	22.	Bird Dog	Everly Brothers
7/21	1	23.	Yakety Yak	Coasters
1/06	2	24.	Great Balls Of Fire	Jerry Lee Lewis
3/10	2	25.	26 Miles (Santa Catalina)	Four Preps
1/13	2	26.	Stood Up	Ricky Nelson
3/17	2	27.	Sweet Little Sixteen	Chuck Berry
10/13	2	28.	Rock-in Robin	Bobby Day
3/31	2	29.	Lollipop	Chordettes
1/06	2	30.	All The Way	Frank Sinatra
4/28	2	31.	Wear My Ring Around Your Neck	Elvis Presley
12/15	2	32.	Problems	Everly Brothers
6/16	3	33.	Secretly	Jimmie Rodgers
10/20	3	34.	Topsy II	Cozy Cole
6/09	3	35.	Big Man	Four Preps
2/10	3	36.	Short Shorts	Royal Teens
8/18	3	37.	My True Love	Jack Scott
3/24	3	38.	Are You Sincere	Andy Williams
8/04	3	39.	Splish Splash	Bobby Darin
3/10	4	40.	A Wonderful Time Up There	Pat Boone

THE TOP 40 HITS
1959

PK DATE	PK POS	RANK	TITLE	ARTIST
10/05	1	1.	Mack The Knife	Bobby Darin
6/01	1	2.	The Battle Of New Orleans	Johnny Horton
3/09	1	3.	Venus	Frankie Avalon
2/09	1	4.	Stagger Lee	Lloyd Price
8/24	1	5.	The Three Bells	Browns
7/13	1	6.	Lonely Boy	Paul Anka
4/13	1	7.	Come Softly To Me	Fleetwoods
1/19	1	8.	Smoke Gets In Your Eyes	Platters
12/14	1	9.	Heartaches By The Number	Guy Mitchell
9/21	1	10.	Sleep Walk	Santo & Johnny
5/18	1	11.	Kansas City	Wilbert Harrison
8/10	1	12.	A Big Hunk O' Love	Elvis Presley
11/16	1	13.	Mr. Blue	Fleetwoods
12/28	1	14.	Why	Frankie Avalon
5/11	1	15.	The Happy Organ	Dave "Baby" Cortez
10/05	2	16.	Put Your Head On My Shoulder	Paul Anka
6/15	2	17.	Personality	Lloyd Price
3/09	2	18.	Charlie Brown	Coasters
2/23	2	19.	Donna	Ritchie Valens
2/09	2	20.	16 Candles	Crests
1/19	2	21.	My Happiness	Connie Francis
5/11	2	22.	Sorry (I Ran All the Way Home)	Impalas
8/24	2	23.	Sea Of Love	Phil Phillips
6/08	2	24.	Dream Lover	Bobby Darin
11/30	2	25.	Don't You Know	Della Reese
8/17	2	26.	There Goes My Baby	Drifters
2/02	2	27.	The All American Boy	Bill Parsons
4/27	2	28.	(Now and Then There's) A Fool Such As I	Elvis Presley
8/03	3	29.	My Heart Is An Open Book	Carl Dobkins, Jr.
4/13	3	30.	Pink Shoe Laces	Dodie Stevens
12/28	3	31.	The Big Hurt	Miss Toni Fisher
9/14	3	32.	I'm Gonna Get Married	Lloyd Price
7/20	3	33.	Tiger	Fabian
3/16	3	34.	Alvin's Harmonica	Chipmunks
4/06	3	35.	It's Just A Matter Of Time	Brook Benton
8/24	3	36.	Lavender-Blue	Sammy Turner
9/21	4	37.	('Til) I Kissed You	Everly Brothers
7/13	4	38.	Waterloo	Stonewall Jackson
10/19	4	39.	Teen Beat	Sandy Nelson
6/01	4	40.	Quiet Village	Exotic Sounds of Martin Denny

------ Pop Records ------

ELVIS PRESLEY
ONE NIGHT (Tranis-Presley, BMI)
I GOT STUNG (Gladys, ASCAP)

"One Night" is a rockaballad that is delivered in the artist's usual smash style. Excellent New Orleans-type backing with the emphasis on plucked strings is effective. Flip, "I Got Stung," is a rockabilly effort that is sung with vigor and drive. Tri-market appeal.

RCA Victor 7210

THE EVERLY BROTHERS
PROBLEMS (Acuff Rose, DMI)
LOVE OF MY LIFE (Acuff-Rose, BMI)

The brothers have another likely two-sided click with their great warbling on these fine sides. "Problems" is a rockabilly, done with a "Bo Diddley" rhythm. "Love" is a warm reading of a Latin-tinged medium-beater. Both tunes are by the Bryants. Top potential.

Cadence 1355

CHUCK BERRY
SWEET LITTLE ROCK AND ROLL (Arc, BMI)
JOE JOE GUN (Arc, BMI)

Berry has two hot sides to follow up "Carol." Top tune is similar to "Sweet Little Sixteen." Berry handles the rocker-blues in his form. Flip, "Joe Joe Gun," is a novelty rocker about a cat who lives in the jungle and has encounters with various beasts. Strong r.&b. prospects also.

Chess 1709

MARTY ROBBINS
AIN'T I THE LUCKY ONE (Acuff-Rose, BMI)
THE LAST TIME I SAW MY HEART (Famous, ASCAP)

Robbins follows his "She Was Only Seventeen" with two sock readings. "Ain't I" is a country-flavored rockabilly which the artist sings against fine string backing. "The Last Time" is a pretty three-quarter melody with a Spanish flavor. Both sides can click in pop and c.&w. marts.

Columbia 41282

LITTLE ANTHONY AND THE IMPERIALS
SO MUCH (January, BMI)
OH YEAH (Real Gone, BMI)

"So Much" is somewhat along the lines of "Tears on My Pillow." Anthony's fine vocal is given listenable group support. Tune is a rockaballad, "Oh Yeah" is a brighter tune in the rocker groove that also has a money sound. Two likely pop-r.&b. clicks. End 1036

BILLY DAWN
SUSIE, WE GOOFED AGAIN (Winneton, BMI)

The new artist has a fine sound on the rockabilly-styled ditty. The side has drive and rhythm. It's already getting action in some areas. Cat could have a winner with his first effort. Flip is "This Is Real." (Roncom, ASCAP.) Coed 504

BILLY GRAMMER
GOTTA TRAVEL ON (Sanga, BMI)

The lad delivers the folkish ballad with feeling. Bright, cheerful backing with banjos featured helps sell the side. Disk is moving well in Southern marts, and it figures to break thru nationally. Flip is "Chasing a Dream" (Combine, BMI). It's being handled thru London Records. Monument 400

FOR WEEK ENDING AUGUST 14

The Billboard HOT 100 ®

STAR PERFORMERS showed the greatest upward progress on Hot 100 this week.
Ⓢ Indicates that 45 r.p.m. stereo single version is available.
Ⓐ Indicates that 33⅓ r.p.m. stereo single version is available.

THIS WEEK	ONE WEEK AGO	TWO WEEKS AGO	THREE WEEKS AGO	TITLE — Artist, Company — Record No.	STEREO	WEEKS ON CHART
1	2	5	10	ITSY BITSY TEENIE WEENIE YELLOW POLKA DOT BIKINI — Brian Hyland, Leader 805		6
2	1	1	1	I'M SORRY — Brenda Lee, Decca 31093		11
3	3	14	44	IT'S NOW OR NEVER — Elvis Presley, RCA Victor 7777		4
4	4	2	4	ONLY THE LONELY — Roy Orbison, Monument 421		9
5	5	3	2	ALLEY-OOP — Hollywood Argyles, Lute 5905		11
6	6	7	14	IMAGE OF A GIRL — Safaris, Eldo 101		10
7	18	39	88	WALK, DON'T RUN — Ventures, Dolton 25		4
8	7	8	9	TELL LAURA I LOVE HER — Ray Peterson, RCA Victor 7745		9
9	8	9	15	PLEASE HELP ME, I'M FALLING — Hank Locklin, RCA Victor 7692		12
10	13	13	13	WALKIN' TO NEW ORLEANS — Fats Domino, Imperial 5675		8
11	49	—	—	TWIST — Chubby Checker, Parkway 811		2
12	11	4	3	EVERYBODY'S SOMEBODY'S FOOL — Connie Francis, M-G-M 12899		14
13	9	6	7	MULE SKINNER BLUES — Fendermen, Soma 1137		12
14	15	25	41	FEEL SO FINE — Johnny Preston, Mercury 71651		8
15	14	17	28	FINGER POPPIN' TIME — Hank Ballard and the Midnighters, King 5341		13
16	16	18	22	LOOK FOR A STAR — Garry Miles, Liberty 55261		8
17	17	12	5	BECAUSE THEY'RE YOUNG — Duane Eddy, Jamie 1156		12
18	24	20	25	MISSION BELL — Donnie Brooks, Era 3018		9
19	22	23	36	QUESTION — Lloyd Price, ABC-Paramount 10123		7
20	20	21	26	TROUBLE IN PARADISE — Crests, Coed 531		9
21	12	11	8	WHEN WILL I BE LOVED — Everly Brothers, Cadence 1380		11
22	23	19	18	JOSEPHINE — Bill Black's Combo, Hi 2022		7
23	41	50	61	IN MY LITTLE CORNER OF THE WORLD — Anita Bryant, Carlton 530		5
24	26	49	62	(YOU WERE MADE FOR) ALL MY LOVE — Jackie Wilson, Brunswick 55167		5
25	58	65	78	OVER THE RAINBOW — Demensions, Mohawk 116		6
26	31	27	37	THIS BITTER EARTH — Dinah Washington, Mercury 71635		8
27	30	48	60	VOLARE (NEL BLU DI PINTO DI BLU) — Bobby Rydell, Cameo 179		4
28	19	24	39	LOOK FOR A STAR — Billy Vaughn, Dot 16106		8
29	34	80	89	A WOMAN, A LOVER, A FRIEND — Jackie Wilson, Brunswick 55167		5
30	21	22	38	DON'T COME KNOCKIN' — Fats Domino, Imperial 5675		7
31	33	41	66	IS THERE ANY CHANCE — Marty Robbins, Columbia 41686		8
32	32	45	51	WHERE ARE YOU — Frankie Avalon, Chancellor 1052		9
33	10	10	6	THAT'S ALL YOU GOTTA DO — Brenda Lee, Decca 31093		10
34	25	15	11	A ROCKIN' GOOD WAY — Dinah Washington and Brook Benton, Mercury 71629	Ⓢ	12
35	29	26	40	LOOK FOR A STAR — Garry Mills, Imperial 8674		8
36	85	96	—	THEME FROM THE APARTMENT — Ferrante and Teicher, United Artists 231		3
37	43	62	65	BAD MAN BLUNDER — Kingston Trio, Capitol 4375		3
38	37	37	35	IS A BLUEBIRD BLUE — Conway Twitty, M-G-M 12911		9
39	57	55	83	HOT ROD LINCOLN — Charlie Ryan, Four Star 1733		11
40	67	58	43	STICKS AND STONES — Ray Charles, ABC-Paramount 10118		7
41	59	86	—	DREAMIN' — Johnny Burnette, Liberty 55258		3
42	28	28	20	ALLEY-OOP — Dante and the Evergreens, Madison 130		11
43	36	29	30	LOOK FOR A STAR — Dean Hawley, Dore 554		8
44	39	35	48	ONE OF US (WILL WEEP TONIGHT) — Patti Page, Mercury 71639	Ⓢ	10
45	35	40	31	THERE IS SOMETHING ON YOUR MIND — Bobby Marchan, Fire 1022		9
46	66	78	95	IN THE STILL OF THE NIGHT — Dion and the Belmonts, Laurie 3059		4
47	44	34	45	I REALLY DON'T WANT TO KNOW — Tommy Edwards, M-G-M 12890		12
48	55	60	70	HEARTBREAK (IT'S HURTIN' ME) — Jon Thomas, ABC-Paramount 10123		7
49	42	38	75	HEARTBREAK (IT'S HURTIN' ME) — Little Willie John, King 5356		10
50	60	69	72	MY TANI — Brothers Four, Columbia 41692		6
51	40	53	—	A MESS OF BLUES — Elvis Presley, RCA Victor 7777		3
52	45	31	16	CATHY'S CLOWN — Everly Brothers, Warner Bros. 5151	Ⓢ	17
53	52	57	73	I SHOT MR. LEE — Bobbettes, Triple-X 104		6
54	27	16	12	MY HOME TOWN — Paul Anka, ABC-Paramount 10106		12
55	61	63	90	TA-TA — Clyde McPhatter, Mercury 71660		4
56	46	33	19	BURNING BRIDGES — Jack Scott, Top Rank 2041		17
57	56	51	59	WAKE ME, SHAKE ME — Coasters, Atco 6168		8
58	76	—	—	RED SAILS IN THE SUNSET — Platters and Tony Williams, Mercury 71656		2
59	—	—	—	KIDDIO — Brook Benton, Mercury 71652		1
60	68	75	79	ONE BOY — Joanie Sommers, Warner Bros. 5157		6
61	47	46	33	RUNAROUND — Fleetwoods, Dolton 22		12
62	78	89	—	LISA — Jeanne Black, Capitol 4396		3
63	79	—	—	HELLO, YOUNG LOVERS — Paul Anka, ABC-Paramount 10132		2
64	77	—	—	MY LOVE — Nat King Cole, Capitol 4393		2
65	48	56	50	HEY, LITTLE ONE — Dorsey Burnette, Era 3019		10
66	50	43	42	I'M GETTIN' BETTER — Jim Reeves, RCA Victor 7756		8
67	54	66	82	PLEASE HELP ME, I'M FALLING — Rusty Draper, Mercury 71634		4
68	38	30	17	WONDERFUL WORLD — Sam Cooke, Keen 82112		14
69	65	52	55	ALL I COULD DO WAS CRY — Etta James, Argo 5359		15
70	69	59	49	CLAP YOUR HANDS — Beau-Marks, Shad 5017		13
71	84	70	71	DO YOU MIND — Andy Williams, Cadence 1381		6
72	86	—	—	FAR FAR AWAY — Don Gibson, RCA Victor 7762		2
73	63	42	21	LOVE YOU SO — Rod Holden, Donna 1317		19
74	88	94	98	MIO AMORE — Flamingos, End 1073		4
75	—	—	—	NEVER ON SUNDAY — Don Costa, United Artists 234		1
76	95	—	—	IT ONLY HAPPENED YESTERDAY — Jack Scott, Top Rank 2055		2
77	91	93	97	BIG BOY PETE — Olympics, Arvee 595		6
78	98	—	—	WRECK OF THE "JOHN B" — Jimmie Rodgers, Roulette 4260		2
79	89	—	—	SWINGING DOWN THE LANE — Jerry Wallace, Challenge 59062		2
80	—	—	—	YOGI — Ivy Three, Shell 720		1
81	—	—	—	ANYMORE — Teresa Brewer, Coral 62219		1
82	100	98	100	NIGHT TRAIN — Viscounts, Madison 133		4
83	93	95	—	HAPPY SHADES OF BLUE — Freddy Cannon, Swan 40578		3
84	—	—	—	LITTLE BITTY PRETTY ONE — Frankie Lymon, Roulette 4257		1
85	87	100	—	COOL WATER — Jack Scott, Top Rank 2055		3
86	73	—	—	I LOVE YOU IN THE SAME OLD WAY — Paul Anka, ABC-Paramount 10132		2
87	—	—	—	YOU MEAN EVERYTHING TO ME — Neil Sedaka, RCA Victor 7781		1
88	94	97	94	I'VE BEEN LOVED BEFORE — Shirley and Lee, Warwick 538		6
89	92	—	—	IF I CAN'T HAVE YOU — Etta James and Harvey, Chess 1760		2
90	—	—	—	BRIGADE OF BROKEN HEARTS — Paul Evans, Guaranteed 210		1
91	83	87	91	THAT'S WHEN I CRIED — Jimmy Jones, Cub 9072		5
92	96	—	—	WE GO TOGETHER — Jan and Dean, Dore 555		2
93	—	—	—	HOT ROD LINCOLN — Johnny Bond, Republic 2005		1
94	90	81	74	BE BOP-A-LULA — Everly Brothers, Cadence 1380		5
95	53	61	87	TWIST — Hank Ballard and the Midnighters, King 5171		4
96	—	—	—	BLUE VELVET — Statues, Liberty 55245		1
97	99	—	—	DEVIL OR ANGEL — Bobby Vee, Liberty 55270		2
98	—	—	—	SHE'S MINE — Conway Twitty, M-G-M 12911		1
99	—	—	—	NO — Dodie Stevens, Dot 16103		1
100	—	—	—	RUN, SAMSON, RUN — Neil Sedaka, RCA Victor 7781		1

THE TOP 40 HITS
1960

PK DATE	PK POS	RANK	TITLE	ARTIST
2/22	1	1.	The Theme From "A Summer Place"	Percy Faith
11/28	1	2.	Are You Lonesome To-night?	Elvis Presley
8/15	1	3.	It's Now Or Never	Elvis Presley
5/23	1	4.	Cathy's Clown	Everly Brothers
4/25	1	5.	Stuck On You	Elvis Presley
7/18	1	6.	I'm Sorry	Brenda Lee
1/18	1	7.	Running Bear	Johnny Preston
10/17	1	8.	Save The Last Dance For Me	Drifters
2/08	1	9.	Teen Angel	Mark Dinning
9/26	1	10.	My Heart Has A Mind Of Its Own	Connie Francis
1/04	1	11.	El Paso	Marty Robbins
6/27	1	12.	Everybody's Somebody's Fool	Connie Francis
9/19	1	13.	The Twist	Chubby Checker
			re entered at #1 in 1962	
8/08	1	14.	Itsy Bitsy Teenie Weenie Yellow Polkadot Bikini	Brian Hyland
7/11	1	15.	Alley-Oop	Hollywood Argyles
10/10	1	16.	Mr. Custer	Larry Verne
10/24	1	17.	I Want To Be Wanted	Brenda Lee
11/21	1	18.	Stay	Maurice Williams & The Zodiacs
11/14	1	19.	Georgia On My Mind	Ray Charles
11/28	2	20.	Last Date	Floyd Cramer
4/18	2	21.	Greenfields	Brothers Four
3/07	2	22.	He'll Have To Go	Jim Reeves
10/03	2	23.	Chain Gang	Sam Cooke
4/04	2	24.	Puppy Love	Paul Anka
2/29	2	25.	Handy Man	Jimmy Jones
8/29	2	26.	Walk -- Don't Run	Ventures
7/25	2	27.	Only The Lonely (Know How I Feel)	Roy Orbison
3/28	2	28.	Wild One	Bobby Rydell
11/14	2	29.	Poetry In Motion	Johnny Tillotson
5/23	3	30.	Good Timin'	Jimmy Jones
6/13	3	31.	Burning Bridges	Jack Scott
12/12	3	32.	A Thousand Stars	Kathy Young with The Innocents
5/02	3	33.	Sixteen Reasons	Connie Stevens
4/25	3	34.	Sink The Bismarck	Johnny Horton
1/11	3	35.	Way Down Yonder In New Orleans	Freddy Cannon
2/08	3	36.	Where Or When	Dion & The Belmonts
11/14	3	37.	You Talk Too Much	Joe Jones
5/09	4	38.	Night	Jackie Wilson
5/30	4	39.	He'll Have To Stay	Jeanne Black
7/04	4	40.	Because They're Young	Duane Eddy & The Rebels

THE TOP 40 HITS
1961

PK DATE	PK POS	RANK	TITLE	ARTIST
7/10	1	1.	Tossin' And Turnin'	Bobby Lewis
11/06	1	2.	Big Bad John	Jimmy Dean
4/24	1	3.	Runaway	Del Shannon
1/09	1	4.	Wonderland By Night	Bert Kaempfert
2/27	1	5.	Pony Time	Chubby Checker
12/18	1	6.	The Lion Sleeps Tonight	Tokens
4/03	1	7.	Blue Moon	Marcels
9/18	1	8.	Take Good Care Of My Baby	Bobby Vee
2/13	1	9.	Calcutta	Lawrence Welk
10/23	1	10.	Runaround Sue	Dion
9/04	1	11.	Michael	Highwaymen
5/29	1	12.	Travelin' Man	Ricky Nelson
6/26	1	13.	Quarter To Three	U.S. Bonds
10/09	1	14.	Hit The Road Jack	Ray Charles
3/20	1	15.	Surrender	Elvis Presley
1/30	1	16.	Will You Love Me Tomorrow	Shirelles
5/22	1	17.	Mother-In-Law	Ernie K-Doe
12/11	1	18.	Please Mr. Postman	Marvelettes
8/28	1	19.	Wooden Heart	Joe Dowell
6/19	1	20.	Moody River	Pat Boone
6/05	1	21.	Running Scared	Roy Orbison
7/10	2	22.	The Boll Weevil Song	Brook Benton
7/31	2	23.	I Like It Like That, Part 1	Chris Kenner
10/23	2	24.	Bristol Stomp	Dovells
4/03	2	25.	Apache	Jorgen Ingmann
9/25	2	26.	The Mountain's High	Dick & DeeDee
1/23	2	27.	Exodus	Ferrante & Teicher
6/26	2	28.	Raindrops	Dee Clark
2/20	2	29.	Shop Around	Miracles
12/25	2	30.	Run To Him	Bobby Vee
10/09	2	31.	Crying	Roy Orbison
5/29	2	32.	Daddy's Home	Shep & The Limelites
3/27	3	33.	Dedicated To The One I Love	Shirelles
5/08	3	34.	A Hundred Pounds Of Clay	Gene McDaniels
12/04	3	35.	Goodbye Cruel World	James Darren
3/06	3	36.	Wheels	String-A-Longs
8/07	3	37.	Last Night	Mar-Keys
11/13	3	38.	Fool #1	Brenda Lee
9/11	3	39.	My True Story	Jive Five
3/20	3	40.	Don't Worry	Marty Robbins

THE TOP 40 HITS
1962

PK DATE	PK POS	RANK	TITLE	ARTIST
6/02	1	1.	I Can't Stop Loving You	Ray Charles
11/17	1	2.	Big Girls Don't Cry	4 Seasons
9/15	1	3.	Sherry	4 Seasons
7/14	1	4.	Roses Are Red (My Love)	Bobby Vinton
1/27	1	5.	Peppermint Twist - Part I	Joey Dee & the Starliters
12/22	1	6.	Telstar	Tornadoes
5/05	1	7.	Soldier Boy	Shirelles
3/10	1	8.	Hey! Baby	Bruce Channel
2/17	1	9.	Duke Of Earl	Gene Chandler
1/13	1	10.	The Twist	Chubby Checker
			re-entry of 1960 hit (POS 1)	
4/07	1	11.	Johnny Angel	Shelley Fabares
11/03	1	12.	He's A Rebel	Crystals
8/11	1	13.	Breaking Up Is Hard To Do	Neil Sedaka
10/20	1	14.	Monster Mash	Bobby "Boris" Pickett & The Crypt-Kickers
4/21	1	15.	Good Luck Charm	Elvis Presley
9/01	1	16.	Sheila	Tommy Roe
5/26	1	17.	Stranger On The Shore	Mr. Acker Bilk
7/07	1	18.	The Stripper	David Rose
3/31	1	19.	Don't Break The Heart That Loves You	Connie Francis
8/25	1	20.	The Loco-Motion	Little Eva
11/17	2	21.	Return To Sender	Elvis Presley
12/22	2	22.	Limbo Rock	Chubby Checker
5/05	2	23.	Mashed Potato Time	Dee Dee Sharp
9/22	2	24.	Ramblin' Rose	Nat King Cole
7/21	2	25.	The Wah Watusi	Orlons
2/03	2	26.	Can't Help Falling In Love	Elvis Presley
2/24	2	27.	The Wanderer	Dion
3/17	2	28.	Midnight In Moscow	Kenny Ball & his Jazzmen
9/08	2	29.	You Don't Know Me	Ray Charles
11/03	2	30.	Only Love Can Break A Heart	Gene Pitney
12/01	3	31.	Bobby's Girl	Marcie Blane
10/20	3	32.	Do You Love Me	Contours
11/10	3	33.	All Alone Am I	Brenda Lee
6/23	3	34.	Palisades Park	Freddy Cannon
7/28	3	35.	Sealed With A Kiss	Brian Hyland
4/14	3	36.	Slow Twistin'	Chubby Checker
2/24	3	37.	Norman	Sue Thompson
9/29	3	38.	Green Onions	Booker T. & The MG's
6/16	3	39.	It Keeps Right On A-Hurtin'	Johnny Tillotson
1/27	3	40.	I Know (You Don't Love Me No More)	Barbara George

THE TOP 40 HITS
1963

PK DATE	PK POS	RANK	TITLE	ARTIST
10/12	1	1.	Sugar Shack	Jimmy Gilmer & The Fireballs
3/30	1	2.	He's So Fine..	Chiffons
12/07	1	3.	Dominique...	Singing Nun
2/09	1	4.	Hey Paula	Paul & Paula
8/31	1	5.	My Boyfriend's Back..	Angels
9/21	1	6.	Blue Velvet..	Bobby Vinton
6/15	1	7.	Sukiyaki	Kyu Sakamoto
4/27	1	8.	I Will Follow Him	Little Peggy March
8/10	1	9.	Fingertips - Pt 2	Little Stevie Wonder
3/02	1	10.	Walk Like A Man..	4 Seasons
1/12	1	11.	Go Away Little Girl	Steve Lawrence
11/23	1	12.	I'm Leaving It Up To You.................................	Dale & Grace
7/20	1	13.	Surf City	Jan & Dean
6/01	1	14.	It's My Party	Lesley Gore
1/26	1	15.	Walk Right In	Rooftop Singers
7/06	1	16.	Easier Said Than Done	Essex
5/18	1	17.	If You Wanna Be Happy	Jimmy Soul
8/03	1	18.	So Much In Love	Tymes
11/16	1	19.	Deep Purple	Nino Tempo & April Stevens
3/23	1	20.	Our Day Will Come	Ruby & The Romantics
12/14	2	21.	Louie Louie	Kingsmen
4/13	2	22.	Can't Get Used To Losing You	Andy Williams
2/23	2	23.	Ruby Baby	Dion
10/12	2	24.	Be My Baby...	Ronettes
8/24	2	25.	Hello Mudduh, Hello Fadduh! (A Letter From Camp)	Allan Sherman
9/28	2	26.	Sally, Go 'Round The Roses	Jaynetts
8/17	2	27.	Blowin' In The Wind..	Peter, Paul & Mary
11/23	2	28.	Washington Square	Village Stompers
8/10	2	29.	Wipe Out...	Surfaris
3/23	2	30.	The End Of The World	Skeeter Davis
5/11	2	31.	Puff The Magic Dragon	Peter, Paul & Mary
9/07	3	32.	If I Had A Hammer..	Trini Lopez
3/16	3	33.	You're The Reason I'm Living	Bobby Darin
2/02	3	34.	The Night Has A Thousand Eyes	Bobby Vee
12/07	3	35.	Everybody...	Tommy Roe
8/10	3	36.	(You're the) Devil In Disguise...........................	Elvis Presley
6/22	3	37.	Hello Stranger...	Barbara Lewis
3/09	3	38.	Rhythm Of The Rain	Cascades
5/25	3	39.	Surfin' U.S.A.	Beach Boys
6/01	3	40.	I Love You Because	Al Martino

THE TOP 40 HITS
1964

PK DATE	PK POS	RANK	TITLE	ARTIST
2/01	1	1.	I Want To Hold Your Hand	Beatles
4/04	1	2.	Can't Buy Me Love	Beatles
1/04	1	3.	There! I've Said It Again	Bobby Vinton
10/31	1	4.	Baby Love	Supremes
9/26	1	5.	Oh, Pretty Woman	Roy Orbison
9/05	1	6.	The House Of The Rising Sun	Animals
6/06	1	7.	Chapel Of Love	Dixie Cups
12/26	1	8.	I Feel Fine	Beatles
3/21	1	9.	She Loves You	Beatles
5/16	1	10.	My Guy	Mary Wells
7/04	1	11.	I Get Around	Beach Boys
12/19	1	12.	Come See About Me	Supremes
8/22	1	13.	Where Did Our Love Go	Supremes
10/17	1	14.	Do Wah Diddy Diddy	Manfred Mann
8/01	1	15.	A Hard Day's Night	Beatles
7/18	1	16.	Rag Doll	4 Seasons
5/09	1	17.	Hello, Dolly!	Louis Armstrong & The All Stars
12/12	1	18.	Mr. Lonely	Bobby Vinton
8/15	1	19.	Everybody Loves Somebody	Dean Martin
6/27	1	20.	A World Without Love	Peter & Gordon
12/05	1	21.	Ringo	Lorne Greene
5/30	1	22.	Love Me Do	Beatles
11/28	1	23.	Leader Of The Pack	Shangri-Las
4/04	2	24.	Twist And Shout	Beatles
2/01	2	25.	You Don't Own Me	Lesley Gore
10/17	2	26.	Dancing In The Street	Martha & The Vandellas
9/19	2	27.	Bread And Butter	Newbeats
7/11	2	28.	Memphis	Johnny Rivers
11/07	2	29.	Last Kiss	J. Frank Wilson & The Cavaliers
12/12	2	30.	She's Not There	Zombies
7/04	2	31.	My Boy Lollipop	Millie Small
5/09	2	32.	Do You Want To Know A Secret	Beatles
2/22	3	33.	Dawn (Go Away)	Four Seasons
4/11	3	34.	Suspicion	Terry Stafford
3/14	3	35.	Please Please Me	Beatles
1/11	3	36.	Popsicles And Icicles	Murmaids
2/01	3	37.	Out Of Limits	Marketts
11/21	3	38.	Come A Little Bit Closer	Jay & The Americans
6/13	3	39.	Love Me With All Your Heart	Ray Charles Singers
8/01	3	40.	The Little Old Lady (From Pasadena)	Jan & Dean

THE TOP 40 HITS
1965

PK DATE	PK POS	RANK	TITLE	ARTIST
7/10	1	1.	(I Can't Get No) Satisfaction	Rolling Stones
10/09	1	2.	Yesterday	Beatles
12/04	1	3.	Turn! Turn! Turn!	Byrds
5/01	1	4.	Mrs. Brown You've Got A Lovely Daughter	Herman's Hermits
8/14	1	5.	I Got You Babe	Sonny & Cher
9/04	1	6.	Help!	Beatles
6/19	1	7.	I Can't Help Myself	Four Tops
2/06	1	8.	You've Lost That Lovin' Feelin'	Righteous Brothers
1/23	1	9.	Downtown	Petula Clark
2/20	1	10.	This Diamond Ring	Gary Lewis & The Playboys
3/27	1	11.	Stop! In The Name Of Love	Supremes
5/29	1	12.	Help Me, Rhonda	Beach Boys
11/06	1	13.	Get Off Of My Cloud	Rolling Stones
11/20	1	14.	I Hear A Symphony	Supremes
4/10	1	15.	I'm Telling You Now	Freddie & The Dreamers
3/13	1	16.	Eight Days A Week	Beatles
3/06	1	17.	My Girl	Temptations
10/02	1	18.	Hang On Sloopy	McCoys
6/26	1	19.	Mr. Tambourine Man	Byrds
9/25	1	20.	Eve Of Destruction	Barry McGuire
12/25	1	21.	Over And Over	Dave Clark Five
5/22	1	22.	Ticket To Ride	Beatles
8/07	1	23.	I'm Henry VIII, I Am	Herman's Hermits
4/24	1	24.	Game Of Love	Wayne Fontana & The Mindbenders
6/12	1	25.	Back In My Arms Again	Supremes
10/30	2	26.	A Lover's Concerto	Toys
6/05	2	27.	Wooly Bully	Sam The Sham & The Pharaohs
3/27	2	28.	Can't You Hear My Heartbeat	Herman's Hermits
9/04	2	29.	Like A Rolling Stone	Bob Dylan
10/16	2	30.	Treat Her Right	Roy Head & The Traits
5/08	2	31.	Count Me In	Gary Lewis & The Playboys
11/20	2	32.	1-2-3	Len Barry
8/21	2	33.	Save Your Heart For Me	Gary Lewis & The Playboys
12/18	3	34.	I Got You (I Feel Good)	James Brown & The Famous Flames
3/20	3	35.	The Birds And The Bees	Jewel Akens
1/16	3	36.	Love Potion Number Nine	Searchers
1/30	3	37.	The Name Game	Shirley Ellis
7/31	3	38.	What's New Pussycat?	Tom Jones
8/28	3	39.	California Girls	Beach Boys
12/11	3	40.	Let's Hang On!	Four Seasons

★ STAR PERFORMERS—Selections registering greatest upward progress this week.

S Indicates that 45 r.p.m. stereo single version is available. △ Indicates that 33⅓ r.p.m. mono single version is available. Indicates that 33⅓ r.p.m. stereo single version is available.

Column headers: THIS WEEK | Wk. Ago | 2 Wks. Ago | 3 Wks. Ago | TITLE — Artist, Label & Number | Weeks On Chart

This	Wk.Ago	2Wk	3Wk	TITLE — Artist, Label & Number	Wks
1	1	1	1	TOSSIN' AND TURNIN' — Bobby Lewis, Beltone 1002	17
2	2	2	5	I LIKE IT LIKE THAT — Chris Kenner, Instant 3229	12
3	3	7	12	LAST NIGHT — Mar-Keys, Satellite 107	7
4	4	4	8	DUM DUM — Brenda Lee, Decca 31272	9
5	9	13	18	WOODEN HEART (Muss I Denn) — Joe Dowell, Smash 1708	8
6	10	23	41	MICHAEL — Highwaymen, United Artists 258	6
7	7	16	24	PRETTY LITTLE ANGEL EYES — Curtis Lee, Dunes 2007	7
8	8	9	10	LET'S TWIST AGAIN — Chubby Checker, Parkway 824	9
9	6	8	9	TOGETHER — Connie Francis, MGM 13019	8
10	16	28	52	SCHOOL IS OUT — Gary (U.S.) Bonds, LeGrand 1009	4
11	15	24	35	YOU DON'T KNOW WHAT YOU'VE GOT (Until You Lose It) — Ral Donner, Gone 5108	6
12	14	19	28	I'LL BE THERE — Damita Jo, Mercury 71840	7
13	13	14	15	NEVER ON SUNDAY — Chordettes, Cadence 1402	9
14	5	5	6	HATS OFF TO LARRY — Del Shannon, Big Top 3075	11
15	20	35	66	HURT — Timi Yuro, Liberty 55343	4
16	25	30	36	DON'T BET MONEY HONEY — Linda Scott, Canadian-American 127	7
17	22	36	56	LET THE FOUR WINDS BLOW — Fats Domino, Imperial 5764	7
18	18	18	21	MY KIND OF GIRL — Matt Monro, Warwick 636	12
19	12	6	3	QUARTER TO THREE — Gary (U.S.) Bonds, LeGrand 1008	13
20	11	3	2	BOLL WEEVIL SONG — Brook Benton, Mercury 71820	14
21	32	59	78	AS IF I DIDN'T KNOW — Adam Wade, Coed 553	4
22	26	31	38	I'M GONNA KNOCK ON YOUR DOOR — Eddie Hodges, Cadence 1397	9
23	17	17	17	CUPID — Sam Cooke, RCA Victor 7883 △	11
24	28	33	37	I FALL TO PIECES — Patsy Cline, Decca 31205	13
25	40	53	61	ONE SUMMER NIGHT — Diamonds, Mercury 71831	7
26	34	61	73	I'M A-TELLING YOU — Jerry Butler, Vee Jay 390	4
27	33	45	49	QUITE A PARTY — Fireballs, Warwick 644	8
28	29	37	47	RUNAROUND — Regents, Gee 1071	6
29	19	11	11	SAN ANTONIO ROSE — Floyd Cramer, RCA Victor 7893 △	11
30	23	15	14	PLEASE STAY — Drifters, Atlantic 2105	11
31	39	43	51	A TEAR — Gene McDaniels, Liberty 55344	7
32	41	46	54	MY TRUE STORY — Jive Five, Beltone 1006	7
33	44	56	57	HILLBILLY HEAVEN — Tex Ritter, Capitol 4567	7
34	21	10	4	YELLOW BIRD — Arthur Lyman, Hi Fi 5024	12
35	24	20	20	SACRED — Castells, Era 3048	12
36	42	52	62	PRINCESS — Frank Gari, Crusade 1022	7
37	27	29	31	THAT'S WHAT GIRLS ARE MADE FOR — Spinners, Tri-Phi 1001	8
38	46	55	74	RIGHT OR WRONG — Wanda Jackson, Capitol 4553	8
39	43	34	33	SEA OF HEARTBREAK — Don Gibson, RCA Victor 7890 △	9
40	75	—	—	DOES YOUR CHEWING GUM LOSE ITS FLAVOR (On the Bedpost Over Night) — Lonnie Donegan, Dot 15911	2
41	87	—	—	TAKE GOOD CARE OF MY BABY — Bobby Vee, Liberty 55354	2
42	51	60	75	I DON'T WANT TO TAKE A CHANCE — Mary Wells, Motown 1011	5
43	62	78	97	I JUST DON'T UNDERSTAND — Ann-Margret, RCA Victor 7894 △	4
44	66	—	—	WHO PUT THE BOMP (In the Bomp, Bomp, Bomp) — Barry Mann, ABC-Paramount 10237	2
45	45	57	59	TIME WAS — Flamingos, End 1092	7
46	52	58	64	A THING OF THE PAST — Shirelles, Scepter 1220	6
47	48	51	55	THE CHARLESTON — Ernie Fields, Rendezvous 150	7
48	58	72	—	AMOR — Ben E. King, Atco 6203	3
49	84	87	—	I'LL NEVER SMILE AGAIN — Platters, Mercury 71847	3
50	31	12	7	RAINDROPS — Dee Clark, Vee Jay 383	16
51	53	62	68	MIGHTY GOOD LOVIN' — Miracles, Tamla 54044	6
52	67	—	—	DON'T CRY BABY — Etta James, Argo 5393	2
53	—	—	83	STARLIGHT, STARBRIGHT — Linda Scott, Canadian-American 127	3
54	61	63	70	NAG — Halos, Seven Arts 709	5
55	50	41	45	NO, NO, NO — Chanters, Deluxe 6191	9
56	57	68	90	I NEVER KNEW — Clyde McPhatter, Mercury 71841	4
57	60	74	98	MR. HAPPINESS — Johnny Maestro, Coed 552	4
58	30	25	27	THE FISH — Bobby Rydell, Cameo 192	7
59	70	77	92	TEARS ON MY PILLOW — McGuire Sisters, Coral 62276	4
60	64	67	69	PEANUTS — Rick and the Keens, Smash 1705	7
61	—	78	—	WITHOUT YOU — Johnny Tillotson, Cadence 1404	2
62	94	95	—	TRANSISTOR SISTER — Freddy Cannon, Swan 4078	3
63	93	85	—	MISSING YOU — Ray Peterson, Dunes 2006	3
64	74	76	—	IT'S GONNA WORK OUT FINE — Ike and Tina Turner, Sue 749	3
65	76	—	—	LET ME BELONG TO YOU — Brian Hyland, ABC-Paramount 10236	2
66	72	73	80	WATER BOY — Don Shirley Trio, Cadence 1392	5
67	—	90	—	A LITTLE BIT OF SOAP — Jarmels, Laurie 3098	2
68	85	90	—	THE MOUNTAIN'S HIGH — Dick and Deedee, Liberty 55350	3
69	71	—	—	CANDY MAN — Roy Orbison, Monument 447	2
70	54	54	60	WHAT A SWEET THING THAT WAS — Shirelles, Scepter 1220	5
71	—	—	—	CRYIN' — Roy Orbison, Monument 447	1
72	88	—	—	LONELY STREET — Clarence Henry, Argo 5395	2
73	—	—	—	LOVER'S ISLAND — Bluejays, Milestone 2008	1
74	79	80	91	THE GUNS OF NAVARONE — Joe Reisman, Landa 674	3
75	81	92	—	RUN, RUN, RUN — Ronny Douglas, Everest 19413	3
76	91	97	—	WHEN WE GET MARRIED — Dreamlovers, Heritage 102	3
77	80	86	—	TEARDROPS IN MY HEART — Joe Barry, Smash 1710	3
78	68	69	95	MY CLAIRE DE LUNE — Steve Lawrence, United Artists 335	4
79	90	—	—	HULLY GULLY AGAIN — Little Caesar & the Romans, Del-Fi 4164	2
80	89	—	—	DON'T CRY NO MORE — Bobby (Blue) Bland, Duke 340	2
81	82	94	—	NOW AND FOREVER — Bert Kaempfert, Decca 31279	3
82	83	84	89	IF — Paragons, Tap 101	5
83	—	—	—	BACK BEAT NO. 1 — Rondells, Amy 825	1
84	98	—	—	SAN-HO-ZAY — Freddy King, Federal 12428	2
85	92	99	—	SUMMER SOUVENIRS — Karl Hammil Jr., Arliss 1007	3
86	86	88	99	HERE IN MY HEART — Al Martino, Capitol 4593	4
87	—	—	—	BLESS YOU — Tony Orlando, Epic 9452	1
88	—	—	—	MAGIC MOON — Rays, XYZ 607	1
89	—	91	—	DEDICATED (To the Songs I Love) — Three Friends, Imperial 5763	2
90	95	—	—	EVERY BREATH I TAKE — Gene Pitney, Musicor 1011	2
91	—	—	—	MEXICO — Bob Moore, Monument 446	1
92	—	—	—	ROLL OVER BEETHOVEN — Velaires, Jamie 1198	1
93	96	—	—	WELL-A, WELL-A — Shirley & Lee, Warwick 664	2
94	—	—	—	IN TIME — Steve Lawrence, United Artists 335	1
95	—	—	—	MUSIC, MUSIC, MUSIC — Sensations, Argo 5391	1
96	—	—	—	STARLIGHT — Preludes Five, Pik 231	1
97	100	—	—	MY HEART'S ON FIRE — Billy Bland, Old Town 1105	2
98	—	—	—	MORE MONEY FOR YOU AND ME — Four Preps, Capitol 4599	1
99	—	—	—	GIRLS, GIRLS, GIRLS — Coasters, Atco 6204	1
100	—	—	—	PITTER PATTER — Four Sportsmen, Sunnybrook 4	1

BUBBLING UNDER THE HOT 100

1. STICK SHIFT — Duals, Sue 745
2. THEME FROM SILVER CITY — Ventures, Dolton 44
3. JOHNNY WILLOW — Fred Darian, JAF 2023
4. BLACKLAND FARMER — Wink Martindale, Dot 16243
5. MR. PAGANINI — Ella Fitzgerald, Verve 10237
6. BABY, YOU'RE RIGHT — James Brown, King 5524
7. I'LL NEVER SMILE AGAIN — Wanderers, Cub 9094
8. LOOK IN MY EYES — Chantels, Carlton 555
9. PRETTY PRETTY GIRL — Time Tones, Atco 6201
10. NOTHIN' BUT GOOD — Hank Ballard and the Midnighters, King 5535
11. DON'T FORGET I LOVE YOU — Butanes, Enrica 1007
12. YOU DON'T KNOW WHAT IT MEANS — Jackie Wilson, Brunswick 55219
13. BIG COLD WIND — Pat Boone, Dot 16244
14. JEREMIAH PEABODY'S POLY UNSATURATED QUICK DISSOLVING FAST ACTING PLEASANT TASTING GREEN AND PURPLE PILLS — Ray Stevens, Mercury 71843
15. A FAR, FAR BETTER THING — Della Reese, RCA Victor 7884
16. THE WAY YOU LOOK TONIGHT — Lettermen, Capitol 4586
17. TENNESSEE WALTZ — Don Robertson, RCA Victor 7909
18. THE BELLS ARE RINGING — Van Dykes, Deluxe 6193
19. SOMEBODY CARES — Zerro, Maxie 702
20. BLACKLAND FARMER — Frankie Miller, Starday 424

HOT 100—A TO Z

Amor 48
As If I Didn't Know 21
Back Beat No. 1 83
Bless You 87
Boll Weevil Song 20
Candy Man 69
Charleston, The 47
Cryin' 71
Cupid 23
Dedicated (To the Songs I Love) 89
Does Your Chewing Gum Lose Its Flavor 40
Don't Bet Money Honey 16
Don't Cry Baby 52
Don't Cry No More 80
Dum Dum 4
Every Breath I Take 90
Fish, The 58
Girls, Girls, Girls 99
Guns of Navarone, The 74
Hats Off to Larry 14
Here in My Heart 86
Hillbilly Heaven 33
Hully Gully Again 79
Hurt 15
I Don't Want to Take a Chance 42
I Fall to Pieces 24
I Just Don't Understand 43
I Like It Like That 2
I Never Knew 56
I'll Be There 12
I'll Never Smile Again 49
I'm A-Telling You 26
I'm Gonna Knock on Your Door 22
It's Gonna Work Out Fine 64
Last Night 3
Let Me Belong to You 65
Let's Twist Again 8
Let the Four Winds Blow 17
Little Bit of Soap, A 67
Lonely Street 72
Lover's Island 73
Magic Moon 88
Mexico 91
Mighty Good Lovin' 51
Missing You 63
More Money for You and Me 98
Mountain's High, The 68
Mr. Happiness 57
Music, Music, Music 95
My Claire de Lune 78
My Kind of Girl 18
My True Story 32
Nag 54
Never on Sunday 13
New and Forever 81
No, No, No 55
One Summer Night 25
Peanuts 60
Pitter Patter 100
Please Stay 30
Pretty Little Angel Eyes 7
Princess 36
Quarter to Three 19
Quite a Party 27
Raindrops 50
Right or Wrong 38
Roll Over Beethoven 92
Run, Run, Run 75
Runaround 28
Sacred 35
San Antonio Rose 29
San-Ho-Zay 84
School Is Out 10
Sea of Heartbreak 39
Starlight 96
Starlight, Starbright 53
Summer Souvenirs 85
Take Good Care of My Baby 41
Tear, A 31
Teardrops in My Heart 77
Tears on My Pillow 59
That's What Girls Are Made For 37
Thing of the Past, A 46
Time Was 45
Together 9
Tossin' and Turnin' 1
Transistor Sister 62
Water Boy 66
Well-A, Well-A 93
What a Sweet Thing That Was 70
When We Get Married 76
Who Put the Bomp 44
Wooden Heart 5
Yellow Bird 34
You Don't Know What You've Got 11

Billboard

For Week Ending October 12, 1963

HOT 100 ®

★ STAR performer—Sides registering greatest proportionate upward progress this week.

This Wk.	Last Wk.	2 Wks. Ago	3 Wks. Ago	TITLE, Artist, Label & Number	Wks. on Chart
1	4	19	65	SUGAR SHACK — Jimmy Gilmer and the Fireballs, Dot 16487	4
2	3	3	12	BE MY BABY — Ronettes, Philles 116	7
3	1	1	1	BLUE VELVET — Bobby Vinton, Epic 9614	10
4	5	9	10	CRY BABY — Garnet Mimms & the Enchanters, United Artists 629	9
5	2	2	5	SALLY, GO 'ROUND THE ROSES — Jaynetts, Tuff 369	6
6	9	13	23	BUSTED — Ray Charles, ABC-Paramount 10481	6
7	6	5	2	MY BOYFRIEND'S BACK — Angels, Smash 1834	11
8	16	32	50	MEAN WOMAN BLUES — Roy Orbison, Monument 824	6
9	8	4	4	HEAT WAVE — Martha & the Vandellas, Gordy 7022	11
10	17	33	52	DONNA THE PRIMA DONNA — Dion Di Muci, Columbia 42852	5
11	13	20	27	HONOLULU LULU — Jan & Dean, Liberty 55613	6
12	7	7	11	WONDERFUL! WONDERFUL! — Tymes, Parkway 884	9
13	28	35	53	THAT SUNDAY, THAT SUMMER — Nat King Cole, Capitol 5027	7
14	21	34	51	DON'T THINK TWICE IT'S ALL RIGHT — Peter, Paul & Mary, Warner Bros. 5385	5
15	14	11	7	SURFER GIRL — Beach Boys, Capitol 5009	11
16	10	6	6	THEN HE KISSED ME — Crystals, Philles 115	9
17	11	8	8	MICKEY'S MONKEY — Miracles, Tamla 54083	9
18	23	29	40	I CAN'T STAY MAD AT YOU — Skeeter Davis, RCA Victor 8219	6
19	19	24	26	PART TIME LOVE — Little Johnny Taylor, Galaxy 722	6
20	33	58	74	DEEP PURPLE — Nino Tempo & April Stevens, Atco 6273	6
21	26	31	57	TALK TO ME — Sunny and the Sunglows, Tear Drop 3014	6
22	12	12	14	A WALKIN' MIRACLE — Essex, Roulette 4515	8
23	38	69	100	WASHINGTON SQUARE — Village Stompers, Epic 9617	4
24	18	16	19	MARTIAN HOP — Ran-Dells, Chairman 4403	11
25	27	30	41	BUST OUT — Busters, Arlen 735	6
26	34	46	64	FOOLS RUSH IN — Rick Nelson, Decca 31533	5
27	15	10	3	IF I HAD A HAMMER — Trini Lopez, Reprise 20198	12
28	31	38	48	HELLO HEARTACHE, GOODBYE LOVE — Little Peggy March, RCA Victor 8221	6
29	32	41	55	I'LL TAKE YOU HOME — Drifters, Atlantic 2201	6
30	20	15	22	LITTLE DEUCE COUPE — Beach Boys, Capitol 5009	9
31	41	45	70	BLUE BAYOU — Roy Orbison, Monument 824	5
32	54	66	99	MARIA ELENA — Los Indios Tabajaras, RCA Victor 8216	4
33	22	14	13	THE MONKEY TIME — Major Lance, Okeh 7175	14
34	36	47	56	TWO TICKETS TO PARADISE — Brook Benton, Mercury 72177	6
35	58	86	—	IT'S ALL RIGHT — Impressions, ABC-Paramount 10487	3
36	46	74	—	THE GRASS IS GREENER — Brenda Lee, Decca 31539	3
37	25	35	35	ONLY IN AMERICA — Jay & the Americans, United Artists 626	9
38	29	17	21	THE KIND OF BOY YOU CAN'T FORGET — Raindrops, Jubilee 5455	10
39	50	70	—	YOU LOST THE SWEETEST BOY — Mary Wells, Motown 1048	3
40	24	26	32	WHAM — Lonnie Mack, Fraternity 912	8
41	30	21	15	PAINTED, TAINTED ROSE — Al Martino, Capitol 5000	12
42	48	59	75	A LOVE SO FINE — Chiffons, Laurie 3195	6
43	37	23	18	YOU CAN NEVER STOP ME LOVING YOU — Johnny Tillotson, Cadence 1437	10
44	42	42	45	MORE — Vic Dana, Dolton 81	10
45	56	82	—	CROSSFIRE! — Orlons, Cameo 295	3
46	59	81	—	SHE'S A FOOL — Lesley Gore, Mercury 72180	3
47	35	22	16	HEY GIRL — Freddie Scott, Colpix 692	12
48	40	43	44	BIRTHDAY PARTY — Pixies Three, Mercury 72130	9
49	63	—	—	WORKOUT STEVIE, WORKOUT — Little Stevie Wonder, Tamla 54086	2
50	51	53	60	BETTY IN BERMUDAS — Dovells, Parkway 882	7
51	39	28	17	MOCKINGBIRD — Inez Foxx, Symbol 919	17
52	43	44	46	TREAT MY BABY GOOD — Bobby Darin, Capitol 5019	8
53	65	73	82	RED SAILS IN THE SUNSET — Fats Domino, ABC-Paramount 10484	4
54	62	71	79	SEPTEMBER SONG — Jimmy Durante, Warner Bros. 5382	4
55	53	55	59	WHAT DOES A GIRL DO — Shirelles, Scepter 1259	6
56	69	—	—	MISTY — Lloyd Price, Double L 722	2
57	61	80	92	CRY TO ME — Betty Harris, Jubilee 4556	4
58	60	67	78	I'M CONFESSIN' — Frank Ifield, Capitol 5032	5
59	66	—	—	MONKEY-SHINE — Bill Black's Combo, Hi 2069	2
60	57	48	34	MORE — Kai Winding, Verve 10295	14
61	73	87	90	BABY GET IT (And Don't Quit It) — Jackie Wilson, Brunswick 55250	4
62	67	72	77	HE'S MINE — Alice Wonder Land, Bardell 774	4
63	74	—	—	TWO SIDES (To Every Story) — Etta James, Argo 5452	2
64	68	75	76	ELEPHANT WALK — Donald Jenkins & the Daylighters, Cortland 109	4
65	89	—	—	I'M LEAVING IT UP TO YOU — Dale & Grace, Montel-Michele 921	2
66	78	83	91	DOWN THE AISLE — Patty LaBelle & the Blue Belles, Newtown 2777	5
67	70	76	81	ENAMORADO — Keith Colley, Unical 3006	5
68	—	—	—	EVERYBODY — Tommy Roe, ABC-Paramount 10478	1
69	80	—	—	WALKING THE DOG — Rufus Thomas, Stax 140	2
70	79	—	—	FIRST DAY BACK AT SCHOOL — Paul & Paula, Philips 40142	2
71	96	—	—	500 MILES AWAY FROM HOME — Bobby Bare, RCA Victor 8238	2
72	85	93	—	NIGHT LIFE — Rusty Draper, Monument 823	3
73	82	90	—	(Down at) PAPA JOE'S — Dixiebelles, Sound Stage 7 2507	3
74	87	99	—	POINT PANIC — Surfaris, Decca 31538	3
75	76	78	87	MY BABE — Righteous Brothers, Moonglow 223	6
76	72	84	88	CINDY'S GONNA CRY — Johnny Crawford, Del-Fi 4231	6
77	83	97	—	LITTLE EEEFIN ANNIE — Joe Perkins, Sound Stage 7 2511	3
78	81	91	—	BLUE GUITAR — Richard Chamberlain, MGM 13170	3
79	94	—	—	NEW MEXICAN ROSE — 4 Seasons, Vee Jay 562	2
80	91	96	—	SWEET IMPOSSIBLE YOU — Brenda Lee, Decca 31529	3
81	—	—	—	SPEED BALL — Ray Stevens, Mercury 72189	1
82	84	89	—	STRANGE FEELING — Billy Stewart, Chess 1868	3
83	90	—	—	WILD! — Dee Dee Sharp, Cameo 274	2
84	86	94	—	JENNY BROWN — Smothers Brothers, Mercury 72182	3
85	95	—	—	TOYS IN THE ATTIC — Joe Sherman, World Artists 1008	2
86	—	—	—	YOUR TEEN-AGE DREAMS — Johnny Mathis, Mercury 72184	1
87	75	77	80	TEENAGE CLEOPATRA — Tracey Dey, Liberty 55604	5
88	88	98	—	EVERYBODY GO HOME — Eydie Gorme, Columbia 42854	3
89	—	—	—	BETTER TO GIVE THAN RECEIVE — Joe Hinton, Back Beat 539	1
90	—	—	—	DETROIT CITY NO. 2 — Ben Colder, MGM 13167	1
91	99	—	—	THAT'S THE WAY IT GOES — 4 Seasons, Vee Jay 562	2
92	—	—	—	COME BACK — Johnny Mathis, Mercury 72184	1
93	—	—	—	CUANDO CALIENTA EL SOL — Steve Allen, Dot 16507	1
94	—	—	—	GOTTA TRAVEL ON — Timi Yuro, Liberty 55634	1
95	—	—	—	COWBOY BOOTS — Dave Dudley, Golden Ring 3020	1
96	—	—	—	SIGNED, SEALED AND DELIVERED — James Brown & the Famous Flames, King 5803	1
97	—	—	93	LONELY DRIFTER — O'Jays, Imperial 3976	2
98	—	—	—	TWO-TEN, SIX-EIGHTEEN — Jimmie Rodgers, Dot 16527	1
99	—	—	—	DON'T WAIT TOO LONG — Tony Bennett, Columbia 42866	1
100	—	—	—	HEY LONELY ONE — Baby Washington, Sue 794	1

THE TOP 40 HITS
1966

PK DATE	PK POS	RANK	TITLE	ARTIST
12/31	1	1.	I'm A Believer	Monkees
3/05	1	2.	The Ballad Of The Green Berets	SSgt Barry Sadler
12/03	1	3.	Winchester Cathedral	New Vaudeville Band
4/09	1	4.	(You're My) Soul And Inspiration	Righteous Brothers
5/07	1	5.	Monday, Monday	Mamas & The Papas
1/08	1	6.	We Can Work It Out	Beatles
8/13	1	7.	Summer In The City	Lovin' Spoonful
9/24	1	8.	Cherish	Association
9/10	1	9.	You Can't Hurry Love	Supremes
7/30	1	10.	Wild Thing	Troggs
6/11	1	11.	Paint It, Black	Rolling Stones
10/15	1	12.	Reach Out I'll Be There	Four Tops
5/28	1	13.	When A Man Loves A Woman	Percy Sledge
2/05	1	14.	My Love	Petula Clark
11/19	1	15.	You Keep Me Hangin' On	Supremes
7/16	1	16.	Hanky Panky	Tommy James & The Shondells
1/01	1	17.	The Sounds Of Silence	Simon & Garfunkel
6/25	1	18.	Paperback Writer	Beatles
10/29	1	19.	96 Tears	? (Question Mark) & The Mysterians
11/05	1	20.	Last Train To Clarksville	Monkees
11/12	1	21.	Poor Side Of Town	Johnny Rivers
2/26	1	22.	These Boots Are Made For Walkin'	Nancy Sinatra
12/10	1	23.	Good Vibrations	Beach Boys
4/30	1	24.	Good Lovin'	Young Rascals
7/02	1	25.	Strangers In The Night	Frank Sinatra
9/03	1	26.	Sunshine Superman	Donovan
2/19	1	27.	Lightnin' Strikes	Lou Christie
12/31	2	28.	Snoopy Vs. The Red Baron	Royal Guardsmen
12/10	2	29.	Mellow Yellow	Donovan
3/19	2	30.	19th Nervous Breakdown	Rolling Stones
8/06	2	31.	Lil' Red Riding Hood	Sam The Sham & The Pharaohs
4/09	2	32.	Daydream	Lovin' Spoonful
8/20	2	33.	Sunny	Bobby Hebb
6/11	2	34.	Did You Ever Have To Make Up Your Mind?	Lovin' Spoonful
5/28	2	35.	A Groovy Kind Of Love	Mindbenders
1/29	2	36.	Barbara Ann	Beach Boys
7/09	2	37.	Red Rubber Ball	Cyrkle
4/23	2	38.	Bang Bang (My Baby Shot Me Down)	Cher
9/17	2	39.	Yellow Submarine	Beatles
5/21	2	40.	Rainy Day Women #12 & 35	Bob Dylan

THE TOP 40 HITS
1967

PK DATE	PK POS	RANK	TITLE	ARTIST
10/21	1	1.	To Sir With Love	Lulu
12/02	1	2.	Daydream Believer	Monkees
7/01	1	3.	Windy	Association
8/26	1	4.	Ode To Billie Joe	Bobbie Gentry
4/15	1	5.	Somethin' Stupid	Nancy Sinatra & Frank Sinatra
5/20	1	6.	Groovin'	Young Rascals
9/23	1	7.	The Letter	Box Tops
7/29	1	8.	Light My Fire	Doors
3/25	1	9.	Happy Together	Turtles
12/30	1	10.	Hello Goodbye	Beatles
6/03	1	11.	Respect	Aretha Franklin
2/18	1	12.	Kind Of A Drag	Buckinghams
11/25	1	13.	Incense And Peppermints	Strawberry Alarm Clock
3/11	1	14.	Love Is Here And Now You're Gone	Supremes
3/04	1	15.	Ruby Tuesday	Rolling Stones
8/19	1	16.	All You Need Is Love	Beatles
5/13	1	17.	The Happening	Supremes
3/18	1	18.	Penny Lane	Beatles
12/16	2	19.	I Heard It Through The Grapevine	Gladys Knight & The Pips
11/04	2	20.	Soul Man	Sam & Dave
3/25	2	21.	Dedicated To The One I Love	Mamas & The Papas
7/08	2	22.	Little Bit O'Soul	Music Explosion
12/02	2	23.	The Rain, The Park & Other Things	Cowsills
2/04	2	24.	Georgy Girl	Seekers
10/07	2	25.	Never My Love	Association
7/29	2	26.	I Was Made To Love Her	Stevie Wonder
9/09	2	27.	Reflections	Diana Ross & The Supremes
7/22	2	28.	Can't Take My Eyes Off You	Frankie Valli
1/28	2	29.	Tell It Like It Is	Aaron Neville
5/13	2	30.	Sweet Soul Music	Arthur Conley
4/29	2	31.	A Little Bit Me, A Little Bit You	Monkees
9/09	3	32.	Come Back When You Grow Up	Bobby Vee
5/27	3	33.	I Got Rhythm	Happenings
11/04	3	34.	It Must Be Him	Vikki Carr
8/19	3	35.	Pleasant Valley Sunday	Monkees
3/11	3	36.	Baby I Need Your Lovin'	Johnny Rivers
6/17	3	37.	She'd Rather Be With Me	Turtles
4/15	3	38.	This Is My Song	Petula Clark
5/27	4	39.	Release Me (And Let Me Love Again)	Engelbert Humperdinck
7/01	4	40.	San Francisco (Be Sure To Wear Flowers In Your Hair)	Scott McKenzie

THE TOP 40 HITS
1968

PK DATE	PK POS	RANK	TITLE	ARTIST
9/28	1	1.	Hey Jude	Beatles
12/14	1	2.	I Heard It Through The Grapevine	Marvin Gaye
2/10	1	3.	Love Is Blue	Paul Mauriat
4/13	1	4.	Honey	Bobby Goldsboro
8/17	1	5.	People Got To Be Free	Rascals
3/16	1	6.	(Sittin' On) The Dock Of The Bay	Otis Redding
6/22	1	7.	This Guy's In Love With You	Herb Alpert
6/01	1	8.	Mrs. Robinson	Simon & Garfunkel
11/30	1	9.	Love Child	Diana Ross & The Supremes
5/18	1	10.	Tighten Up	Archie Bell & The Drells
8/03	1	11.	Hello, I Love You	Doors
1/20	1	12.	Judy In Disguise (With Glasses)	John Fred & His Playboy Band
7/20	1	13.	Grazing In The Grass	Hugh Masekela
9/21	1	14.	Harper Valley P.T.A.	Jeannie C. Riley
2/03	1	15.	Green Tambourine	Lemon Pipers
2/24	2	16.	(Theme From) Valley Of The Dolls	Dionne Warwick
4/06	2	17.	Young Girl	Union Gap featuring Gary Puckett
11/02	2	18.	Those Were The Days	Mary Hopkin
6/29	2	19.	The Horse	Cliff Nobles & Co.
8/24	2	20.	Born To Be Wild	Steppenwolf
12/28	2	21.	For Once In My Life	Stevie Wonder
1/20	2	22.	Chain Of Fools	Aretha Franklin
4/27	2	23.	Cry Like A Baby	Box Tops
8/03	2	24.	Classical Gas	Mason Williams
7/20	2	25.	Lady Willpower	Gary Puckett & The Union Gap
10/26	2	26.	Little Green Apples	O.C. Smith
6/01	2	27.	The Good, The Bad And The Ugly	Hugo Montenegro
10/19	2	28.	Fire	Crazy World Of Arthur Brown
6/22	2	29.	MacArthur Park	Richard Harris
7/27	3	30.	Stoned Soul Picnic	5th Dimension
2/10	3	31.	Spooky	Classics IV
7/06	3	32.	Jumpin' Jack Flash	Rolling Stones
8/31	3	33.	Light My Fire	Jose Feliciano
5/25	3	34.	A Beautiful Morning	Rascals
3/30	3	35.	Valleri	Monkees
11/30	3	36.	Magic Carpet Ride	Steppenwolf
6/15	3	37.	Mony Mony	Tommy James & The Shondells
3/09	4	38.	Simon Says	1910 Fruitgum Co.
1/13	4	39.	Woman, Woman	Union Gap featuring Gary Puckett
4/20	4	40.	Lady Madonna	Beatles

THE TOP 40 HITS
1969

PK DATE	PK POS	RANK	TITLE	ARTIST
4/12	1	1.	Aquarius/Let The Sunshine In	5th Dimension
7/12	1	2.	In The Year 2525	Zager & Evans
5/24	1	3.	Get Back	Beatles
9/20	1	4.	Sugar, Sugar	Archies
8/23	1	5.	Honky Tonk Women	Rolling Stones
2/15	1	6.	Everyday People	Sly & The Family Stone
3/15	1	7.	Dizzy	Tommy Roe
11/08	1	8.	Wedding Bell Blues	5th Dimension
10/18	1	9.	I Can't Get Next To You	Temptations
2/01	1	10.	Crimson And Clover	Tommy James & The Shondells
12/06	1	11.	Na Na Hey Hey Kiss Him Goodbye	Steam
6/28	1	12.	Love Theme From Romeo & Juliet	Henry Mancini
12/20	1	13.	Leaving On A Jet Plane	Peter, Paul & Mary
11/29	1	14.	Come Together/Something	Beatles
12/27	1	15.	Someday We'll Be Together	Diana Ross & The Supremes
11/01	1	16.	Suspicious Minds	Elvis Presley
7/26	2	17.	Crystal Blue Persuasion	Tommy James & The Shondells
3/08	2	18.	Proud Mary	Creedence Clearwater Revival
7/05	2	19.	Spinning Wheel	Blood, Sweat & Tears
8/23	2	20.	A Boy Named Sue	Johnny Cash
4/12	2	21.	You've Made Me So Very Happy	Blood, Sweat & Tears
5/10	2	22.	Hair	Cowsills
1/11	2	23.	I'm Gonna Make You Love Me	Diana Ross & The Supremes & The Temptations
10/18	2	24.	Hot Fun In The Summertime	Sly & The Family Stone
10/04	2	25.	Jean	Oliver
5/31	2	26.	Love (Can Make You Happy)	Mercy
9/27	2	27.	Green River	Creedence Clearwater Revival
11/22	2	28.	Take A Letter Maria	R.B. Greaves
5/03	2	29.	It's Your Thing	Isley Brothers
11/29	2	30.	And When I Die	Blood, Sweat & Tears
6/28	2	31.	Bad Moon Rising	Creedence Clearwater Revival
3/29	2	32.	Traces	Classics IV featuring Dennis Yost
2/22	3	33.	Build Me Up Buttercup	Foundations
10/04	3	34.	Little Woman	Bobby Sherman
2/01	3	35.	Worst That Could Happen	Brooklyn Bridge
3/29	3	36.	Time Of The Season	Zombies
7/12	3	37.	Good Morning Starshine	Oliver
1/11	3	38.	Wichita Lineman	Glen Campbell
12/20	3	39.	Down On The Corner	Creedence Clearwater Revival
2/15	3	40.	Touch Me	Doors

THE TOP 40 HITS
1970

PK DATE	PK POS	RANK	TITLE	ARTIST
2/28	1	1.	Bridge Over Troubled Water	Simon & Garfunkel
10/27	1	2.	I'll Be There	Jacksons
1/03	1	3.	Raindrops Keep Fallin' On My Head	B.J. Thomas
7/25	1	4.	(They Long To Be) Close To You	Carpenters
12/26	1	5.	My Sweet Lord	George Harrison
11/21	1	6.	I Think I Love You	Partridge Family
9/19	1	7.	Ain't No Mountain High Enough	Diana Ross
5/09	1	8.	American Woman	Guess Who
8/29	1	9.	War	Edwin Starr
4/11	1	10.	Let It Be	Beatles
12/12	1	11.	The Tears Of A Clown	Smokey Robinson & The Miracles
7/11	1	12.	Mama Told Me (Not To Come)	Three Dog Night
4/25	1	13.	ABC	Jackson 5
6/27	1	14.	The Love You Save	Jackson 5
2/14	1	15.	Thank You (Falettinme Be Mice Elf Agin)	Sly & The Family Stone
5/30	1	16.	Everything Is Beautiful	Ray Stevens
6/13	1	17.	The Long And Winding Road	Beatles
8/22	1	18.	Make It With You	Bread
1/31	1	19.	I Want You Back	Jackson 5
2/07	1	20.	Venus	Shocking Blue
10/10	1	21.	Cracklin' Rosie	Neil Diamond
10/31	2	22.	We've Only Just Begun	Carpenters
12/26	2	23.	One Less Bell To Answer	5th Dimension
6/06	2	24.	Which Way You Goin' Billy?	Poppy Family featuring Susan Jacks
3/07	2	25.	Travelin' Band	Creedence Clearwater Revival
10/03	2	26.	Lookin' Out My Back Door	Creedence Clearwater Revival
2/21	2	27.	Hey There Lonely Girl	Eddie Holman
3/21	2	28.	The Rapper	Jaggerz
5/23	2	29.	Vehicle	Ides Of March
6/27	3	30.	Ball Of Confusion (That's What The World Is Today)	Temptations
10/31	3	31.	Fire And Rain	James Taylor
4/18	3	32.	Spirit In The Sky	Norman Greenbaum
3/28	3	33.	Instant Karma (We All Shine On)	John Ono Lennon
12/05	3	34.	Gypsy Woman	Brian Hyland
10/03	3	35.	Candida	Dawn
10/17	3	36.	Green-Eyed Lady	Sugarloaf
8/08	3	37.	Signed, Sealed, Delivered I'm Yours	Stevie Wonder
5/30	3	38.	Love On A Two-Way Street	Moments
7/25	3	39.	Band Of Gold	Freda Payne
8/22	3	40.	Spill The Wine	Eric Burdon & War

THE TOP 40 HITS
1971

PK DATE	PK POS	RANK	TITLE	ARTIST
4/17	1	1.	Joy To The World	Three Dog Night
10/02	1	2.	Maggie May	Rod Stewart
6/19	1	3.	It's Too Late	Carole King
2/13	1	4.	One Bad Apple	Osmonds
8/07	1	5.	How Can You Mend A Broken Heart	Bee Gees
1/23	1	6.	Knock Three Times	Dawn
12/25	1	7.	Brand New Key	Melanie
9/11	1	8.	Go Away Little Girl	Donny Osmond
12/04	1	9.	Family Affair	Sly & The Family Stone
11/06	1	10.	Gypsys, Tramps & Thieves	Cher
4/03	1	11.	Just My Imagination (Running Away With Me)	Temptations
11/20	1	12.	Theme From Shaft	Isaac Hayes
3/20	1	13.	Me And Bobby McGee	Janis Joplin
5/29	1	14.	Brown Sugar	Rolling Stones
7/24	1	15.	Indian Reservation (The Lament Of The Cherokee Reservation Indian)	Raiders
7/31	1	16.	You've Got A Friend	James Taylor
9/04	1	17.	Uncle Albert/Admiral Halsey	Paul & Linda McCartney
6/12	1	18.	Want Ads	Honey Cone
4/10	2	19.	What's Going On	Marvin Gaye
5/08	2	20.	Never Can Say Goodbye	Jackson 5
8/14	2	21.	Mr. Big Stuff	Jean Knight
10/16	2	22.	Superstar	Carpenters
6/19	2	23.	Rainy Days And Mondays	Carpenters
9/11	2	24.	Spanish Harlem	Aretha Franklin
2/27	2	25.	Mama's Pearl	Jackson 5
8/28	2	26.	Take Me Home, Country Roads	John Denver with Fat City
3/20	2	27.	She's A Lady	Tom Jones
5/01	2	28.	Put Your Hand In The Hand	Ocean
10/16	3	29.	Yo-Yo	Osmonds
12/11	3	30.	Have You Seen Her	Chi-Lites
7/03	3	31.	Treat Her Like A Lady	Cornelius Brothers & Sister Rose
3/13	3	32.	For All We Know	Carpenters
2/13	3	33.	Rose Garden	Lynn Anderson
9/04	3	34.	Smiling Faces Sometimes	Undisputed Truth
9/18	3	35.	Ain't No Sunshine	Bill Withers
11/13	3	36.	Imagine	John Lennon/Plastic Ono Band
11/27	3	37.	Baby I'm-A Want You	Bread
10/02	3	38.	The Night They Drove Old Dixie Down	Joan Baez
1/30	3	39.	Lonely Days	Bee Gees
8/28	3	40.	Signs	Five Man Electrical Band

★ STAR performer—Sides registering greatest proportionate upward progress this week.

Record Industry Association of America seal of certification as million selling single.

TW	LW	2WA	3WA	TITLE, Artist, Label & Number	Wks on Chart
1	5	6	10	RINGO — Lorne Greene, RCA Victor 8444	6
2	6	11	21	MR. LONELY — Bobby Vinton, Epic 9730	6
3	1	2	2	LEADER OF THE PACK — Shangri-Las, Red Bird 10-014	9
4	4	5	9	SHE'S NOT THERE — Zombies, Parrot 9695	8
5	2	1	1	BABY LOVE — Supremes, Motown 1066	10
6	8	10	18	TIME IS ON MY SIDE — Rolling Stones, London 9708	8
7	7	8	13	YOU REALLY GOT ME — Kinks, Reprise 0306	11
8	13	31	66	COME SEE ABOUT ME — Supremes, Motown 1068	4
9	10	19	33	MOUNTAIN OF LOVE — Johnny Rivers, Imperial 66075	6
10	11	12	19	I'M GONNA BE STRONG — Gene Pitney, Musicor 1045	7
11	3	3	4	COME A LITTLE BIT CLOSER — Jay & the Americans, United Artists 759	13
12	12	14	22	ASK ME — Elvis Presley, RCA Victor 8440	9
13	15	29	54	DANCE, DANCE, DANCE — Beach Boys, Capitol 5306	4
14	16	22	31	RIGHT OR WRONG — Ronnie Dove, Diamond 173	7
15	19	20	28	I'M INTO SOMETHING GOOD — Herman's Hermits, MGM 13280	8
16	9	4	3	LAST KISS — J. Frank Wilson & the Cavaliers, Josie 923	14
17	24	36	56	GOIN' OUT OF MY HEAD — Little Anthony & the Imperials, DCP 1119	5
18	18	24	29	EVERYTHING'S ALRIGHT — Newbeats, Hickory 1282	7
19	28	47	71	SHA LA LA — Manfred Mann, Ascot 2165	3
20	22	27	53	BIG MAN IN TOWN — 4 Seasons, Philips 40238	5
21	26	59	73	THE JERK — Larks, Money 106	4
22	—	—	—	I FEEL FINE — Beatles, Capitol 5327	1
23	29	34	47	WALKING IN THE RAIN — Ronettes, Philles 123	7
24	30	61	82	SATURDAY NIGHT AT THE MOVIES — Drifters, Atlantic 2260	4
25	27	32	42	SIDEWALK SURFIN' — Jan & Dean, Liberty 55727	6
26	20	23	30	REACH OUT FOR ME — Dionne Warwick, Scepter 1285	7
27	25	16	17	AIN'T THAT LOVING YOU BABY — Elvis Presley, RCA Victor 8440	9
28	14	7	5	HAVE I THE RIGHT? — Honeycombs, Interphon 7707	12
29	17	17	20	IS IT TRUE — Brenda Lee, Decca 31690	8
30	40	52	70	MY LOVE FORGIVE ME (Amore, Scusami) — Robert Goulet, Columbia 43131	7
31	46	63	78	ANY WAY YOU WANT IT — Dave Clark Five, Epic 9739	4
32	44	51	52	GONE, GONE, GONE — Everly Brothers, Warner Bros. 5478	8
33	41	53	68	OH NO, NOT MY BABY — Maxine Brown, Wand 162	7
34	21	13	11	OH, PRETTY WOMAN — Roy Orbison, Monument 851	15
35	23	9	6	THE DOOR IS STILL OPEN TO MY HEART — Dean Martin, Reprise 0307	11
36	39	46	58	SHE UNDERSTANDS ME — Johnny Tillotson, MGM 13284	6
37	51	81	—	THE WEDDING — Julie Rogers, Mercury 72332	3
38	50	60	74	TOO MANY FISH IN THE SEA — Marvelettes, Tamla 54105	5
39	35	38	45	SLAUGHTER ON 10TH AVE. — Ventures, Dolton 300	7
40	36	33	34	WHO CAN I TURN TO — Tony Bennett, Columbia 43141	7
41	43	48	59	WE COULD — Al Martino, Capitol 5293	5
42	38	44	55	SHAGGY DOG — Mickey Lee Lane, Swan 4183	9
43	59	96	—	AMEN — Impressions, ABC-Paramount 10602	3
44	55	79	94	WILLOW WEEP FOR ME — Chad & Jeremy, World Artists 1034	4
45	47	50	60	AIN'T IT THE TRUTH — Mary Wells, 20th Century-Fox 544	6
46	—	—	—	SHE'S A WOMAN — Beatles, Capitol 5327	1
47	42	42	48	DON'T EVER LEAVE ME — Connie Francis, MGM 13287	4
48	63	71	90	RUN, RUN, RUN — Gestures, Soma 1417	4
49	65	88	—	HOW SWEET IT IS — Marvin Gaye, Tamla 54107	3
50	81	—	—	AS TEARS GO BY — Marianne Faithfull, London 9697	2
51	68	—	—	WITHOUT THE ONE YOU LOVE — Four Tops, Motown 1069	2
52	77	94	—	THOU SHALT NOT STEAL — Dick & Deedee, Warner Bros. 5482	3
53	78	—	—	DEAR HEART — Andy Williams, Columbia 43180	2
54	64	73	89	ONE MORE TIME — Ray Charles Singers, Command 4057	4
55	71	87	—	KEEP SEARCHIN' — Del Shannon, Amy 915	3
56	56	67	67	S-W-I-M — Bobby Freeman, Autumn 5	6
57	75	—	—	DEAR HEART — Jack Jones, Kapp 635	2
58	58	64	79	IT AIN'T ME, BABE — Johnny Cash, Columbia 43145	6
59	62	78	99	SINCE I DON'T HAVE YOU — Chuck Jackson, Wand 169	4
60	53	45	46	NEEDLE IN A HAYSTACK — Velvelettes, V.I.P. 25007	8
61	83	—	—	LOVE POTION NUMBER NINE — Searchers, Kapp Winner's Circle 27	2
62	79	—	—	WALK AWAY — Matt Monro, Liberty 55745	2
63	—	—	—	WILD ONE — Martha & the Vandellas, Gordy 7036	1
64	66	70	72	OPPORTUNITY — Jewels, Dimension 1034	9
65	69	74	75	LISTEN LONELY GIRL — Johnny Mathis, Mercury 72339	7
66	60	69	81	FOUR STRONG WINDS — Bobby Bare, RCA Victor 8443	6
67	67	77	96	ALMOST THERE — Andy Williams, Columbia 43128	4
68	76	—	—	THE PRICE — Solomon Burke, Atlantic 2259	2
69	82	97	—	THE 81 — Candy & the Kisses, Cameo 336	3
70	86	—	—	MY LOVE (Roses Are Red) — "You Know Who" Group, 4 Corners 112	2
71	96	—	—	DO-WACKA-DO — Roger Miller, Smash 1947	2
72	73	75	83	IF YOU WANT THIS LOVE — Sonny Knight, Aura 403	4
73	89	—	—	(There's) ALWAYS SOMETHING THERE TO REMIND ME — Sandie Shaw, Reprise 0320	2
74	90	—	—	I'M GONNA LOVE YOU TOO — Hullaballoos, Roulette 4587	2
75	72	72	80	CALIFORNIA BOUND — Ronny & the Daytonas, Mala 490	5
76	92	—	—	DON'T FORGET I STILL LOVE YOU — Bobbi Martin, Coral 63426	2
77	80	99	—	IT'S ALL OVER — Walter Jackson, Okeh 7204	3
78	—	—	—	WHAT NOW — Gene Chandler, Constellation 141	1
79	—	—	—	SMILE — Betty Everett & Jerry Butler, Vee Jay 633	1
80	—	—	—	LEADER OF THE LAUNDROMAT — Detergents, Roulette 4590	1
81	—	—	—	HAWAII TATTOO — Waikikis, Kapp Winner's Circle 30	1
82	84	85	97	DO ANYTHING YOU WANNA — Harold Betters, Gateway 747	4
83	98	—	—	GETTING MIGHTY CROWDED — Betty Everett, Vee Jay 628	2
84	85	—	—	A WOMAN'S LOVE — Carla Thomas, Atlantic 2258	2
85	88	—	—	HEY, LITTLE ONE — J. Frank Wilson & the Cavaliers, Josie 926	2
86	94	95	—	SCRATCHY — Travis Wammack, Ara 204	3
87	—	—	—	PARTY GIRL — Tommy Roe, ABC-Paramount 10604	1
88	—	—	—	SOMETIMES I WONDER — Major Lance, Okeh 7209	1
89	—	—	—	BOOM, BOOM — Animals, MGM 13298	1
90	—	—	—	LOVIN' PLACE — Gale Garnett, RCA Victor 8472	1
91	99	—	—	A HAPPY GUY — Rick Nelson, Decca 31703	2
92	93	93	—	HERE SHE COMES — Tymes, Parkway 934	3
93	95	98	—	I WON'T FORGET YOU — Jim Reeves, RCA Victor 8461	3
94	97	—	—	YOU'RE THE ONLY WORLD I KNOW — Sonny James, Capitol 5280	2
95	—	—	—	TALK TO ME BABY — Barry Mann, Red Bird 10-015	1
96	—	—	—	ENDLESS SLEEP — Hank Williams Jr., MGM 13278	1
97	—	—	—	PRETEND YOU DON'T SEE HER — Bobby Vee, Liberty 55751	1
98	—	—	—	FIDDLER ON THE ROOF — Village Stompers, Epic 9740	1
99	—	—	—	ROME WILL NEVER LEAVE YOU — Richard Chamberlain, MGM 13285	1
100	—	—	—	I DON'T WANT TO WALK WITHOUT YOU — Phyllis McGuire, Reprise 0310	1

ELTON JOHN—CROCODILE ROCK (3:56)

(prod: Gus Dudgeon) (writers: John-Taupin) (James, BMI) Followup to his top 10 winner "Honky Cat" is a clever easy beat rocker with a sound and flavor of the 50's hits. First on the label change from Uni to MCA. Flip: "Elderberry Wine" (3:34) (James, BMI) **MCA** 40000

THE TOP 40 HITS
1972

PK DATE	PK POS	RANK	TITLE	ARTIST
4/15	1	1.	The First Time Ever I Saw Your Face	Roberta Flack
7/29	1	2.	Alone Again (Naturally)	Gilbert O'Sullivan
1/15	1	3.	American Pie - Parts I & II	Don McLean
2/19	1	4.	Without You	Nilsson
11/04	1	5.	I Can See Clearly Now	Johnny Nash
3/25	1	6.	A Horse With No Name	America
9/23	1	7.	Baby Don't Get Hooked On Me	Mac Davis
12/16	1	8.	Me And Mrs. Jones	Billy Paul
6/10	1	9.	The Candy Man	Sammy Davis, Jr.
7/08	1	10.	Lean On Me	Bill Withers
10/21	1	11.	My Ding-A-Ling	Chuck Berry
8/26	1	12.	Brandy (You're A Fine Girl)	Looking Glass
2/12	1	13.	Let's Stay Together	Al Green
12/09	1	14.	I Am Woman	Helen Reddy
6/03	1	15.	I'll Take You There	Staple Singers
3/18	1	16.	Heart Of Gold	Neil Young
5/27	1	17.	Oh Girl	Chi-Lites
10/14	1	18.	Ben	Michael Jackson
12/02	1	19.	Papa Was A Rollin' Stone	Temptations
7/01	1	20.	Song Sung Blue	Neil Diamond
9/16	1	21.	Black & White	Three Dog Night
5/06	2	22.	I Gotcha	Joe Tex
9/02	2	23.	Long Cool Woman (In A Black Dress)	Hollies
7/15	2	24.	Too Late To Turn Back Now	Cornelius Brothers & Sister Rose
4/22	2	25.	Rockin' Robin	Michael Jackson
11/04	2	26.	Nights In White Satin	Moody Blues
12/30	2	27.	Clair	Gilbert O'Sullivan
2/26	2	28.	Hurting Each Other	Carpenters
11/18	2	29.	I'd Love You To Want Me	Lobo
10/14	2	30.	Use Me	Bill Withers
7/08	2	31.	Outa-Space	Billy Preston
10/28	2	32.	Burning Love	Elvis Presley
3/11	3	33.	The Lion Sleeps Tonight	Robert John
8/05	3	34.	(If Loving You Is Wrong) I Don't Want To Be Right	Luther Ingram
2/26	3	35.	Precious And Few	Climax
12/23	3	36.	You Ought To Be With Me	Al Green
9/02	3	37.	I'm Still In Love With You	Al Green
12/09	3	38.	If You Don't Know Me By Now	Harold Melvin & The Bluenotes
11/18	3	39.	I'll Be Around	Spinners
9/23	3	40.	Saturday In The Park	Chicago

THE TOP 40 HITS
1973

PK DATE	PK POS	RANK	TITLE	ARTIST
2/24	1	1.	Killing Me Softly With His Song	Roberta Flack
4/21	1	2.	Tie A Yellow Ribbon Round The Ole Oak Tree	Dawn featuring Tony Orlando
6/02	1	3.	My Love	Paul McCartney & Wings
1/06	1	4.	You're So Vain	Carly Simon
2/03	1	5.	Crocodile Rock	Elton John
9/08	1	6.	Let's Get It On	Marvin Gaye
11/10	1	7.	Keep On Truckin' (Part 1)	Eddie Kendricks
10/27	1	8.	Midnight Train To Georgia	Gladys Knight & The Pips
7/21	1	9.	Bad, Bad Leroy Brown	Jim Croce
12/01	1	10.	Top Of The World	Carpenters
8/25	1	11.	Brother Louie	Stories
7/07	1	12.	Will It Go Round In Circles	Billy Preston
10/06	1	13.	Half-Breed	Cher
4/07	1	14.	The Night The Lights Went Out In Georgia	Vicki Lawrence
12/29	1	15.	Time In A Bottle	Jim Croce
12/15	1	16.	The Most Beautiful Girl	Charlie Rich
8/04	1	17.	The Morning After	Maureen McGovern
8/18	1	18.	Touch Me In The Morning	Diana Ross
9/15	1	19.	Delta Dawn	Helen Reddy
5/26	1	20.	Frankenstein	Edgar Winter Group
5/19	1	21.	You Are The Sunshine Of My Life	Stevie Wonder
10/20	1	22.	Angie	Rolling Stones
6/30	1	23.	Give Me Love (Give Me Peace On Earth)	George Harrison
9/29	1	24.	We're An American Band	Grand Funk
1/27	1	25.	Superstition	Stevie Wonder
3/24	1	26.	Love Train	O'Jays
11/24	1	27.	Photograph	Ringo Starr
2/24	2	28.	Dueling Banjos	Eric Weissberg & Steve Mandell
12/08	2	29.	Goodbye Yellow Brick Road	Elton John
8/11	2	30.	Live And Let Die	Wings
6/16	2	31.	Playground In My Mind	Clint Holmes
7/07	2	32.	Kodachrome	Paul Simon
4/07	2	33.	Neither One Of Us (Wants To Be The First To Say Goodbye)	Gladys Knight & The Pips
4/28	2	34.	The Cisco Kid	War
10/06	2	35.	Loves Me Like A Rock	Paul Simon with The Dixie Hummingbirds
6/02	2	36.	Daniel	Elton John
10/13	2	37.	Ramblin Man	Allman Brothers Band
7/28	2	38.	Yesterday Once More	Carpenters
3/31	2	39.	Also Sprach Zarathustra (2001)	Deodato
5/05	3	40.	Little Willy	Sweet

THE TOP 40 HITS
1974

PK DATE	PK POS	RANK	TITLE	ARTIST
2/02	1	1.	The Way We Were	Barbra Streisand
3/02	1	2.	Seasons In The Sun	Terry Jacks
5/18	1	3.	The Streak	Ray Stevens
8/24	1	4.	(You're) Having My Baby	Paul Anka
12/07	1	5.	Kung Fu Fighting	Carl Douglas
6/15	1	6.	Billy, Don't Be A Hero	Bo Donaldson & The Heywoods
7/27	1	7.	Annie's Song	John Denver
5/04	1	8.	The Loco-Motion	Grand Funk
4/20	1	9.	TSOP (The Sound Of Philadelphia)	MFSB featuring The Three Degrees
11/23	1	10.	I Can Help	Billy Swan
7/13	1	11.	Rock Your Baby	George McCrae
10/05	1	12.	I Honestly Love You	Olivia Newton-John
4/13	1	13.	Bennie And The Jets	Elton John
1/12	1	14.	The Joker	Steve Miller Band
10/26	1	15.	Then Came You	Dionne Warwicke & Spinners
2/09	1	16.	Love's Theme	Love Unlimited Orchestra
1/19	1	17.	Show And Tell	Al Wilson
11/02	1	18.	You Haven't Done Nothin	Stevie Wonder
10/19	1	19.	Nothing From Nothing	Billy Preston
4/06	1	20.	Hooked On A Feeling	Blue Swede
3/30	1	21.	Sunshine On My Shoulders	John Denver
6/08	1	22.	Band On The Run	Paul McCartney & Wings
1/26	1	23.	You're Sixteen	Ringo Starr
6/29	1	24.	Sundown	Gordon Lightfoot
9/28	1	25.	Rock Me Gently	Andy Kim
12/28	1	26.	Angie Baby	Helen Reddy
8/10	1	27.	Feel Like Makin' Love	Roberta Flack
12/21	1	28.	Cat's In The Cradle	Harry Chapin
3/23	1	29.	Dark Lady	Cher
8/17	1	30.	The Night Chicago Died	Paper Lace
11/09	1	31.	You Ain't Seen Nothing Yet	Bachman-Turner Overdrive
7/06	1	32.	Rock The Boat	Hues Corporation
9/14	1	33.	I Shot The Sheriff	Eric Clapton
9/21	1	34.	Can't Get Enough Of Your Love, Babe	Barry White
11/16	1	35.	Whatever Gets You Thru The Night	John Lennon with The Plastic Ono Nuclear Band
5/18	2	36.	Dancing Machine	Jackson 5
6/15	2	37.	You Make Me Feel Brand New	Stylistics
11/16	2	38.	Do It ('Til You're Satisfied)	B.T. Express
3/09	2	39.	Boogie Down	Eddie Kendricks
7/27	2	40.	Don't Let The Sun Go Down On Me	Elton John

THE TOP 40 HITS
1975

PK DATE	PK POS	RANK	TITLE	ARTIST
6/21	1	1.	Love Will Keep Us Together	Captain & Tennille
11/29	1	2.	Fly, Robin, Fly	Silver Convention
11/01	1	3.	Island Girl	Elton John
5/03	1	4.	He Don't Love You (Like I Love You)	Tony Orlando & Dawn
10/11	1	5.	Bad Blood	Neil Sedaka
9/06	1	6.	Rhinestone Cowboy	Glen Campbell
4/12	1	7.	Philadelphia Freedom	Elton John Band
11/22	1	8.	That's The Way (I Like It)	KC & The Sunshine Band
8/09	1	9.	Jive Talkin'	Bee Gees
9/20	1	10.	Fame	David Bowie
1/04	1	11.	Lucy In The Sky With Diamonds	Elton John
8/02	1	12.	One Of These Nights	Eagles
9/27	1	13.	I'm Sorry	John Denver
5/31	1	14.	Before The Next Teardrop Falls	Freddy Fender
3/22	1	15.	My Eyes Adored You	Frankie Valli
4/05	1	16.	Lovin' You	Minnie Riperton
2/01	1	17.	Laughter In The Rain	Neil Sedaka
4/26	1	18.	(Hey Won't You Play) Another Somebody Done Somebody Wrong Song	B.J. Thomas
3/29	1	19.	Lady Marmalade	Patti LaBelle
2/22	1	20.	Pick Up The Pieces	AWB (Average White Band)
7/26	1	21.	The Hustle	Van McCoy & The Soul City Symphony
3/15	1	22.	Black Water	Doobie Brothers
12/27	1	23.	Let's Do It Again	Staple Singers
3/08	1	24.	Have You Never Been Mellow	Olivia Newton-John
7/19	1	25.	Listen To What The Man Said	Wings
3/01	1	26.	Best Of My Love	Eagles
8/23	1	27.	Fallin' In Love	Hamilton, Joe Frank & Reynolds
6/07	1	28.	Thank God I'm A Country Boy	John Denver
5/24	1	29.	Shining Star	Earth, Wind & Fire
1/25	1	30.	Please Mr. Postman	Carpenters
1/18	1	31.	Mandy	Barry Manilow
2/15	1	32.	You're No Good	Linda Ronstadt
2/08	1	33.	Fire	Ohio Players
6/14	1	34.	Sister Golden Hair	America
8/30	1	35.	Get Down Tonight	K.C. & The Sunshine Band
7/26	2	36.	I'm Not In Love	10cc
6/21	2	37.	When Will I Be Loved	Linda Ronstadt
1/04	2	38.	You're The First, The Last, My Everything	Barry White
11/08	2	39.	Lyin' Eyes	Eagles
10/18	3	40.	Miracles	Jefferson Starship

THE TOP 40 HITS
1976

PK DATE	PK POS	RANK	TITLE	ARTIST
11/13	1	1.	Tonight's The Night (Gonna Be Alright)	Rod Stewart
5/22	1	2.	Silly Love Songs	Wings
8/07	1	3.	Don't Go Breaking My Heart	Elton John & Kiki Dee
4/03	1	4.	Disco Lady	Johnnie Taylor
9/18	1	5.	Play That Funky Music	Wild Cherry
3/13	1	6.	December, 1963 (Oh, What a Night)	Four Seasons
2/07	1	7.	50 Ways To Leave Your Lover	Paul Simon
7/24	1	8.	Kiss And Say Goodbye	Manhattans
10/23	1	9.	If You Leave Me Now	Chicago
5/29	1	10.	Love Hangover	Diana Ross
7/10	1	11.	Afternoon Delight	Starland Vocal Band
9/11	1	12.	(Shake, Shake, Shake) Shake Your Booty	KC & The Sunshine Band
10/09	1	13.	A Fifth Of Beethoven	Walter Murphy & The Big Apple Band
10/16	1	14.	Disco Duck (Part 1)	Rick Dees & His Cast Of Idiots
1/17	1	15.	I Write The Songs	Barry Manilow
1/31	1	16.	Love Rollercoaster	Ohio Players
5/15	1	17.	Boogie Fever	Sylvers
1/24	1	18.	Theme From Mahogany (Do You Know Where You're Going To)	Diana Ross
9/04	1	19.	You Should Be Dancing	Bee Gees
5/01	1	20.	Let Your Love Flow	Bellamy Brothers
1/10	1	21.	Convoy	C.W. McCall
5/08	1	22.	Welcome Back	John Sebastian
3/06	1	23.	Love Machine (Part 1)	Miracles
2/28	1	24.	Theme From S.W.A.T.	Rhythm Heritage
1/03	1	25.	Saturday Night	Bay City Rollers
11/06	1	26.	Rock'n Me	Steve Miller
12/04	2	27.	The Rubberband Man	Spinners
6/12	2	28.	Get Up And Boogie (That's Right)	Silver Convention
3/27	2	29.	Dream Weaver	Gary Wright
3/06	2	30.	All By Myself	Eric Carmen
9/25	2	31.	I'd Really Love To See You Tonight	England Dan & John Ford Coley
5/01	2	32.	Right Back Where We Started From	Maxine Nightingale
9/04	2	33.	You'll Never Find Another Love Like Mine	Lou Rawls
7/31	2	34.	Love Is Alive	Gary Wright
2/07	2	35.	Love To Love You Baby	Donna Summer
11/20	2	36.	The Wreck Of The Edmund Fitzgerald	Gordon Lightfoot
11/20	3	37.	Love So Right	Bee Gees
6/12	3	38.	Misty Blue	Dorthy Moore
8/14	3	39.	Let 'Em In	Wings
2/07	3	40.	You Sexy Thing	Hot Chocolate

THE TOP 40 HITS
1977

PK DATE	PK POS	RANK	TITLE	ARTIST
10/15	1	1.	You Light Up My Life	Debby Boone
8/20	1	2.	Best Of My Love	Emotions
7/30	1	3.	I Just Want To Be Your Everything	Andy Gibb
12/24	1	4.	How Deep Is Your Love	Bee Gees
3/05	1	5.	Love Theme From "A Star Is Born" (Evergreen)	Barbra Streisand
5/21	1	6.	Sir Duke	Stevie Wonder
2/05	1	7.	Torn Between Two Lovers	Mary MacGregor
3/26	1	8.	Rich Girl	Daryl Hall & John Oates
10/01	1	9.	Star Wars Theme/Cantina Band	Meco
6/25	1	10.	Got To Give It Up - Pt. 1	Marvin Gaye
1/29	1	11.	Car Wash	Rose Royce
1/08	1	12.	You Don't Have To Be A Star (To Be In My Show)	Marilyn McCoo & Billy Davis, Jr.
4/23	1	13.	Don't Leave Me This Way	Thelma Houston
4/09	1	14.	Dancing Queen	Abba
4/30	1	15.	Southern Nights	Glen Campbell
2/19	1	16.	Blinded By The Light	Manfred Mann's Earth Band
5/07	1	17.	Hotel California	Eagles
1/22	1	18.	I Wish	Stevie Wonder
7/02	1	19.	Gonna Fly Now (Theme From "Rocky")	Bill Conti
7/09	1	20.	Undercover Angel	Alan O'Day
1/15	1	21.	You Make Me Feel Like Dancing	Leo Sayer
5/14	1	22.	When I Need You	Leo Sayer
4/16	1	23.	Don't Give Up On Us	David Soul
6/18	1	24.	Dreams	Fleetwood Mac
2/26	1	25.	New Kid In Town	Eagles
7/16	1	26.	Da Doo Ron Ron	Shaun Cassidy
6/11	1	27.	I'm Your Boogie Man	KC & The Sunshine Band
7/23	1	28.	Looks Like We Made It	Barry Manilow
11/26	2	29.	Don't It Make My Brown Eyes Blue	Crystal Gayle
10/22	2	30.	Nobody Does It Better	Carly Simon
10/01	2	31.	Keep It Comin' Love	KC & The Sunshine Band
7/30	2	32.	I'm In You	Peter Frampton
11/12	2	33.	Boogie Nights	Heatwave
3/12	2	34.	Fly Like An Eagle	Steve Miller
9/17	2	35.	Float On	Floaters
9/10	2	36.	(Your Love Has Lifted Me) Higher And Higher	Rita Coolidge
12/17	3	37.	Blue Bayou	Linda Ronstadt
1/29	3	38.	Dazz	Brick
10/22	3	39.	That's Rock 'N' Roll	Shaun Cassidy
9/24	3	40.	Don't Stop	Fleetwood Mac

PETER FRAMPTON
"I'm In You"
THE NEW SINGLE.

FROM THE SOON-TO-BE-RELEASED NEW ALBUM, "I'M IN YOU."
PRODUCED BY PETER FRAMPTON
DIRECTION: DEE ANTHONY/BANDANA ENTERPRISES, LTD.

AM 1941

On A&M Records and Tapes

PETER FRAMPTON—I'm In You (3:57); producer: Peter Frampton; writer: Peter Frampton; publishers: Almo/Fram-Dee, ASCAP. A&M 1941. A lavish orchestration featuring strings, synthesizers romantic piano and sleek Frampton guitar break envelopes the artists soft sensitive vocal in a grandly contemporary rock ballad with a direct but touching lyric. The first product from Frampton since his multiple-platinum live album.

Billboard

For Week Ending July 30, 1966

HOT 100 ®

★ STAR performer—Sides registering greatest proportionate upward progress this week.

Record Industry Association of America seal of certification as million selling single.

THIS WEEK	Last Wk.	2 Wks. Ago	TITLE, Artist (Producer), Label & Number	Wks. on Chart
Billboard Award				
1	2 2 6		WILD THING — Troggs (Page One-York Pala), Atco 6415; Fontana 1548	6
2	1 1 4		HANKY PANKY — Tommy James & the Shondells (Jeff Barry & Ellie Greenwich), Roulette 4686	9
3	3 9 12		LIL' RED RIDING HOOD — Sam the Sham & the Pharaohs (Stan Kesler), MGM 13506	8
4	4 12 22		THE PIED PIPER — Crispian St. Peters (David Nicolson), Jamie 1320	8
5	9 14 19		I SAW HER AGAIN — Mama's & the Papa's (Lou Adler), Dunhill 4031	5
6	7 10 15		HUNGRY — Paul Revere & the Raiders (Terry Melcher), Columbia 43678	4
7	21 53		SUMMER IN THE CITY — Lovin' Spoonful (Erik-Jacobsen), Kama Sutra 211	3
8	10 15 24		SWEET PEA — Tommy Roe, ABC Records 10762	8
9	17 38 70		MOTHER'S LITTLE HELPER — Rolling Stones (Andrew Loog Oldham), London 902	4
10	14 21 35		SOMEWHERE MY LOVE — Ray Conniff & the Singers (Ernie Altschuler), Columbia 43625	7
11	50 — —		THEY'RE COMING TO TAKE ME AWAY, HA-HAAA! — Napoleon XIV (Jepolena Prod.), Warner Bros. 5831	2
12	6 5		PAPERBACK WRITER — Beatles (George Martin), Capitol 5651	8
13	8 3 2		RED RUBBER BALL — Cyrkle (John Simon), Columbia 43589	11
14	25 50 64		SUNNY — Bobby Hebb (Jerry Ross), Philips 40365	6
15	5 4 5		YOU DON'T HAVE TO SAY YOU LOVE ME — Dusty Springfield, Philips 40371	11
16	32 56 78		THIS DOOR SWING BOTH WAYS — Herman's Hermits (Mickie Most), MGM 13548	4
17	23 39 54		OVER UNDER SIDEWAYS DOWN — Yardbirds (Samwell-Smith, Napier-Bell), Epic 10035	6
18	18 25 39		THE WORK SONG — Herb Alpert & the Tijuana Brass (Herb Alpert), A & M 805	5
19	19 26 40		LOVE LETTERS — Elvis Presley, RCA Victor 8870	5
20	24 34 51		I WANT YOU — Bob Dylan (Bob Johnston), Columbia 43683	5
21	13 8 8		LITTLE GIRL — Syndicate of Sound (Gary Thompson), Bell 640	8
22	12 6 3		STRANGERS IN THE NIGHT — Frank Sinatra (Jimmy Bowen), Reprise 0470	13
23	26 48 61		SWEET DREAMS — Tommy McLain (Floyd Soileau & Huey Meaux), MSL 197	4
24	15 13 14		AIN'T TOO PROUD TO BEG — Temptations (N. Whitfield), Gordy 7054	10
25	30 35 56		TRAINS AND BOATS AND PLANES — Dionne Warwick (Bacharach-David), Scepter 12153	5
26	46 73		I COULDN'T LIVE WITHOUT YOUR LOVE — Petula Clark (Tony Hatch), Warner Bros. 5835	3
27	27 30 38		HAPPY SUMMER DAYS — Ronnie Dove (Phil Kahl), Diamond 205	5
28	29 32 47		WHERE WERE YOU WHEN I NEEDED YOU — Grass Roots (Sloan & Barri), Dunhill 4029	7
29	11 7 10		ALONG COMES MARY — Association (C. Boettcher), Valiant 741	8
30	41 67 83		SEE YOU IN SEPTEMBER — Happenings (Bright Tunes Prod.), B. T. Puppy 520	4
31	16 11 11		DIRTY WATER — Standells (Ed Cobb), Tower 185	15
32	38 45 60		PRETTY FLAMINGO — Manfred Mann (John Burgess), United Artists 50040	5
33	52 58 58		SEARCHING FOR MY LOVE — Bobby Moore & the Rhythm Aces (Rick Hall), Checker 1129	4
34	37 43 50		BILLY AND SUE — B. J. Thomas, Hickory 1395	7
35	35 40 48		THE IMPOSSIBLE DREAM — Jack Jones (David Kapp), Kapp 755	5
36	48 55 77		FRIDAY'S CHILD — Nancy Sinatra (Lee Hazlewood), Reprise 0491	4
37	20 20 30		YOU BETTER RUN — Young Rascals (Young Rascals), Atlantic 2338	6
38	36 16 7		COOL JERK — Capitols (Ollie McLaughlin), Karen 1524	14
39	22 19 25		I WASHED MY HANDS IN MUDDY WATER — Johnny Rivers (Lou Adler), Imperial 66175	8
40	68 —		BLOWIN' IN THE WIND — Stevie Wonder (C. Paul), Tamla 54136	2
41	28 24 21		POPSICLE — Jan & Dean (Jan Berry), Liberty 55886	9
42	42 52 62		YOU WOULDN'T LISTEN — Ides of March (Mike Considine), Parrot 304	6
43	40 47 57		YOU CAN'T ROLLER SKATE IN A BUFFALO HERD — Roger Miller (Jerry Kennedy), Smash 2043	6
44	54 74		5 D (Fifth Dimension) — Byrds (Allen Stanton), Columbia 43702	3
45	55 78 98		DISTANT SHORES — Chad & Jeremy (Larry Marks), Columbia 43682	4
46	47 49 59		WHOLE LOT OF SHAKIN' IN MY HEART (Since I Met You) — Miracles (Frank Wilson), Tamla 54134	7
47	62 72		THE JOKER WENT WILD — Brian Hyland (Snuff Garrett & Leon Russell), Philips 40377	4
48	78 —		WARM AND TENDER LOVE — Percy Sledge (Marlin Greene & Quin Ivy), Atlantic 2342	2
49	56 66 74		CAN I TRUST YOU? — Bachelors (Dick Rowe), London 20010	5
50	64 82 84		MISTY — Groove Holmes (Cal Lampley), Prestige 401	4
51	83 —		LADY JANE — Rolling Stones (Andrew Loog Oldham), London 902	2
52	69 81 93		LOOK AT ME GIRL — Bobby Vee (Dallas Smith), Liberty 55877	4
53	61 68 79		TAR AND CEMENT — Verdelle Smith (Vance-Pockriss Prod.), Capitol 5632	6
54	4 89 —		ALMOST PERSUADED — David Houston (Billy Sherrill), Epic 10025	3
55	75 90 —		YOU YOU YOU — Mel Carter (Nik de Caro), Imperial 66182	3
56	80 —		MAKE ME BELONG TO YOU — Barbara Lewis (Jerry Wexler & Ollie McLaughlin), Atlantic 2346	2
57	82 97		SUMMERTIME — Billy Stewart (Billy Davis), Chess 1966	3
58	57 64 65		I'M A NUT — Leroy Pullins (Lisauer-Wheeler), Kapp 758	6
59	79 —		THE TIP OF MY FINGER — Eddy Arnold (Chet Atkins), RCA Victor 8869	2
60	59 63 69		PAST, PRESENT AND FUTURE — Shangri-Las (Shadow Morton), Red Bird 10068	4
61	— —		GUANTANAMERA — Sandpipers (Tommy LiPuma), A&M 806	1
62	— —		ALFIE — Cher (Sonny Bono), Imperial 66192	1
63	93 —		BORN A WOMAN — Sandy Posey (Chip Moman), MGM 13501	3
64	90 —		WORKING IN THE COAL MINE — Lee Dorsey (A. Toussaint-M. Sehorn), Amy 958	2
65	89 99 100		WADE IN THE WATER — Ramsey Lewis (Esmond Edwards), Cadet 5541	4
66	100 — —		A MILLION AND ONE — Dean Martin (Jimmy Bowen), Reprise 0500	2
67	63 69 73		I LOVE ONIONS — Susan Christie (John Hill), Columbia 43595	8
68	65 76 82		LARA'S THEME FROM "DR. ZHIVAGO" — Roger Williams, Kapp 758	6
69	70 85 88		LONELY SOLDIER — Mike Williams (Prod. by Staff), Atlantic 2339	4
70	73 88 —		I GUESS I'LL ALWAYS LOVE YOU — Isley Brothers (Holland & Dozier), Tamla 54135	3
71	66 70 76		TEENAGER'S PRAYER — Joe Simon (J.R. Enterprises), Sound Stage 7 2564	7
72	71 71 68		I LOVE YOU 1,000 TIMES — Platters (Luther Dixon), Musicor 1166	14
73	98 —		BUS STOP — Hollies (Ron Richardson), Imperial 66186	2
74	— —		(YOU MAKE ME FEEL) SO GOOD — McCoys (Feldman, Goldstein, Gottehrer), Bang 527	1
75	— —		MY HEART'S SYMPHONY — Gary Lewis & the Playboys (Snuff Garrett), Liberty 55898	1
76	— —		LAND OF 1,000 DANCES — Wilson Pickett (Jerry Wexler & Rick Hall), Atlantic 2348	1
77	88 —		I BELIEVE I'M GONNA MAKE IT — Joe Tex (Buddy Killen), Dial 4033	3
78	76 77 92		HEY YOU LITTLE BOO-GA-LOO — Chubby Checker (Dave Appell), Parkway 989	5
79	— —		MONEY WON'T CHANGE YOU — James Brown & the Famous Flames (James Brown Prod.), King 6048	1
80	92 —		SUGAR AND SPICE — Cryan Shames (MG Prod.), Destination 624	2
81	99 —		OPEN THE DOOR TO YOUR HEART — Darrell Banks, Revilot 201	2
82	— —		BRING BACK THE TIME — The Platters (Luther Dixon), Scepter 12154	1
83	— —		LIVIN' ABOVE YOUR HEAD — Jay & the Americans (Jerry Granahan), United Artists 50046	1
84	— —		WOULDN'T IT BE NICE — Beach Boys (Brian Wilson), Capitol 5706	1
85	85 91		UPTIGHT — Nancy Wilson (David Cavanaugh), Capitol 5673	3
86	— —		LONELY SUMMER — Shades of Blue (John Rhys), Impact 1014	1
87	84 84 80		STOP! GET A TICKET — Clefs of Lavender Hill (Steven Palmer), Date 1510	6
88	84 84 80		WIPE OUT — Surfaris, Dot 144	17
89	— —		7 AND 7 IS — Love (Jac Holzman), Elektra 45605	1
90	— —		SUNSHINE SUPERMAN — Donovan (Mickey Most), Epic 10045	1
91	— —		LET'S CALL IT A DAY GIRL — Razor's Edge (Bob Feldman), POW 101	1
92	— —		I PUT A SPELL ON YOU — Alan Price Set (Alan Price), Parrot 3001	1
93	94 95		DRIVE MY CAR — Bob Kuban & the In-Men (Mel Friedman), Musicland, U.S.A. 20007	3
94	95 —		GEORGIA ROSE — Tony Bennett (Ernie Altschuler), Columbia 43715	2
95	96 98		(We'll Be) UNITED — Intruders, Gamble 201	3
96	— —		THE PHILLY FREEZE — Alvin Cash & the Registers, Mar-v-Lus 6012	1
97	— —		HOW SWEET IT IS — Jr. Walker & the All-Stars (J. Bristol-H. Fuqua), Soul 30054	1
98	— —		TO SHOW I LOVE YOU — Peter & Gordon (John Burgess), Capitol 5684	1
99	— —		LOVE ATTACK — James Carr (Q. Claunch), Goldwax 309	1
100	— —		TAKIN' ALL I CAN GET — Mitch Ryder & the Detroit Wheels (Bob Crewe), New Voice 814	1

THE TOP 40 HITS
1978

PK DATE	PK POS	RANK	TITLE	ARTIST
3/18	1	1.	Night Fever	Bee Gees
6/17	1	2.	Shadow Dancing	Andy Gibb
12/09	1	3.	Le Freak	Chic
2/04	1	4.	Stayin' Alive	Bee Gees
9/30	1	5.	Kiss You All Over	Exile
9/09	1	6.	Boogie Oogie Oogie	Taste Of Honey
1/14	1	7.	Baby Come Back	Player
11/11	1	8.	MacArthur Park	Donna Summer
3/04	1	9.	(Love Is) Thicker Than Water	Andy Gibb
8/12	1	10.	Three Times A Lady	Commodores
12/02	1	11.	You Don't Bring Me Flowers	Barbra Streisand & Neil Diamond
8/26	1	12.	Grease	Frankie Valli
5/20	1	13.	With A Little Luck	Wings
5/13	1	14.	If I Can't Have You	Yvonne Elliman
10/28	1	15.	Hot Child In The City	Nick Gilder
6/10	1	16.	You're The One That I Want	John Travolta & Olivia Newton-John
8/05	1	17.	Miss You	Rolling Stones
11/04	1	18.	You Needed Me	Anne Murray
6/03	1	19.	Too Much, Too Little, Too Late	Johnny Mathis/Deniece Williams
6/24	2	20.	Baker Street	Gerry Rafferty
1/28	2	21.	Short People	Randy Newman
5/13	2	22.	The Closer I Get To You	Roberta Flack with Donny Hathaway
11/18	2	23.	Double Vision	Foreigner
4/01	3	24.	Lay Down Sally	Eric Clapton
4/22	3	25.	Can't Smile Without You	Barry Manilow
11/18	3	26.	How Much I Feel	Ambrosia
3/18	3	27.	Emotion	Samantha Sang
2/18	3	28.	Just The Way You Are	Billy Joel
3/04	3	29.	Sometimes When We Touch	Dan Hill
9/23	3	30.	Hopelessly Devoted To You	Olivia Newton-John
7/08	3	31.	Take A Chance On Me	Abba
9/09	3	32.	Hot Blooded	Foreigner
8/12	3	33.	Last Dance	Donna Summer
10/28	3	34.	Reminiscing	Little River Band
6/24	3	35.	It's A Heartache	Bonnie Tyler
1/14	3	36.	Here You Come Again	Dolly Parton
2/04	4	37.	We Are The Champions	Queen
1/14	4	38.	You're In My Heart (The Final Acclaim)	Rod Stewart
12/09	4	39.	I Just Wanna Stop	Gino Vannelli
7/08	4	40.	Use Ta Be My Girl	O'Jays

THE TOP 40 HITS
1979

PK DATE	PK POS	RANK	TITLE	ARTIST
8/25	1	1.	My Sharona	Knack
7/14	1	2.	Bad Girls	Donna Summer
2/10	1	3.	Da Ya Think I'm Sexy?	Rod Stewart
5/05	1	4.	Reunited	Peaches & Herb
6/02	1	5.	Hot Stuff	Donna Summer
3/10	1	6.	I Will Survive	Gloria Gaynor
12/22	1	7.	Escape (The Pina Colada Song)	Rupert Holmes
6/30	1	8.	Ring My Bell	Anita Ward
12/08	1	9.	Babe	Styx
1/06	1	10.	Too Much Heaven	Bee Gees
10/20	1	11.	Rise	Herb Alpert
3/24	1	12.	Tragedy	Bee Gees
11/24	1	13.	No More Tears (Enough Is Enough)	Barbra Streisand/ Donna Summer
11/17	1	14.	Still	Commodores
11/03	1	15.	Pop Muzik	M
10/06	1	16.	Sad Eyes	Robert John
4/14	1	17.	What A Fool Believes	Doobie Brothers
8/18	1	18.	Good Times	Chic
11/10	1	19.	Heartache Tonight	Eagles
4/28	1	20.	Heart Of Glass	Blondie
4/21	1	21.	Knock On Wood	Amii Stewart
10/13	1	22.	Don't Stop 'Til You Get Enough	Michael Jackson
6/09	1	23.	Love You Inside Out	Bee Gees
2/03	2	24.	Y.M.C.A.	Village People
11/10	2	25.	Dim All The Lights	Donna Summer
9/15	2	26.	After The Love Has Gone	Earth, Wind & Fire
2/24	2	27.	Fire	Pointer Sisters
6/16	2	28.	We Are Family	Sister Sledge
8/11	3	29.	The Main Event/Fight	Barbra Streisand
1/06	3	30.	My Life	Billy Joel
2/17	3	31.	A Little More Love	Olivia Newton-John
9/15	3	32.	The Devil Went Down To Georgia	Charlie Daniels Band
5/19	3	33.	In The Navy	Village People
5/05	3	34.	Music Box Dancer	Frank Mills
12/22	4	35.	Send One Your Love	Stevie Wonder
3/17	4	36.	Heaven Knows	Donna Summer with Brooklyn Dreams
5/12	4	37.	Stumblin' In	Suzi Quatro & Chris Norman
10/13	4	38.	Sail On	Commodores
4/07	4	39.	Sultans Of Swing	Dire Straits
6/16	4	40.	Just When I Needed You Most	Randy Vanwarmer

THE TOP 40 HITS
1980

PK DATE	PK POS	RANK	TITLE	ARTIST
11/15	1	1.	Lady	Kenny Rogers
4/19	1	2.	Call Me	Blondie
12/27	1	3.	(Just Like) Starting Over	John Lennon
9/06	1	4.	Upside Down	Diana Ross
3/22	1	5.	Another Brick In The Wall (Part II)	Pink Floyd
2/23	1	6.	Crazy Little Thing Called Love	Queen
1/19	1	7.	Rock With You	Michael Jackson
8/02	1	8.	Magic	Olivia Newton-John
5/31	1	9.	Funkytown	Lipps, Inc.
10/04	1	10.	Another One Bites The Dust	Queen
10/25	1	11.	Woman In Love	Barbra Streisand
6/28	1	12.	Coming Up (Live at Glasgow)	Paul McCartney & Wings
7/19	1	13.	It's Still Rock And Roll To Me	Billy Joel
2/16	1	14.	Do That To Me One More Time	Captain & Tennille
1/05	1	15.	Please Don't Go	KC & The Sunshine Band
8/30	1	16.	Sailing	Christopher Cross
12/06	2	17.	More Than I Can Say	Leo Sayer
9/13	2	18.	All Out Of Love	Air Supply
4/26	2	19.	Ride Like The Wind	Christopher Cross
3/29	2	20.	Working My Way Back To You/Forgive Me, Girl	Spinners
3/01	2	21.	Yes, I'm Ready	Teri DeSario with K.C.
3/15	2	22.	Longer	Dan Fogelberg
7/19	3	23.	Little Jeannie	Elton John
1/26	3	24.	Coward Of The County	Kenny Rogers
5/03	3	25.	Lost In Love	Air Supply
6/28	3	26.	The Rose	Bette Midler
6/07	3	27.	Biggest Part Of Me	Ambrosia
11/15	3	28.	The Wanderer	Donna Summer
10/25	3	29.	He's So Shy	Pointer Sisters
9/06	3	30.	Emotional Rescue	Rolling Stones
8/16	3	31.	Take Your Time (Do It Right) Part 1	S.O.S. Band
3/08	4	32.	Desire	Andy Gibb
2/02	4	33.	Cruisin'	Smokey Robinson
4/19	4	34.	With You I'm Born Again	Billy Preston & Syreeta
7/19	4	35.	Cupid/I've Loved You For A Long Time	Spinners
5/24	4	36.	Don't Fall In Love With A Dreamer	Kenny Rogers with Kim Carnes
9/27	4	37.	Give Me The Night	George Benson
9/13	4	38.	Fame	Irene Cara
12/27	5	39.	Hungry Heart	Bruce Springsteen
12/06	5	40.	Master Blaster (Jammin')	Stevie Wonder

THE TOP 40 HITS
1981

PK DATE	PK POS	RANK	TITLE	ARTIST
11/21	1	1.	Physical	Olivia Newton-John
5/16	1	2.	Bette Davis Eyes	Kim Carnes
8/15	1	3.	Endless Love	Diana Ross & Lionel Richie
10/17	1	4.	Arthur's Theme (Best That You Can Do)	Christopher Cross
4/11	1	5.	Kiss On My List	Daryl Hall & John Oates
8/01	1	6.	Jessie's Girl	Rick Springfield
2/28	1	7.	I Love A Rainy Night	Eddie Rabbitt
2/21	1	8.	9 To 5	Dolly Parton
11/07	1	9.	Private Eyes	Daryl Hall & John Oates
3/28	1	10.	Rapture	Blondie
2/07	1	11.	Celebration	Kool & The Gang
5/02	1	12.	Morning Train (Nine To Five)	Sheena Easton
1/31	1	13.	The Tide Is High	Blondie
3/21	1	14.	Keep On Loving You	REO Speedwagon
6/20	1	15.	Stars on 45 [medley]	Stars on 45
7/25	1	16.	The One That You Love	Air Supply
11/28	2	17.	Waiting For A Girl Like You	Foreigner
3/21	2	18.	Woman	John Lennon
10/31	2	19.	Start Me Up	Rolling Stones
8/29	2	20.	Slow Hand	Pointer Sisters
5/02	2	21.	Just The Two Of Us	Grover Washington, Jr./ Bill Withers
1/10	2	22.	Love On The Rocks	Neil Diamond
5/23	2	23.	Being With You	Smokey Robinson
7/04	2	24.	All Those Years Ago	George Harrison
9/19	2	25.	Queen Of Hearts	Juice Newton
8/15	2	26.	Theme From "Greatest American Hero" (Believe It or Not)	Joey Scarbury
9/05	3	27.	Stop Draggin' My Heart Around	Stevie Nicks with Tom Petty
12/19	3	28.	Let's Groove	Earth, Wind & Fire
3/21	3	29.	The Best Of Times	Styx
6/13	3	30.	Sukiyaki	Taste Of Honey
8/15	3	31.	I Don't Need You	Kenny Rogers
1/10	3	32.	Guilty	Barbra Streisand & Barry Gibb
12/05	3	33.	Every Little Thing She Does Is Magic	Police
9/05	4	34.	Urgent	Foreigner
5/02	4	35.	Angel Of The Morning	Juice Newton
10/17	4	36.	For Your Eyes Only	Sheena Easton
12/05	4	37.	Oh No	Commodores
10/03	4	38.	Who's Crying Now	Journey
6/20	4	39.	A Woman Needs Love (Just Like You Do)	Ray Parker Jr. & Raydio
9/05	5	40.	(There's) No Gettin' Over Me	Ronnie Milsap

THE TOP 40 HITS
1982

PK DATE	PK POS	RANK	TITLE	ARTIST
3/20	1	1.	I Love Rock 'N Roll	Joan Jett & The Blackhearts
5/15	1	2.	Ebony And Ivory	Paul McCartney & Stevie Wonder
7/24	1	3.	Eye Of The Tiger	Survivor
2/06	1	4.	Centerfold	J. Geils Band
12/18	1	5.	Maneater	Daryl Hall & John Oates
10/02	1	6.	Jack & Diane	John Cougar
7/03	1	7.	Don't You Want Me	Human League
11/06	1	8.	Up Where We Belong	Joe Cocker & Jennifer Warnes
9/04	1	9.	Abracadabra	Steve Miller Band
9/11	1	10.	Hard To Say I'm Sorry	Chicago
11/27	1	11.	Truly	Lionel Richie
1/30	1	12.	I Can't Go For That (No Can Do)	Daryl Hall & John Oates
12/11	1	13.	Mickey	Toni Basil
10/30	1	14.	Who Can It Be Now?	Men At Work
5/08	1	15.	Chariots Of Fire - Titles	Vangelis
2/27	2	16.	Open Arms	Journey
7/03	2	17.	Rosanna	Toto
8/07	2	18.	Hurt So Good	John Cougar
5/22	2	19.	Don't Talk To Strangers	Rick Springfield
11/27	2	20.	Gloria	Laura Branigan
4/10	2	21.	We Got The Beat	Go-Go's
11/06	3	22.	Heart Attack	Olivia Newton-John
10/16	3	23.	Eye In The Sky	Alan Parsons Project
5/22	3	24.	I've Never Been To Me	Charlene
2/13	3	25.	Harden My Heart	Quarterflash
7/24	4	26.	Hold Me	Fleetwood Mac
4/10	4	27.	Freeze-Frame	J. Geils Band
3/20	4	28.	That Girl	Stevie Wonder
5/22	4	29.	867-5309/Jenny	Tommy Tutone
2/27	4	30.	Shake It Up	Cars
10/23	4	31.	I Keep Forgettin' (Every Time You're Near)	Michael McDonald
6/26	4	32.	Heat Of The Moment	Asia
6/12	4	33.	The Other Woman	Ray Parker Jr.
11/13	5	34.	Heartlight	Neil Diamond
6/12	5	35.	Always On My Mind	Willie Nelson
9/18	5	36.	You Should Hear How She Talks About You	Melissa Manchester
4/03	5	37.	Make A Move On Me	Olivia Newton-John
9/04	5	38.	Even The Nights Are Better	Air Supply
3/20	5	39.	Sweet Dreams	Air Supply
7/17	5	40.	Let It Whip	Dazz Band

THE TOP 40 HITS
1983

PK DATE	PK POS	RANK	TITLE	ARTIST
7/09	1	1.	Every Breath You Take	Police
3/05	1	2.	Billie Jean	Michael Jackson
5/28	1	3.	Flashdance...What A Feeling	Irene Cara
12/10	1	4.	Say Say Say	Michael Jackson/ Paul McCartney
11/12	1	5.	All Night Long (All Night)	Lionel Richie
10/01	1	6.	Total Eclipse Of The Heart	Bonnie Tyler
1/15	1	7.	Down Under	Men At Work
4/30	1	8.	Beat It	Michael Jackson
10/29	1	9.	Islands In The Stream	Kenny Rogers & Dolly Parton
2/19	1	10.	Baby, Come To Me	Patti Austin & James Ingram
9/10	1	11.	Maniac	Michael Sembello
5/21	1	12.	Let's Dance	David Bowie
9/03	1	13.	Sweet Dreams (Are Made of This)	Eurythmics
9/24	1	14.	Tell Her About It	Billy Joel
2/05	1	15.	Africa	Toto
4/23	1	16.	Come On Eileen	Dexys Midnight Runners
7/02	2	17.	Electric Avenue	Eddy Grant
12/17	2	18.	Say It Isn't So	Daryl Hall & John Oates
2/26	2	19.	Shame On The Moon	Bob Seger & The Silver Bullet Band
1/08	2	20.	The Girl Is Mine	Paul McCartney & Michael Jackson
3/26	2	21.	Do You Really Want To Hurt Me	Culture Club
10/08	2	22.	Making Love Out Of Nothing At All	Air Supply
6/18	2	23.	Time (Clock Of The Heart)	Culture Club
5/07	2	24.	Jeopardy	Greg Kihn
11/12	3	25.	Uptown Girl	Billy Joel
9/10	3	26.	The Safety Dance	Men Without Hats
1/29	3	27.	Sexual Healing	Marvin Gaye
1/08	3	28.	Dirty Laundry	Don Henley
3/26	3	29.	Hungry Like The Wolf	Duran Duran
8/06	3	30.	She Works Hard For The Money	Donna Summer
12/24	3	31.	Union Of The Snake	Duran Duran
2/26	3	32.	Stray Cat Strut	Stray Cats
4/16	3	33.	Mr. Roboto	Styx
10/08	3	34.	King Of Pain	Police
6/04	3	35.	Overkill	Men At Work
7/09	4	36.	Never Gonna Let You Go	Sergio Mendes
10/08	4	37.	True	Spandau Ballet
9/03	4	38.	Puttin' On The Ritz	Taco
3/26	4	39.	You Are	Lionel Richie
11/05	4	40.	One Thing Leads To Another	Fixx

Billboard HOT 100

FOR WEEK ENDING NOVEMBER 16, 1968

®

★ STAR PERFORMER—Sides registering greatest proportionate upward progress this week. ⓡ Record Industry Association of America seal of certification as million selling single.

This Week	2 Wks. Ago	3 Wks. Ago	Wks. on Chart	TITLE Artist (Producer), Label & Number
1	1	1	10	HEY JUDE — Beatles (George Martin), Apple 2276
2	2	4	7	THOSE WERE THE DAYS — Mary Hopkin (Paul McCartney), Apple 1801
3	9	19	5	LOVE CHILD — Diana Ross & Supremes (Clan), Motown 1135
4	7	12	7	MAGIC CARPET RIDE — Steppenwolf (Gabriel Mekler), Dunhill 4160
5	5	8	10	HOLD ME TIGHT — Johnny Nash (Johnny Nash & Arthur Jenkins), JAD 207
6	6	10	15	WHITE ROOM — Cream (Felix Pappalardi), Atco 6617
7	4	3	14	LITTLE GREEN APPLES — O. C. Smith (Jerry Fuller), Columbia 44616
8	21	29	4	WHO'S MAKING LOVE — Johnnie Taylor (Don Davis), Stax 0009
9	18	35	66	ABRAHAM, MARTIN AND JOHN — Dion (Laurie Prod.-Phil Gernhard Prod.), Laurie 3464
10	8	6	9	ELENORE — Turtles (Chip Douglas), White Whale 276
11	9	4	3	FIRE — Crazy World of Arthur Brown (Kit Lambert), Track 2556
12	11	7	7	OVER YOU — Gary Puckett & the Union Gap (Jerry Fuller), Columbia 44644
13	13	21	27	SWEET BLINDNESS — Fifth Dimension (Bones Howe), Soul City 768
14	35	79	—	FOR ONCE IN MY LIFE — Stevie Wonder (Henry Cosby), Tamla 54174
15	10	5	6	MIDNIGHT CONFESSIONS — Grassroots (Steve Barri), Dunhill 4144
16	17	18	11	HEY, WESTERN UNION MAN — Jerry Butler (Gamble-Huff), Mercury 72850
17	36	36	48	CHEWY CHEWY — Ohio Express (Kasenetz-Katz Associates), Buddah 70
18	37	57	54	ALWAYS TOGETHER — Dells (Bobby Miller), Cadet 5621
19	14	11	12	SUZIE Q — Creedence Clearwater Revival (Saul Zaentz), Fantasy 616
20	19	19	17	REVOLUTION — Beatles (George Martin), Apple 2276
21	16	15	5	GIRL WATCHER — O'Kaysions (North State Music), ABC 11094
22	23	23	23	FOOL FOR YOU — Impressions (Curtis Mayfield), Curtom 1932
23	67	75	—	WICHITA LINEMAN — Glen Campbell (Al de Lory), Capitol 2302
24	24	34	36	KEEP ON LOVIN' ME, HONEY — Marvin Gaye & Tammi Terrell (Ashford & Simpson), Tamla 54173
25	26	27	34	HI-HEEL SNEAKERS — Jose Feliciano (Rick Jarrard), RCA Victor 47-9641
26	47	64	—	I LOVE HOW YOU LOVE ME — Bobby Vinton (Billy Sherrill), Epic 10397
27	27	28	42	BANG-SHANG-A-LANG — Archies (Don Kirshner), Calendar 63-1006
28	20	20	16	SAY IT LOUD (I'm Black and I'm Proud) — James Brown & His Famous Flames (James Brown), King 6187
29	12	13	13	PIECE OF MY HEART — Big Brother & the Holding Company, Columbia 44626
30	42	50	64	BRING IT ON HOME TO ME — Eddie Floyd (Steve Cropper), Stax 0012
31	40	57	65	LITTLE ARROWS — Leapy Lee (Gordon Mills), Decca 32380
32	25	26	28	COURT OF LOVE — Unifics (Guy Draper), Kapp 935
33	57	67	80	STORMY — Classics IV (Buddy Buie), Imperial 66328
34	34	41	43	QUICK JOEY SMALL (Run Joey Run) — Kasenetz-Katz Singing Orchestral Circus (Kasenetz-Katz Associates), Buddah 64
35	15	14	8	HARPER VALLEY P.T.A. — Jeannie C. Riley (Shelby S. Singleton Jr.), Plantation 3
36	29	25	20	ALL ALONG THE WATCHTOWER — Jimi Hendrix Experience (Jimi Hendrix), Reprise 0767
37	43	43	70	CYCLES — Frank Sinatra (Don Costa), Reprise 0764
38	38	38	38	TAKE ME FOR A LITTLE WHILE — Vanilla Fudge (Shadow Morton), Atco 6616
39	46	47	47	THE FUNKY JUDGE — Bull & The Matadors (Sherrel-Cross Prod.), Toddlin' Town 108
40	22	22	22	SHAPE OF THINGS TO COME — Max Frost & the Troopers (Mike Curb), Tower 419
41	48	66	—	PROMISES, PROMISES — Dionne Warwick (Burt Bacharach-Hal David), Scepter 12231
42	56	56	72	PICKIN' WILD MOUNTAIN BERRIES — Peggy Scott & Jo Jo Benson (Shelby S. Singleton Jr. & Bob McKee), SSS Int'l 748
43	45	46	68	LES BICYCLETTES DE BELSIZE — Engelbert Humperdinck (Peter Sullivan), Parrot 40032
44	32	32	33	CHAINED — Marvin Gaye (Frank Wilson), Tamla 54170
45	—	—	—	CLOUD NINE — Temptations (Norman Whitfield), Gordy 7081
46	74	—	—	BOTH SIDES NOW — Judy Collins (Mark Abramson), Elektra 45639
47	73	—	—	TOO WEAK TO FIGHT — Clarence Carter (Rick Hall & Staff), Atlantic 2569
48	53	53	53	BATTLE HYMN OF THE REPUBLIC — Andy Williams with the St. Charles Borromeo Choir (Andy Williams), Columbia 44650
49	54	54	75	THE STRAIGHT LIFE — Bobby Goldsboro (Bob Montgomery & Bobby Goldsboro), United Artists 50461
50	60	60	67	CINNAMON — Derek (George Tobin & Johnny Cymbal), Bang 558
51	49	67	84	SHAME, SHAME — Magic Lanterns (Steve Rowland), Atlantic 2560
52	52	52	79	1432 FRANKLIN PIKE CIRCLE HERO — Bobby Russell (Buzz Cason & Bobby Russell), Elf 90030
53	68	72	89	GOODY GOODY GUMDROPS — 1910 Fruitgum Co. (Kasenetz-Katz Associates), Buddah 71
54	65	89	—	THE STAR-SPANGLED BANNER — Jose Feliciano, RCA Victor 47-9665
55	59	59	50	DO SOMETHING TO ME — Tommy James & the Shondells (Tommy James), Roulette 7026
56	63	63	60	I LOVE YOU MADLY — Fantastic Four (Mike Hanks), Soul 3505
57	64	65	76	FROM THE TEACHER TO THE PREACHER — Gene Chandler & Barbara Acklin (Carl Davis), Brunswick 55387
58	72	76	93	PEACE BROTHER PEACE — Bill Medley (Medley Prod.), MGM 14000
59	58	58	58	CINDERELLA SUNSHINE — Paul Revere & the Raiders, featuring Mark Lindsay (Mark Lindsay), Columbia 44655
60	75	—	—	GOODBYE MY LOVE — James Brown (James Brown), King 6198
61	87	—	—	KENTUCKY WOMAN — Deep Purple (Derek Lawrence), Tetragrammaton 1508
62	62	62	62	PORPOISE SONG — Monkees (Gerry Goffin), Colgems 66-1031
63	84	87	—	FIRE — Five by Five (Gene Kent), Paula 302
64	81	97	—	THE YARD WENT ON FOREVER — Richard Harris (Jimmy Webb), Dunhill 4171
65	89	96	—	TALKING ABOUT MY BABY — Gloria Walker (Eugene Davis), Flaming Arrow 35
66	94	—	—	HANG 'EM HIGH — Booker T. & M.G.'s (Booker T. & M.G.'s), Stax 0013
67	77	78	78	HARPER VALLEY P.T.A. (Later That Day) — Ben Colder (Jack Clement), MGM 13997
68	71	71	74	SHAKE — Shadows of Knight (Kasenetz-Katz Associates), Team 520
69	79	93	—	NOT ENOUGH INDIANS — Dean Martin (Jimmy Bowen), Reprise 0780
70	78	80	—	FOR ONCE IN MY LIFE — Jackie Wilson (Carl Davis), Brunswick 55392
71	91	91	—	CROWN OF CREATION — Jefferson Airplane (Al Schmitt), RCA Victor 47-9644
72	76	—	—	SLOW DRAG — Intruders (Gamble-Huff), Gamble 221
73	80	81	—	EVERYBODY GOT TO BELIEVE IN SOMEBODY — Sam & Dave (Isaac Hayes & David Porter), Atlantic 2568
74	95	—	—	SUNDAY SUN — Neil Diamond (Tom Catalano & Neil Diamond), UNI 55084
75	97	—	—	LET'S MAKE A PROMISE — Peaches & Herb (Gamble-Huff), Date 1633
76	—	—	—	SCARBOROUGH FAIR — Sergio Mendes & Brasil '66 (Sergio Mendes), A&M 983
77	—	—	—	ROCKIN' IN THE SAME OLD BOAT — Bobby Bland, Duke 440
78	98	—	—	A MAN AND A HALF — Wilson Pickett (Tom Dowd), Atlantic 2575
79	—	—	—	STAND BY YOUR MAN — Tammy Wynette (Billy Sherrill), Epic 10398
80	86	86	—	SWEET DARLIN' — Martha Reeves & the Vandellas (Richard Morris), Gordy 7079
81	—	—	—	PUT YOUR HEAD ON MY SHOULDER — Lettermen (Al de Lory), Capitol 2324
82	82	84	95	MORNIN' GLORY — Bobbie Gentry & Glen Campbell (Kelly Gordon & Al de Lory), Capitol 2314
83	83	83	83	DO WHAT YOU GOTTA DO — Nina Simone (Stroud Prod.), RCA Victor 47-9602
84	—	—	—	PEOPLE — Tymes (Jimmy "Wiz" Wisner), Columbia 44630
85	93	94	94	AUNT DORA'S LOVE SOUL SHACK — Arthur Conley (Tom Dowd), Atco 6622
86	—	—	—	WITH A LITTLE HELP FROM MY FRIENDS — Joe Cocker (Denny Cordell), A&M 991
87	—	—	—	(She's) SOME KIND OF WONDERFUL — Fantastic Johnny C (Jesse James), Phil L.A. of Soul 320
88	88	90	90	I WALK ALONE — Marty Robbins (Bob Johnston), Columbia 44633
89	—	—	—	JUST AIN'T NO LOVE — Barbara Acklin (Carl Davis-Eugene Record), Brunswick 55388
90	90	95	—	CALIFORNIA EARTHQUAKE — Mama Cass (John Simon), Dunhill 4164
91	—	—	—	BABY LET'S WAIT — Royal Guardsmen (Gernard-Brandige-Fuller), Laurie 3461
92	92	92	—	BILLY, YOU'RE MY FRIEND — Gene Pitney (Bob Schwartz), Musicor 1331
93	—	—	—	BALLAD OF TWO BROTHERS — Autry Inman (Glenn Sutton & Billy Sherrill), Epic 10389
94	—	—	—	HARD TO HANDLE — Patti Drew (Carl Davis), Capitol 2379
95	—	—	—	I'VE GOT LOVE FOR MY BABY — Young Hearts (Bobby Sanders & Soultown Prod.), Minit 32045
96	96	—	—	I PUT A SPELL ON YOU — Creedence Clearwater Revival (Saul Zaentz), Fantasy 617
97	—	—	—	HOOKED ON A FEELING — B. J. Thomas (Chips Moman), Scepter 12230
98	—	—	—	I WORRY ABOUT YOU — Joe Simon (J. R. Ent.), Sound Stage 7 2617
99	99	100	—	COME ON, REACT — Fireballs (Norman Petty), Atco 6614
100	100	—	—	A WHITER SHADE OF PALE — Hesitations (P. Robinson, T. Wiltshire, L. Banks), Kapp 948

Compiled from national retail sales and radio station airplay by the Music Popularity Dept. of Record Market Research, Billboard.

Billboard HOT 100 ®

★ STAR PERFORMER — Records showing greatest increase in retail sales activity over the previous week, based on accrual market reports.

⊛ Record Industry Association Of America seal of certification as "million seller." ●

THIS WEEK	LAST WEEK	TITLE, Artist (Producer) Label, Number (Distributing Label)
1	1	(They Long to Be) CLOSE TO YOU — Carpenters (Jack Daugherty), A&M 1183
2	5	MAKE IT WITH YOU — Bread (David Gates), Elektra 45686
3	2	MAMA TOLD ME (Not to Come) ● — Three Dog Night (Richard Podolor), Dunhill 4239 (Capitol)
4	4	BAND OF GOLD ● — Freda Payne (Holland-Dozier) Invictus 9075
5	9	SIGNED, SEALED, DELIVERED (I'm Yours) — Stevie Wonder (Stevie Wonder), Tamla 54196 (Motown)
6	4	THE LOVE YOU SAVE/I FOUND THAT GIRL — Jackson 5 (Corporation), Motown 1166
7	14	SPILL THE WINE — Eric Burdon & War (Jerry Goldstein), MGM 14118
8	6	BALL OF CONFUSION (That's What the World Is Today) — Temptations (Norman Whitfield), Gordy 7099 (Motown)
9	11	TIGHTER, TIGHTER — Alive & Kicking (Tommy James-Bob King), Roulette 7078
10	8	O-O-H CHILD — 5 Stairsteps (Stan Vincent), Buddah 165
11	7	RIDE CAPTAIN RIDE — Blues Image (Richard Podolor), Atco 6746
12	25	WAR ● — Edwin Starr (Norman Whitfield) Gordy 7101 (Motown)
13	12	HITCHIN' A RIDE — Vanity Fare (Roger Easterby & Des Champ) Page One 21029 (Bell)
14	15	ARE YOU READY? — Pacific Gas & Electric (John Hill), Columbia 4-45158
15	10	LAY DOWN (Candles in the Rain) — Melanie with the Edwin Hawkins Singers (Peter Schekeryk) Buddah 167
16	16	TEACH YOUR CHILDREN — Crosby, Stills, Nash & Young (D. Crosby, S. Stills, G. Nash & N. Young), Atlantic 2735
17	18	OHIO — Crosby, Stills, Nash & Young (D. Crosby, S. Stills, G. Nash & N. Young), Atlantic 2740
18	20	I JUST CAN'T HELP BELIEVING — B.J. Thomas (Chips Moman), Scepter 12283
19	24	LAY A LITTLE LOVIN' ON ME — Robin McNamara (Jeff Barry), Steed 724 (Paramount)
20	19	A SONG OF JOY — Miguel Rios (Hispavox), A&M 1193
21	26	(If You Let Me Make Love to You Then) WHY CAN'T I TOUCH YOU? — Ronnie Dyson (Billy Jackson) Columbia 4-45110
22	32	IN THE SUMMERTIME — Mungo Jerry (Barry Murray), Janus 125
23	13	GIMME DAT DING — Pipkins (John Burgess), Capitol 2819
24	17	THE WONDER OF YOU/MAMA LIKED THE ROSES — Elvis Presley, RCA Victor 47-9835
25	28	SILVER BIRD — Mark Lindsay (Jerry Fuller), Columbia 4-45180
26	30	WESTBOUND #9 — Flaming Ember (Stagecoach Prod.), Hot Wax 7003 (Buddah)
27	39	TELL IT ALL BROTHER — Kenny Rogers & the First Edition (Jimmy Bowen & Kenny Rogers), Reprise 0911
28	41	OVERTURE FROM TOMMY — Assembled Multitude (Bill Buster), Atlantic 2737
29	60	PATCHES — Clarence Carter (Rick Hall), Atlantic 2748
30	57	GET UP I FELL LIKE BEING A SEX MACHINE (Part I & Part II) — James Brown (James Brown), King 6318
31	29	MISSISSIPPI QUEEN — Mountain (Felix Pappalardi), Windfall 532 (Bell)
32	31	LOVE LAND — Charles Wright & the Watts 103rd Street Rhythm Band (Charles Wright), Warner Bros. 7365
33	47	SUMMERTIME BLUES — Who (Kit Lambert-Chris Stamp), Decca 32708

THIS WEEK	LAST WEEK	TITLE, Artist (Producer) Label, Number (Distributing Label)
34	44	THE SLY, THE SLICK AND THE WICKED — Lost Generation (Eugene Record), Brunswick 55436 (Decca)
35	38	MAYBE — Three Degrees (Richard Barrett), Roulette 7079
36	35	MISSISSIPPI — John Phillips (Lou Adler), Dunhill 4236
37	43	EVERYBODY'S GOT THE RIGHT TO LOVE — Supremes (Frank Wilson), Motown 1167
38	50	25 OR 6 TO 4 — Chicago (James William Guercio), Columbia 4-45194
39	56	DO YOU SEE MY LOVE (For You Growing) — Jr. Walker & the All Stars (Jimmy Bristol), Soul 35073 (Motown)
40	34	CHECK OUT YOUR MIND — Impressions (Curtis Mayfield), Curtom 1951 (Buddah)
41	27	SAVE THE COUNTRY — 5th Dimension (Bones Howe), Bell 895
42	51	BIG YELLOW TAXI — Neighborhood (Jimmy Bryant), Big Tree 102
43	46	MY MARIE — Engelbert Humperdinck (Peter Sullivan), Parrot 40049 (London)
44	36	GO BACK — Crabby Appleton (Don Gallucci), Elektra 45687
45	49	PAPER MACHE — Dionne Warwick (Burt Bacharach-Hal David), Scepter 12285
46	37	STEAL AWAY — Johnnie Taylor (Don Davis), Stax 0063
47	52	I WANT TO TAKE YOU HIGHER — Ike & Tina Turner & the Ikettes (Ike Turner), Liberty 56177
48	48	HOW ABOUT A LITTLE HAND (For the Boys in the Band) — Boys In the Band (Bob Feldman-Herman Griffin) Spring 103 (Polydor)
49	69	HAND ME DOWN WORLD — Guess Who (Jack Richardson & Nimbus 9), RCA 74-0367
50	53	PEARL — Tommy Roe (Steve Barri), ABC 11266
51	71	AMERICA, COMMUNICATE WITH ME — Ray Stevens (Ray Stevens), Barnaby 2016 (Columbia)
52	45	WHEN WE GET MARRIED — Intruders (Gamble-Huff Productions), Gamble 4004
53	54	I'LL BE RIGHT HERE — Tyrone Davis (Willie Henderson), Dakar 618 (Atlantic)
54	61	EVERYTHING A MAN COULD EVER NEED — Glen Campbell (Al DeLory), Capitol 2843
55	55	CINNAMON GIRL — Neil Young & Crazy Horse (David Briggs & Neil Young), Reprise 0911
56	59	COTTAGE CHEESE — Crow (B. Monaco), Amaret 119
57	62	SUNSHINE — Archies (Jeff Barry), Kirshner 63-1009 (RCA)
58	40	TRYING TO MAKE A FOOL OF ME — Delfonics (Stan & Bell Prod.), Philly Groove (Bell) 162
59	74	WIGWAM — Bob Dylan (Bob Johnston), Columbia 4-45199
60	64	SOLITARY MAN — Neil Diamond (Jeff Barry-Ellie Greenwich), Bang 578
61	—	(I Know) I'M LOSING YOU — Rare Earth (Norman Whitfield), Rare Earth 5017 (Motown)
62	65	GROOVY SITUATION — Gene Chandler (Gene Chandler), Mercury 73083
63	63	STEALING IN THE NAME OF THE LORD — Paul Kelly (Buddy Killen), Happy Tiger 541
64	67	YOU'VE BEEN MY INSPIRATION — Main Ingredient (Silverstein-Simmons-McPherson), RCA 74-0340
65	72	HELLO DARLIN' — Conway Twitty (Owen Bradley), Decca 32661
66	77	GLORY GLORY — Rascals with the Sweet Inspirations (Rascals & Arif Mardin), Atlantic 2743
67	90	SING A SONG FOR FREEDOM — Frijid Pink (Pink Unlimited), Parrot 349 (London)

THIS WEEK	LAST WEEK	TITLE, Artist (Producer) Label, Number (Distributing Label)
68	68	THAT SAME OLD FEELING — Pickettywitch (John MacLeod), Janus 118
69	80	SNOWBIRD — Anne Murray (Brian Ahern), Capitol 2738
70	70	SONG FROM M*A*S*H — Al DeLory (Phil Wright), Capitol 2811
71	—	JULIE, DO YA LOVE ME — Bobby Sherman (Jackie Mills), Metromedia 194
72	—	HI-DE-HO — Blood, Sweat & Tears (Roy Halee & Bobby Colomby), Columbia 4-45204
73	73	SUPERMAN — Ides of March (Frank Rand & Bob Destocki), Warner Bros. 7403
74	75	LONG LONELY NIGHTS — Dells (Bobby Miller), Cadet 5672 (Chess)
75	76	GIRLS WILL BE GIRLS, BOYS WILL BE BOYS — Isley Brothers (R. Isley, O. Isley, R. Isley), T-Neck 921 (Buddah)
76	99	IT'S A SHAME — Spinners (Stevie Wonder), V.I.P. 25057 (Motown)
77	86	QUE SERA, SERA (Whatever Will Be, Will Be) — Mary Hopkin (Paul McCartney), Apple 1823 (Capitol)
78	85	HUMPHREY THE CAMEL — Jack Blanchard & Misty Morgan (Little Richie Johnson), Wayside 013 (Mercury)
79	88	HUMMINGBIRD — B.B. King (Bill Szymczyk), ABC 11268
80	83	DOWN BY THE RIVER — Buddy Miles & the Freedom Express (Robin McBride & Buddy Miles), Mercury 73086
81	81	APARTMENT #21 — Bobbie Gentry (Rick Hall), Capitol 2849
82	82	DROP BY MY PLACE — Little Carl Carlton (Mike Terry), Back Beat 613
83	84	BLACK FOX — Freddy Robinson (Higgins & Ervin), Pacific Jazz 88155 (Liberty/United Artists)
84	78	LET THE MUSIC TAKE YOUR MIND — Kool & the Gang (Gene Redd), De-Lite 529
85	—	I'VE LOST YOU/THE NEXT STEP IS LOVE — Elvis Presley, RCA Victor 47-9873
86	87	SOMETHING — Booker T. & the MG's (Booker T. & the MG's), Stax 0073
87	96	YELLOW RIVER — Christie (Mike Smith), Epic 5-10626 (Columbia)
88	97	CANDIDA — Dawn (Tokens & Dave Appell), Bell 903
89	98	MORNING MUCH BETTER — Ten Wheel Drive with Genya Ravan (Guy Draper), Polydor 14037
90	92	IT'S YOUR LIFE — Andy Kim (Jeff Barry), Steed 727 (Paramount)
91	100	BIG YELLOW TAXI — Joni Mitchell (Joni Mitchell), Reprise 0906
92	—	MILL VALLEY — Miss Abrams & the Strawberry Point School Third Grade Class (Erik Jacobsen & Rita Abrams), Reprise 0928
93	94	NO ARMS CAN EVER HOLD YOU — Bobby Vinton (Billy Sherrill), Epic 5-10629 (Columbia)
94	—	BLACK HANDS WHITE COTTON — Caboose (Larry Rogers), Enterprise 9015 (Stax/Volt)
95	—	ONLY YOU KNOW AND I KNOW — Dave Mason (Tommy LiPuma & Dave Mason), Blue Thumb 114
96	—	EVERYTHING'S TUESDAY — Chairmen of the Board (Holland-Dozier-Holland), Invictus 9079 (Capitol)
97	—	YOURS LOVE — Joe Simon (John R.), Sound Stage 7 2664 (Monument)
98	—	BALL AND CHAIN — Tommy James (Tommy James & Bob King), Roulette 7084
99	—	A SONG THAT NEVER COMES — Mama Cass Elliot (Steve Barri), Dunhill 4244
100	—	BRING IT ON HOME — Lou Rawls (Rick Hall & David Axelrod), Capitol 2856

THE TOP 40 HITS
1984

PK DATE	PK POS	RANK	TITLE	ARTIST
12/22	1	1.	Like A Virgin	Madonna
7/07	1	2.	When Doves Cry	Prince
2/25	1	3.	Jump	Van Halen
3/31	1	4.	Footloose	Kenny Loggins
9/01	1	5.	What's Love Got To Do With It	Tina Turner
4/21	1	6.	Against All Odds (Take A Look At Me Now)	Phil Collins
10/13	1	7.	I Just Called To Say I Love You	Stevie Wonder
8/11	1	8.	Ghostbusters	Ray Parker Jr.
2/04	1	9.	Karma Chameleon	Culture Club
11/17	1	10.	Wake Me Up Before You Go-Go	Wham!
5/12	1	11.	Hello	Lionel Richie
1/21	1	12.	Owner Of A Lonely Heart	Yes
12/08	1	13.	Out Of Touch	Daryl Hall & John Oates
6/09	1	14.	Time After Time	Cyndi Lauper
5/26	1	15.	Let's Hear It For The Boy	Deniece Williams
9/29	1	16.	Let's Go Crazy	Prince & the Revolution
6/23	1	17.	The Reflex	Duran Duran
11/03	1	18.	Caribbean Queen (No More Love On The Run)	Billy Ocean
9/22	1	19.	Missing You	John Waite
6/30	2	20.	Dancing In The Dark	Bruce Springsteen
12/15	2	21.	The Wild Boys	Duran Duran
3/24	2	22.	Somebody's Watching Me	Rockwell
3/10	2	23.	Girls Just Want To Have Fun	Cyndi Lauper
11/17	2	24.	Purple Rain	Prince & the Revolution
2/11	2	25.	Joanna	Kool & The Gang
3/03	2	26.	99 Luftballons	Nena
11/24	3	27.	I Feel For You	Chaka Khan
9/08	3	28.	She Bop	Cyndi Lauper
1/28	3	29.	Talking In Your Sleep	Romantics
9/29	3	30.	Drive	Cars
8/04	3	31.	State Of Shock	Jacksons
7/07	3	32.	Jump (For My Love)	Pointer Sisters
5/05	3	33.	Hold Me Now	Thompson Twins
8/25	3	34.	Stuck On You	Lionel Richie
10/20	3	35.	Hard Habit To Break	Chicago
6/09	3	36.	Oh Sherrie	Steve Perry
3/31	4	37.	Here Comes The Rain Again	Eurythmics
6/30	4	38.	Self Control	Laura Branigan
7/14	4	39.	Eyes Without A Face	Billy Idol
3/03	4	40.	Thriller	Michael Jackson

THE TOP 40 HITS
1985

PK DATE	PK POS	RANK	TITLE	ARTIST
12/21	1	1.	Say You, Say Me	Lionel Richie
4/13	1	2.	We Are The World	USA for Africa
2/16	1	3.	Careless Whisper	Wham! featuring George Michael
3/09	1	4.	Can't Fight This Feeling	REO Speedwagon
9/21	1	5.	Money For Nothing	Dire Straits
8/03	1	6.	Shout	Tears For Fears
12/07	1	7.	Broken Wings	Mr. Mister
2/02	1	8.	I Want To Know What Love Is	Foreigner
8/24	1	9.	The Power Of Love	Huey Lewis & The News
6/08	1	10.	Everybody Wants To Rule The World	Tears For Fears
11/16	1	11.	We Built This City	Starship
9/07	1	12.	St. Elmo's Fire (Man In Motion)	John Parr
5/25	1	13.	Everything She Wants	Wham!
6/22	1	14.	Heaven	Bryan Adams
7/13	1	15.	A View To A Kill	Duran Duran
3/30	1	16.	One More Night	Phil Collins
11/30	1	17.	Separate Lives	Phil Collins & Marilyn Martin
5/11	1	18.	Crazy For You	Madonna
7/27	1	19.	Everytime You Go Away	Paul Young
5/18	1	20.	Don't You (Forget About Me)	Simple Minds
11/02	1	21.	Part-Time Lover	Stevie Wonder
10/19	1	22.	Take On Me	A-Ha
10/26	1	23.	Saving All My Love For You	Whitney Houston
11/09	1	24.	Miami Vice Theme	Jan Hammer
7/06	1	25.	Sussudio	Phil Collins
10/12	1	26.	Oh Sheila	Ready For The World
12/28	2	27.	Party All The Time	Eddie Murphy
9/21	2	28.	Cherish	Kool & The Gang
2/02	2	29.	Easy Lover	Philip Bailey with Phil Collins
11/16	2	30.	You Belong To The City	Glenn Frey
1/12	2	31.	All I Need	Jack Wagner
3/23	2	32.	Material Girl	Madonna
2/23	2	33.	Loverboy	Billy Ocean
7/20	2	34.	Raspberry Beret	Prince & the Revolution
3/16	2	35.	The Heat Is On	Glenn Frey
9/14	2	36.	We Don't Need Another Hero (Thunderdome)	Tina Turner
6/01	3	37.	Axel F	Harold Faltermeyer
4/27	3	38.	Rhythm Of The Night	DeBarge
12/28	3	39.	Alive & Kicking	Simple Minds
1/19	3	40.	You're The Inspiration	Chicago

THE TOP 40 HITS
1986

PK DATE	PK POS	RANK	TITLE	ARTIST
1/18	1	1.	That's What Friends Are For	Dionne Warwick & Friends
6/14	1	2.	On My Own	Patti LaBelle & Michael McDonald
5/17	1	3.	Greatest Love Of All	Whitney Houston
3/29	1	4.	Rock Me Amadeus	Falco
3/01	1	5.	Kyrie	Mr. Mister
4/19	1	6.	Kiss	Prince & The Revolution
2/15	1	7.	How Will I Know	Whitney Houston
5/03	1	8.	Addicted To Love	Robert Palmer
5/10	1	9.	West End Girls	Pet Shop Boys
7/05	1	10.	There'll Be Sad Songs (To Make You Cry)	Billy Ocean
3/15	1	11.	Sara	Starship
7/12	1	12.	Holding Back The Years	Simply Red
3/22	1	13.	These Dreams	Heart
6/07	1	14.	Live To Tell	Madonna
2/01	2	15.	Burning Heart	Survivor
2/15	2	16.	When The Going Gets Tough, The Tough Get Going	Billy Ocean
4/19	2	17.	Manic Monday	Bangles
4/05	2	18.	R.O.C.K. In The U.S.A. (A Salute To 60's Rock)	John Cougar Mellencamp
3/22	3	19.	Secret Lovers	Atlantic Starr
6/21	3	20.	Crush On You	Jets
2/01	3	21.	I'm Your Man	Wham!
6/14	3	22.	I Can't Wait	Nu Shooz
7/05	3	23.	Who's Johnny	El DeBarge
5/17	3	24.	Why Can't This Be Love	Van Halen
7/05	4	25.	No One Is To Blame	Howard Jones
5/17	4	26.	What Have You Done For Me Lately	Janet Jackson
5/31	4	27.	If You Leave	Orchestral Manoeuvres In The Dark
1/25	4	28.	Talk To Me	Stevie Nicks
3/01	4	29.	Living In America	James Brown
4/12	5	30.	What You Need	INXS
5/03	5	31.	Harlem Shuffle	Rolling Stones
3/01	5	32.	The Sweetest Taboo	Sade
6/07	5	33.	All I Need Is A Miracle	Mike + The Mechanics
5/10	6	34.	Your Love	Outfield
3/08	6	35.	Silent Running (On Dangerous Ground)	Mike + The Mechanics
1/25	6	36.	My Hometown	Bruce Springsteen
1/11	7	37.	Tonight She Comes	Cars
5/10	7	38.	Take Me Home	Phil Collins
1/25	7	39.	Walk Of Life	Dire Straits
4/12	7	40.	Let's Go All The Way	Sly Fox

Note: The above ranking includes only those records that peaked on or before the 7/12/86 "Hot 100" chart.

THE ARTISTS

This section lists, alphabetically by artist name, every single listed in the Top 1000 ranking.

Each artist's hits are listed in rank order, showing their Top 1000 ranking, along with the original label and number.

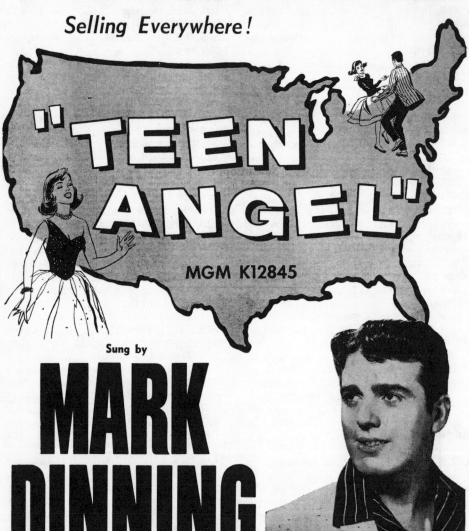

New Hit Streaking Across the Nation!

Selling Everywhere!

"TEEN ANGEL"

MGM K12845

Sung by

MARK DINNING

1540 Broadway, N.Y. 36, N.Y. JU 2-2000

MARK DINNING

BYE NOW, BABY (Acuff-Rose, BMI)—TEEN ANGEL
(Acuff-Rose, BMI)—Dinning has two powerful sides, and
either could step out. "Bye Now, Baby" has Hawaiian
overtones, and it's given a gentle reading. Flip, "Teen
Angel" is folkish, and the vocal is just as salable.
M-G-M 12845

Billboard Hot 100

THIS WEEK	LAST WEEK	TITLE, Weeks On Chart Artist (Producer) Label, Number (Distributing Label)
1	1	CROCODILE ROCK ● 11 Elton John (Gus Dudgeon), MCA 40000
2	2	YOU'RE SO VAIN 12 Carly Simon (Richard Perry), Elektra 45824
3	4	OH BABE, WHAT WOULD YOU SAY 12 Hurricane Smith (Norman Smith), Capitol 3383
4	11	DUELING BANJOS 6 Deliverance (Eric Wiesberg), Warner Bros. 7659
5	15	KILLING ME SOFTLY WITH HIS SONG 4 Roberta Flack (Joel Dorn), Atlantic 45-2940
6	6	DO IT AGAIN 14 Steely Dan (Gary Katz), ABC 11338
7	10	COULD IT BE I'M FALLING IN LOVE 8 Spinners (Thom Bell), Atlantic 45-2927
8	9	DON'T EXPECT ME TO BE YOUR FRIEND 8 Lobo (Phil Gernhard), Big Tree 158 (Bell)
9	3	WHY CAN'T WE LIVE TOGETHER 13 Timmy Thomas (Steve Alaimo for T.K. Prod.), Glades 1703
10	12	ROCKY MOUNTAIN HIGH 13 John Denver (Milton Okun), RCA 74-0829
11	7	THE WORLD IS A GHETTO 14 War (Jerry Goldstein, in association with Lonnie Jordan & Howard Scott/Far Out Prod.), United Artists 50975
12	5	SUPERSTITION 11 Stevie Wonder (Stevie Wonder), Tamla 54226 (Motown)
13	19	LAST SONG 10 Edward Bear (Gene Martynec), Capitol 3452
14	14	DANCING IN THE MOONLIGHT 17 King Harvest (Berjot-Robinson), Perception 515
15	22	LOVE TRAIN 5 O'Jays (Gamble-Huff), Philadelphia International 73524 (Columbia)
16	18	DADDY'S HOME 6 Jermaine Jackson (the Corporation), Motown 1216
17	8	TROUBLE MAN 9 Marvin Gaye (Marvin Gaye), Tamla 54228 (Motown)
18	21	JAMBALAYA (On the Bayou) 8 Blue Ridge Rangers (John Fogerty), Fantasy 689
19	30	THE COVER OF THE ROLLING STONE 12 Dr. Hook & the Medicine Show (Ron Haffkine), Columbia 4-45732
20	16	LOVE JONES 11 Brighter Side of Darkness (Clarence Johnson), 20th Century 2002
21	13	YOUR MAMA DON'T DANCE 9 Ken Loggins & Jim Messina (Jim Messina), Columbia 4-45719
22	26	DO YOU WANT TO DANCE 5 Bette Midler (Joel Dorn), Atlantic 45-2928
23	27	DREIDEL 12 Don McLean (Ed Freeman), United Artists 51100
24	17	HI HI HI 6 Wings (Paul McCartney), Apple 1857
25	50	ALSO SPRACH ZARATHUSTRA (2001) 5 Deodato (Creed Taylor), CTI 12
26	25	YOU TURN ME ON, I'M A RADIO 7 Joni Mitchell, Asylum 11010 (Atlantic)
27	29	REELIN' AND ROCKIN' 6 Chuck Berry (Esmond Edwards), Chess 2136
28	42	I'M JUST A SINGER (In a Rock and Roll Band) 3 Moody Blues (Tony Clark), Threshold 45-67012
29	33	PEACEFUL EASY FEELING 9 Eagles (Glyn Johns), Asylum 11013 (Atlantic)
30	36	I GOT ANTS IN MY PANTS 5 James Brown (James Brown), Polydor 14162
31	20	ME AND MRS. JONES ● 16 Billy Paul (Gamble-Huff), Philadelphia International 73521 (Columbia)
32	34	LIVING TOGETHER GROWING TOGETHER 5 5th Dimension (Bones Howe), Bell 45,310
33	31	HARRY HIPPIE 9 Bobby Womack & Peace (Bobby Womack, Joe Hicks & Muscle Shoals Sound), United Artists 50946
34	38	BIG CITY MISS RUTH ANN 8 Gallery (Mike Theodore, Dennis Coffey), Sussex 248 (Buddah) (London)

THIS WEEK	LAST WEEK	TITLE, Weeks On Chart Artist (Producer) Label, Number (Distributing Label)
35	40	DANNY'S SONG 7 Anne Murray (Brian Ahern), Capitol 3481
36	56	AUBREY 3 Bread (David Gates, James Griffin), Elektra 45832
37	41	JESUS IS JUST ALRIGHT 10 Doobie Brothers (Ted Templeman), Warner Bros. 7661
38	44	HUMMINGBIRD 5 Seals & Crofts (Louie Shelton), Warner Bros. 7671
39	23	SUPERFLY ● 14 Curtis Mayfield (Curtis Mayfield), Curtom 1978 (Buddah)
40	54	NEITHER OF US (Wants to Say Goodbye) 4 Gladys Knight & the Pips (Joe Porter), Soul 35098 (Motown)
41	45	GIVE ME YOUR LOVE 6 Barbara Mason (Curtis Mayfield), Buddah 331
42	53	SPACE ODDITY 3 David Bowie (Gus Dudgeon), RCA 74-0876
43	48	DON'T CROSS THE RIVER 5 America (America), Warner Bros. 7670
44	24	SEPARATE WAYS 7 Elvis Presley, RCA 74-0815
45	49	GOOD MORNING HEARTACHE 6 Diana Ross (Berry Gordy), Motown 1211
46	68	AIN'T NO WOMAN (Like the One I've Got) 3 Four Tops (Steve Barri, Dennis Lambert, Brian Potter), Dunhill 4-339
47	57	DEAD SKUNK 4 Loudon Wainwright III (Thomas Jefferson Kaye), Columbia 4-45726
48	37	I'M NEVER GONNA BE ALONE ANYMORE 8 Cornelius Brothers & Sister Rose (Bob Archibald), United Artists 50996
49	58	SOUL SONG 4 Joe Stampley (Norris Wilson), Dot 17442 (Famous)
50	84	STIR IT UP 3 Johnny Nash (Johnny Nash), Epic 5-10949 (Columbia)
51	46	YOU'VE GOT TO MAKE IT (If You Want It) 9 Main Ingredient (Silvester/Simmons), RCA 74-0856
52	62	ROSALIE 4 Sam Neely (Rudy Durand), Capitol 3510
53	88	BREAK UP TO MAKE UP 4 The Stylistics (Thom Bell), Avco 4611
54	61	TODAY I STARTED LOVING YOU AGAIN 4 Bettye Swann (Rick Hall & Mickey Buckins), Atlantic 45-2921
55	67	KISSING MY LOVE 5 Bill Withers (Bill Withers), Sussex 250 (Buddah)
56	43	PIECES OF APRIL 9 Three Dog Night (Richard Podolor), Dunhill 4331
57	65	HELLO HURRAY 3 Alice Cooper (Bob Ezrin), Warner Bros. 7673
58	64	CONTROL OF ME 6 Les Emmerson (Ted Gerow, Les Emmerson), Lion 141 (MGM)
59	63	TWEEDLE DEE 6 Little Jimmy Osmond (Mike Curb & Don Costa), MGM 14468
60	69	THE MESSAGE 4 Cymande (John Schroeder), Janus 203
61	78	PEACEFUL 3 Helen Reddy (Tom Catalano), Capitol 3527
62	74	ONE LESS SET OF FOOTSTEPS 3 Jim Croce (Terry Cashman & Tommy West), ABC 11346
63	77	MASTER OF EYES 3 Aretha Franklin (Aretha Franklin, Quincy Jones), Atlantic 45-2941
64	51	DAYTIME, NIGHTTIME 9 Keith Hampshire (Pig-Weed Productions), A&M 1403
65	76	KEEP ON SINGING 3 Austin Roberts (Danny Jansen, Bobby Hart, Austin Roberts), Chelsea 0110 (RCA)
66	71	LOVE IS WHAT YOU MAKE IT 4 Grass Roots (Steve Barri, Bob Grill, Waren Entner), Dunhill 4335
67	72	PALACE GUARD 3 Rick Nelson and the Stone Canyon Band (Rick Nelson), MCA 40001

THIS WEEK	LAST WEEK	TITLE, Weeks On Chart Artist (Producer) Label, Number (Distributing Label)
68	70	BOOGIE WOOGIE MAN 9 Paul Davis (Chips Moman & Paul Davis), Bang 599
69	85	A LETTER TO MYSELF 2 The Chi-Lites (Eugene Record), Brunswick 55491
70	73	HAPPY (Love Theme from "Lady Sings the Blues") 7 Bobby Darin (Bob Crewe), Motown 1217
71	75	HOT WIRE 3 Al Green (P. James, C. Rodgers), Bell 6076
72	81	FOLLOW YOUR DAUGHTER HOME 3 Guess Who (Jack Richardson), RCA 74-0880
73	—	CALL ME (Come Back Home) 1 Al Green (Willie Mitchell), Hi 45-2235 (London)
74	80	HOW CAN I TELL YOU 5 Travis Wammack (Rick Hall), United Artists
75	83	LOST HORIZON 2 Shawn Phillips (Burt Bacharach), A&M 1045
76	90	COOK WITH HONEY 3 Judy Collins (Mark Abramson & Judy Collins), Elektra 45831
77	86	LITTLE WILLIE 5 The Sweet (Phil Wainman for New Productions Ltd.), Bell 45-251
78	82	SLOW MOTION, Part 1 4 Johnny Williams (Gamble-Huff), Philadelphia International 73518 (Columbia)
79	—	BITTER BAD 1 Melanie (Peter Schekeryk), Neighborhood 4210 (Famous)
80	—	TIE A YELLOW RIBBON ROUND THE OLD OAK TREE 1 Dawn (Hank Medress, Dave Appel & the Tokens), Bell 45318
81	87	DO IT IN THE NAME OF LOVE 3 Candi Staton (Rick Hall), Fame 91009 (United Artists)
82	92	MAGIC WOMAN TOUCH 2 The Hollies (Hollies), Epic 5-10951 (Columbia)
83	89	DON'T BURN ME 4 Paul Kelly (Buddy Killen), Warner Bros. 7657
84	—	BOO BOO DON'T 'CHA BE BLUE 1 Tommy James (Tommy James & Bob King), Media Sound 7140 (Roulette)
85	—	PARDON ME SIR 1 Joe Cocker (Denny Cordell), A&M 1407
86	—	STEP BY STEP 1 Joe Simon (Raeford Gerald for Guardian Productions), Spring 133 (Polydor)
87	—	DREAM ME HOME 1 Mac Davis (Rick Hall), Columbia 4-45773
88	—	DAISY A DAY 1 Jud Strunk (Mike Curb & Don Costa), MGM 14463
89	—	ONE MAN BAND (Plays All Alone) 1 Ronnie Dyson (Thom Bell), Columbia 4-45776
90	100	THE NIGHT THE LIGHTS WENT OUT IN GEORGIA 2 Vicki Lawrence (Snuff Garrett), Bell 45-303
91	—	BREAKING UP SOMEONE'S HOME 1 Albert King (Allen Jones & Henry Bush), Stax 0147 (Columbia)
92	—	WALK ON THE WILD SIDE 1 Lou Reed (David Bowie), RCA 74-0887
93	95	WISH THAT I COULD TALK TO YOU 3 Sylvers (Jerry Butler, Meg Johnson, Michael Viner), Pride 1019 (MGM)
94	94	SOMEBODY LOVES YOU 4 Whispers (Ron Carson for GRT Corporation), Janus 200
95	97	GOOD MORNING 2 Michael Redway (Redway/Field), Philips 40720 (Phonogram)
96	—	BELL BOTTOM BLUES 1 Eric Clapton (The Dominos & Tom Dowd), Polydor 15056
97	99	TOSSIN' AND TURNIN' 2 Bunny Sigler (Gamble-Huff), Philadelphia International 73523 (Columbia)
98	98	LOVE MUSIC 3 Raiders (Mark Lindsay), Columbia 4-45759
99	—	WILDFLOWER 1 Skylark (Eirik the Norwegian), Capitol 6626
100	—	SHE'S GOT TO BE A SAINT 3 Ray Price (Don Law Productions), Columbia 4-45724

Compiled from national retail sales and radio airplay by the Music Popularity Charts Dept. of Billboard.

RANK	Title . . . Label & No.

BELLAMY BROTHERS
566 Let Your Love Flow ....Warner 8169
BROOK BENTON
723 The Boll Weevil Song .... Mercury 71820
CHUCK BERRY
409 My Ding-A-Ling..................Chess 2131
734 Sweet Little Sixteen ....Chess 1683
973 School Day........................Chess 1653
MR. ACKER BILK
445 Stranger On The Shore ....Atco 6217
MARCIE BLANE
957 Bobby's Girl ....Seville 120
BLONDIE
44 Call Me..........................Chrysalis 2414
347 Rapture ....Chrysalis 2485
450 The Tide Is High..............Chrysalis 2465
539 Heart Of Glass ....Chrysalis 2295
BLOOD, SWEAT & TEARS
733 Spinning Wheel ....Columbia 44871
745 You've Made Me So Very Happy........
.... Columbia 44776
901 And When I Die.............. Columbia 45008
BLUE SWEDE
548 Hooked On A Feeling .... EMI 3627
U.S. BONDS
358 Quarter To Three..............Legrand 1008
DEBBY BOONE
4 You Light Up My Life ....Warner 8455
PAT BOONE
18 Love Letters In The Sand....... Dot 15570
38 April Love ....Dot 15660
92 I Almost Lost My Mind .... Dot 15472
259 Ain't That A Shame..............Dot 15377
441 Don't Forbid Me ....Dot 15521
626 Moody River ....Dot 16209
DAVID BOWIE
397 Fame...............................RCA 10320
456 Let's Dance .... EMI America 8158
BOX TOPS
145 The Letter ....Mala 565
833 Cry Like A Baby ....Mala 593
LAURA BRANIGAN
702 Gloria ....Atlantic 4048
BREAD
460 Make It With You..............Elektra 45686
BROTHERS FOUR
681 Greenfields...................Columbia 41571
BROTHERS JOHNSON
997 I'll Be Good To You ....A&M 1806
ARTHUR BROWN
904 Fire..............................Atlantic 2556
BROWNS
117 The Three Bells...................RCA 7555
B.T. EXPRESS
799 Do It ('Til You're Satisfied) ....
..........................Roadshow 12395
BUCKINGHAMS
391 Kind Of A Drag ...................U.S.A. 860

RANK	Title . . . Label & No.

BYRDS
225 Turn! Turn! Turn!............ Columbia 43424
592 Mr. Tambourine Man....... Columbia 43271

C

GLEN CAMPBELL
293 Rhinestone Cowboy ....Capitol 4095
503 Southern Nights ....Capitol 4376
CAPTAIN & TENNILLE
150 Love Will Keep Us Together ... A&M 1672
429 Do That To Me One More Time ....
............................Casablanca 2215
986 Lonely Night (Angel Face) ...... A&M 1782
IRENE CARA
37 Flashdance...What A Feeling.............
...........................Casablanca 811440
ERIC CARMEN
738 All By Myself .... Arista 0165
KIM CARNES
7 Bette Davis Eyes .... EMI America 8077
CARPENTERS
109 (They Long To Be) Close To You ....
...........................A&M 1183
337 Top Of The World.................A&M 1468
643 Please Mr. Postman..............A&M 1646
682 We've Only Just Begun ....A&M 1217
789 Superstar.........................A&M 1289
818 Rainy Days And Mondays ...... A&M 1260
842 Hurting Each Other ....A&M 1322
922 Yesterday Once More............A&M 1446
CATHY CARR
863 Ivory Tower ....Fraternity 734
CARS
995 Drive ....Elektra 69706
JOHNNY CASH
735 A Boy Named Sue .... Columbia 44944
SHAUN CASSIDY
564 Da Doo Ron Ron...............Warner 8365
CHAMPS
64 Tequila ....Challenge 1016
GENE CHANDLER
224 Duke Of Earl.....................Vee-Jay 416
BRUCE CHANNEL
222 Hey! Baby ....Smash 1731
HARRY CHAPIN
620 Cat's In The Cradle............Elektra 45203
RAY CHARLES
68 I Can't Stop Loving You . ABC-Para. 10330
362 Hit The Road Jack.........ABC-Para. 10244
648 Georgia On My Mind......ABC-Para. 10135
939 You Don't Know Me.......ABC-Para. 10345
CHUBBY CHECKER
153 The Twist..........................Parkway 811
209 Pony Time........................Parkway 818
755 Limbo Rock ....Parkway 849
CHER
308 Gypsys, Tramps & Thieves.....Kapp 2146
346 Half-Breed.........................MCA 40102

RANK	Title . . . Label & No.	RANK	Title . . . Label & No.

BOBBY DARIN
5 Mack The Knife .... Atco 6147
867 Dream Lover .... Atco 6140

MAC DAVIS
198 Baby Don't Get Hooked On Me ....
.... Columbia 45618

SAMMY DAVIS, JR.
232 The Candy Man .... MGM 14320

SKEETER DAVIS
914 The End Of The World .... RCA 8098

DAWN
107 Tie A Yellow Ribbon Round The Ole
Oak Tree .... Bell 45318
172 Knock Three Times .... Bell 938
256 He Don't Love You (Like I Love You) ..
.... Elektra 45240

BOBBY DAY
757 Rock-in Robin .... Class 229

DORIS DAY
693 Whatever Will Be, Will Be (Que Sera,
Sera) .... Columbia 40704

JIMMY DEAN
77 Big Bad John .... Columbia 42175

JOEY DEE & THE STARLITERS
173 Peppermint Twist .... Roulette 4401

KIKI DEE - see ELTON JOHN

RICK DEES
451 Disco Duck .... RSO 857

JOHN DENVER
381 Annie's Song .... RCA 0295
487 I'm Sorry .... RCA 10353
556 Sunshine On My Shoulders .... RCA 0213
636 Thank God I'm A Country Boy ....
.... RCA 10239
875 Take Me Home, Country Roads ....
.... RCA 0445

DEODATO
926 Also Sprach Zarathustra (2001) ... CTI 12

TERI DeSARIO with K.C.
797 Yes, I'm Ready .... Casablanca 2227

DEXYS MIDNIGHT RUNNERS
601 Come On Eileen .... Mercury 76189

NEIL DIAMOND
284 You Don't Bring Me Flowers ....
.... Columbia 10840
Barbra Streisand & Neil Diamond
549 Cracklin' Rosie .... Uni 55250
627 Song Sung Blue .... Uni 55326
704 Love On The Rocks .... Capitol 4939

DIAMONDS
661 Little Darlin' .... Mercury 71060

DICK & DEEDEE
860 The Mountain's High .... Liberty 55350

MARK DINNING
285 Teen Angel .... MGM 12845

DION
326 Runaround Sue .... Laurie 3110
744 Ruby Baby .... Columbia 42662

891 The Wanderer .... Laurie 3115

DIRE STRAITS
214 Money For Nothing .... Warner 28950

DIXIE CUPS
245 Chapel Of Love .... Red Bird 001

CARL DOBKINS, JR.
991 My Heart Is An Open Book . Decca 30803

BILL DOGGETT
691 Honky Tonk (Parts 1 & 2) .... King 4950

FATS DOMINO
692 Blueberry Hill .... Imperial 5407

BO DONALDSON & THE HEYWOODS
375 Billy, Don't Be A Hero .... ABC 11435

DONOVAN
591 Sunshine Superman .... Epic 10045
726 Mellow Yellow .... Epic 10098

DOOBIE BROTHERS
483 What A Fool Believes .... Warner 8725
568 Black Water .... Warner 8062

DOORS
194 Light My Fire .... Elektra 45615
333 Hello, I Love You .... Elektra 45635

JIMMY DORSEY
670 So Rare .... Fraternity 755

CARL DOUGLAS
354 Kung Fu Fighting .... 20th Century 2140

DOVELLS
769 Bristol Stomp .... Parkway 827

JOE DOWELL
570 Wooden Heart .... Smash 1708

DRIFTERS
195 Save The Last Dance For Me ....
.... Atlantic 2071
908 There Goes My Baby .... Atlantic 2025

DURAN DURAN
340 The Reflex .... Capitol 5345
405 A View To A Kill .... Capitol 5475
685 The Wild Boys .... Capitol 5417
971 Hungry Like The Wolf .... Harvest 5195

BOB DYLAN
854 Like A Rolling Stone .... Columbia 43346
942 Rainy Day Women #12 & 35 ....
.... Columbia 43592

E

EAGLES
457 One Of These Nights .... Asylum 45257
489 Heartache Tonight .... Asylum 46545
505 Hotel California .... Asylum 45386
563 New Kid In Town .... Asylum 45373
604 Best Of My Love .... Asylum 45218
839 Lyin' Eyes .... Asylum 45279

EARTH, WIND & FIRE
637 Shining Star .... Columbia 10090
771 After The Love Has Gone ..... ARC 11033
949 Let's Groove .... ARC 02536

RANK	Title . . . Label & No.

G

MARVIN GAYE
29 I Heard It Through The Grapevine ......
.... Tamla 54176
263 Let's Get It On .... Tamla 54234
477 Got To Give It Up - Pt. 1..... Tamla 54280
722 What's Going On .... Tamla 54201
968 Sexual Healing .... Columbia 03302
CRYSTAL GAYLE
703 Don't It Make My Brown Eyes Blue ....
.... United Art. 1016
GLORIA GAYNOR
160 I Will Survive.................... Polydor 14508
J. GEILS BAND
43 Centerfold .... EMI America 8102
BOBBIE GENTRY
134 Ode To Billie Joe................ Capitol 5950
ANDY GIBB
21 Shadow Dancing .... RSO 893
91 I Just Want To Be Your Everything.....
.... RSO 872
267 (Love Is) Thicker Than Water... RSO 883
NICK GILDER
464 Hot Child In The City........Chrysalis 2226
JIMMY GILMER & THE FIREBALLS
78 Sugar Shack...................... Dot 16487
GO–GO'S
712 We Got The Beat................ I.R.S. 9903
BOBBY GOLDSBORO
79 Honey .... United Art. 50283
LESLEY GORE
385 It's My Party .... Mercury 72119
752 You Don't Own Me .... Mercury 72206
CHARLIE GRACIE
349 Butterfly........................... Cameo 105
GRAND FUNK RAILROAD
398 The Loco-Motion............... Capitol 3840
611 We're An American Band..... Capitol 3660
EDDY GRANT
669 Electric Avenue .... Portrait 03793
GOGI GRANT
12 The Wayward Wind............... Era 1013
R.B. GREAVES
892 Take A Letter Maria .... Atco 6714
AL GREEN
479 Let's Stay Together .... Hi 2202
NORMAN GREENBAUM
985 Spirit In The Sky .... Reprise 0885
LORNE GREENE
593 Ringo .... RCA 8444
GUESS WHO
212 American Woman .... RCA 0325

H

BILL HALEY & His Comets
11 Rock Around The Clock...... Decca 29124

DARYL HALL & JOHN OATES
98 Maneater .... RCA 13354
205 Kiss On My List .... RCA 12142
295 Private Eyes .... RCA 12296
299 Out Of Touch..................... RCA 13916
400 Rich Girl .... RCA 10860
438 I Can't Go For That (No Can Do)........
.... RCA 12357
678 Say It Isn't So.................... RCA 13654
HAMILTON, JOE FRANK & REYNOLDS
622 Fallin' In Love .... Playboy 6024
JAN HAMMER
551 Miami Vice Theme .... MCA 52666
RICHARD HARRIS
936 MacArthur Park................. Dunhill 4134
GEORGE HARRISON
122 My Sweet Lord .... Apple 2995
588 Give Me Love (Give Me Peace On
Earth)........................... Apple 1862
742 All Those Years Ago ..... Dark Horse 49725
WILBERT HARRISON
356 Kansas City .... Fury 1023
**DONNY HATHAWAY - see ROBERTA
FLACK**
ISAAC HAYES
329 Theme From Shaft.......... Enterprise 9038
ROY HEAD
855 Treat Her Right ....Back Beat 546
HEART
607 These Dreams .... Capitol 5541
HEATWAVE
764 Boogie Nights .... Epic 50370
BOBBY HEBB
836 Sunny............................ Philips 40365
DON HENLEY
969 Dirty Laundry .... Asylum 69894
HERMAN'S HERMITS
247 Mrs. Brown You've Got A Lovely
Daughter....................... MGM 13341
635 I'm Henry VIII, I Am .... MGM 13367
835 Can't You Hear My Heartbeat............
.... MGM 13310
**EDDIE HEYWOOD - see HUGO
WINTERHALTER**
HIGHWAYMEN
331 Michael.......................... United Art. 258
HOLLIES
786 Long Cool Woman (In A Black Dress) .
.... Epic 10871
BUDDY HOLLY
972 Peggy Sue .... Coral 61885
HOLLYWOOD ARGYLES
524 Alley-Oop........................... Lute 5905
EDDIE HOLMAN
921 Hey There Lonely Girl .... ABC 11240
CLINT HOLMES
775 Playground In My Mind......... Epic 10891

RANK	Title . . . Label & No.

RUPERT HOLMES
180 Escape (The Pina Colada Song) .... Infinity 50035

HONEY CONE
612 Want Ads .... Hot Wax 7011

MARY HOPKIN
730 Those Were The Days .... Apple 1801

JOHNNY HORTON
41 The Battle Of New Orleans............... .... Columbia 41339

HOT CHOCOLATE
979 You Sexy Thing............... Big Tree 16047

THELMA HOUSTON
497 Don't Leave Me This Way ... Tamla 54278

WHITNEY HOUSTON
236 Greatest Love Of All .... Arista 9466
395 How Will I Know.................. Arista 9434
534 Saving All My Love For You .. Arista 9381

HUES CORPORATION
645 Rock The Boat..................... RCA 0232

HUMAN LEAGUE
162 Don't You Want Me .... A&M 2397

TAB HUNTER
42 Young Love......................... Dot 15533

BRIAN HYLAND
519 Itsy Bitsy Teenie Weenie Yellow Polkadot Bikini.................. Leader 805

I

IDES OF MARCH
937 Vehicle ....Warner 7378

IMPALAS
812 Sorry (I Ran All the Way Home)..............................Cub 9022

JORGEN INGMANN
847 Apache............................. Atco 6184

JAMES INGRAM - see PATTI AUSTIN

ISLEY BROTHERS
896 It's Your Thing .... T-Neck 901

J

TERRY JACKS
206 Seasons In The Sun .... Bell 45432

JACKSON 5
65 I'll Be There..................... Motown 1171
327 ABC............................... Motown 1163
328 The Love You Save .... Motown 1166
472 I Want You Back .... Motown 1157
736 Never Can Say Goodbye..... Motown 1179
765 Dancing Machine.............. Motown 1286
858 Mama's Pearl .... Motown 1177

MICHAEL JACKSON
28 Billie Jean .... Epic 03509
40 Say Say Say .... Columbia 04168
Paul McCartney & Michael Jackson

RANK	Title . . . Label & No.

124 Rock With You.................... Epic 50797
176 Beat It .... Epic 03759
582 Ben............................Motown 1207
619 Don't Stop 'Til You Get Enough .... Epic 50742
707 The Girl Is Mine .... Epic 03288
Michael Jackson/Paul McCartney
794 Rockin' Robin ....Motown 1197

JAGGERZ
924 The Rapper .... Kama Sutra 502

SONNY JAMES
434 Young Love......................Capitol 3602

TOMMY JAMES & THE SHONDELLS
273 Crimson And Clover.......... Roulette 7028
419 Hanky Panky .... Roulette 4686
715 Crystal Blue Persuasion..... Roulette 7050

JAN & DEAN
384 Surf City ....Liberty 55580

JAYNETTS
845 Sally, Go 'Round The Roses .... Tuff 369

JEFFERSON STARSHIP - see STARSHIP

JOAN JETT & THE BLACKHEARTS
24 I Love Rock 'N Roll.......... Boardwalk 135

BILLY JOEL
268 It's Still Rock And Roll To Me............ .... Columbia 11276
537 Tell Her About It............. Columbia 04012
948 Uptown Girl .... Columbia 04149
967 My Life .... Columbia 10853

ELTON JOHN
142 Don't Go Breaking My Heart ....Rocket 40585
Elton John & Kiki Dee
196 Crocodile Rock ....MCA 40000
240 Island Girl ....MCA 40461
296 Philadelphia Freedom...........MCA 40364
415 Lucy In The Sky With Diamonds......... ....MCA 40344
473 Bennie And The Jets............MCA 40198
729 Goodbye Yellow Brick Road ..MCA 40148
853 Don't Let The Sun Go Down On Me ... .MCA 40259
894 Daniel...............................MCA 40046
950 Little Jeannie ....MCA 41236

ROBERT JOHN
463 Sad Eyes .... EMI America 8015
987 The Lion Sleeps Tonight..... Atlantic 2846

JIMMY JONES
868 Handy Man.........................Cub 9049
1000 Good Timin'.........................Cub 9067

TOM JONES
882 She's A Lady .... Parrot 40058

JANIS JOPLIN
357 Me And Bobby McGee .... Columbia 45314

JOURNEY
663 Open Arms.................... Columbia 02687

BRENDA LEE
Does it again!

"I WANT TO BE WANTED"

"JUST A LITTLE"

DECCA
9-31149

a New World of Sound...

DECCA
Records

BRENDA LEE
I WANT TO BE WANTED (Leeds, ASCAP) (3:00)—
JUST A LITTLE (Champion, BMI) (2:23)—The petite
thrush has two more tremendous sides here, the top one
a ballad, and the second side a rhythm tune. On each
she comes thru with a heartfelt vocal.　**Decca 31149**

FOR WEEK ENDING JULY 28, 1973

Billboard HOT 100®

● Records Industry Association Of America seal of certification as "million seller." (Seal indicated by bullet.) •

★ STAR PERFORMER: Star designates records showing greatest upward movement compared to previous week's position.

*Chart Bound

FREE RIDE—Edgar Winter Group (Epic 5-11024)
PEACEMAKER—Albert Hammond (Mums 6021)
TWISTIN' THE NIGHT AWAY—Rod Stewart, (Mercury 73412)

SEE TOP SINGLE PICKS REVIEWS, page 58

THIS WEEK	LAST WEEK	WEEKS ON CHART	TITLE—Artist (Producer) Writer, Label & Number (Distributing Label)	
1	1	15	BAD, BAD LEROY BROWN—Jim Croce (Terry Cashman, Tommy West), Jim Croce, ABC 11359	B-3
2	3	9	YESTERDAY ONCE MORE—Carpenters (Richard & Karen Carpenter), Richard Carpenter, John Bettis, A&M 1446	NAK
3	4	11	SHAMBALA—Three Dog Night (Richard Podolor), Daniel Moore, Dunhill 4352	WCP
★4	7	10	SMOKE ON THE WATER—Deep Purple (Deep Purple), Richie Blackmore, Ian Gillan, Roger Glover, Jon Lord, Ian Paice, Warner Bros. 7710	B-3
5	2	18	WILL IT GO ROUND IN CIRCLES—Billy Preston ● (Billy Preston), Billy Preston, Bruce Fisher, A&M 1411	NAK
★6	11	12	DIAMOND GIRL—Seals & Crofts (Louie Shelton), Jim Seals, Dash Crofts, Warner Brothers 7708	WBM
7	5	11	KODACHROME—Paul Simon (Paul Simon & the Muscle Shoals Sound Rhythm Section), Paul Simon, Columbia 4-45859	B-B
8	8	12	BOOGIE WOOGIE BUGLE BOY—Bette Midler (Barry Manilow), Don Raye, Hughie Prince, Atlantic 45-2964	MCA
★9	20	6	THE MORNING AFTER—Maureen McGovern (Carl Maduri), Al Kasha, Joel Hirshhorn, 20th Century 2010	WCP
10	6	11	GIVE ME LOVE (Give Me Peace On Earth)—George Harrison (George Harrison), George Harrison, Apple 1862	HAN
★11	17	9	TOUCH ME IN THE MORNING—Diana Ross (Michael Masser, Tom Baird), Michael Masser, Ron Miller, Motown 1239	WCP
★12	16	16	MONSTER MASH—Bobby (Boris) Pickett & the Crypt Kickers (Gary Paxton), B. Pickett, L. Capizzi, Parrot 348 (London)	SGC
13	14	11	MONEY—Pink Floyd (Pink Floyd), Roger Waters, Harvest 3609 (Capitol)	
14	9	19	PLAYGROUND IN MY MIND—Clint Holmes ● (Paul Vance & Lee Pockriss), Paul Vance & Lee Pockriss, Epic 5-10891 (Columbia)	B-3
15	10	15	NATURAL HIGH—Bloodstone ● (Mike Vernon), McCormick, London 45-1046	
16	19	6	FEELIN' STRONGER EVERY DAY—Chicago (James William Guercio), Peter Cetera & James Pankow, Columbia 4-45880	
17	18	13	SO VERY HARD TO GO—Tower of Power (Tower of Power), S. Kupka, E. Castillo, Warner Brothers 7687	WBM
★18	22	6	GET DOWN—Gilbert O'Sullivan (Gordon Mills), Gilbert O'Sullivan, MAM 3629 (London)	MCA
★19	26	6	I BELIEVE IN YOU (You Believe in Me)—Johnnie Taylor (Don Davis), Don Davis; Stax 0161 (Columbia)	SGC
★20	24	6	BROTHER LOUIE—Stories (Kenny Kerner, Richie Wise) Michael Brown, Kama Sutra 577 (Buddah)	
★21	29	4	LIVE AND LET DIE—Wings (George Martin), Paul McCartney, Apple 1863	B-3
22	23	9	MISDEMEANOR—Foster Sylvers (Keg Johnson, Mike Viner), Leon Sylvers III, MGM 14580	
★23	30	5	UNEASY RIDER—Charlie Daniels (Charlie Daniels) Charlie Daniels, Kama Sutra 576 (Buddah)	
★24	33	4	HERE I AM (Come and Take Me)—Al Green (Willie Mitchell, Al Green), Al Green, M. Hodges, Hi 2247 (London)	SGC
25	27	5	IF YOU WANT ME TO STAY—Sly & the Family Stone (Sly Stone for Fresh) Sylvester Stewart, Epic 5-11017 (Columbia)	
26	12	15	LONG TRAIN RUNNING—Doobie Brothers (Ted Templeman), Tom Johnston, Warner Brothers 7698	WBM
27	15	14	BEHIND CLOSED DOORS—Charlie Rich (Billy Sherrill), Kenny O'Dell, Epic 5-10950 (Columbia)	SGC
28	31	7	WHERE PEACEFUL WATERS FLOW—Gladys Knight & the Pips (Tony Camillo, Gladys Knight and the Pips) Jim Weatherly, Buddah 363	SGC
★29	35	6	HOW CAN I TELL HER—Lobo (Phil Gernhard), Lobo, Big Tree 16,004 (Bell)	
★30	38	4	ANGEL—Aretha Franklin (Quincy Jones & Aretha Franklin), C. Franklin, S. Saunders, Atlantic 45-2969	SGC
31	21	16	MY LOVE—Paul McCartney & Wings ● (The Gramophone Company), Paul McCartney, Apple 1861	HAN
★32	41	6	DELTA DAWN—Helen Reddy (Tom Catalano), A. Harvey, L. Collins, Capitol 3645	B-3
33	13	16	RIGHT PLACE, WRONG TIME—Dr. John (Allen Toussaint), Mac Rebennack, Atco 6914	WBM
34	25	9	DOIN' IT TO DEATH—Fred Wesley & the J.B.'s (James Brown), James Brown, People 621 (Polydor)	
35	37	6	SOUL MAKOSSA—Manu Dibango (No Producer Listed), Manu Dibango, Atlantic 45-2971	
★36	50	3	LET'S GET IT ON—Marvin Gaye (Marvin Gaye, Ed Townsend) Ed Townsend, Tamla 54234 (Motown)	WCP
37	32	14	ONE OF A KIND (Love Affair)—Spinners ● (Thom Bell), Joseph B. Jefferson, Atlantic 45-2962	B-B
★38	47	6	ARE YOU MAN ENOUGH—Four Tops (Steve Barri, Dennis Lambert & Brian Potter), Dennis Lambert, Dunhill 4354	B-3/WCP
★39	51	3	SAY, HAS ANYBODY SEEN MY SWEET GYPSY ROSE—Dawn featuring Tony Orlando (Hank Medress, Dave Appell and the Tokens) Irwin Levine & L. Russell Brown, Bell 45,374	
40	36	9	I'LL ALWAYS LOVE MY MAMA—Intruders (Gamble-Huff), K. Gamble, L. Huff, J. Whitehead, G. McFadden, Gamble 2506 (Columbia)	B-B
41	34	16	I'M GONNA LOVE YOU JUST A LITTLE MORE BABY—Barry White (Barry White), Barry White, 20th Century 2018	CPI
42	44	14	ROLL OVER BEETHOVEN—Electric Light Orchestra (Jeff Lynne), Chuck Berry, United Artists 173	WBM
★43	60	4	THE HURT—Cat Stevens (Cat Stevens), Cat Stevens, A&M 1418	WCP
44	53	7	NOBODY WANTS YOU WHEN YOU'RE DOWN & OUT—Bobby Womack (Bobby Womack) J. Cox, United Artists 255	MCA
45	46	8	THERE'S NO ME WITHOUT YOU—Manhattans (Bobby Martin), E. Bivins, Columbia 4-45838	
★46	66	2	GYPSY MAN—War (Jerry Goldstein), D. Allen, H. Brown, B. Dickerson, L. Jordan, C. Miller, L. Oaskar, H. Scott, United Artists 281	
47	39	14	DADDY COULD SWEAR I DECLARE—Gladys Knight & the Pips (Johnny Bristol), John Bristol, M. Knight, Gladys Knight, Soul 35105 (Motown)	WCP
48	28	12	SATIN SHEETS—Jeanne Pruett (Walter Haynes), John E. Volinkaty, MCA 40015	MCA
★49	69	3	YOUNG LOVE/A MILLION TO ONE—Donny Osmond (Mike Curb & Don Costa) Joyer, Contey, MGM 14583	SGC
50	42	17	WHY ME—Kris Kristofferson (Fred Foster, Dennis Linde), Kris Kristofferson, Monument 8571 (Columbia)	CHA
51	57	6	OVER THE HILL & FAR AWAY—Led Zeppelin (Jimmy Page), James Patrick Page, Atlantic 2970	
★52	67	3	BELIEVE IN HUMANITY/YOU LIGHT UP MY LIFE—Carole King (Lou Adler) Carole King, Ode 66035 (A&M	SGC
★53	65	3	CLOUDS—David Gates (David Gates) David Gates, Elektra 45857	SGC
54	49	8	SOUL MAKOSSA—Afrique (No Producer Listed), Manu Dibango, Mainstream 5542	
55	43	19	PILLOW TALK—Sylvia ● (Sylvia Robinson & Michael Burton), Sylvia Robinson, Michael Burton, Vibration 521 (All Platinum)	SGC
56	48	7	WATERGRATE—Dickie Goodman (Dickie Goodman) Dickie Goodman, Rainy Wednesday 202	
57	68	3	MEET THAT LADY—Isley Brothers (The Isleys) The Isleys, T-Neck 72251 (Columbia)	
★58	87	3	EVERYONE'S AGREED THAT EVERYTHING WILL TURN OUT FINE—Stealers Wheel (Lieber-Stoller) Joe Egan, Gerry Rafferty, A&M 1450	
59	59	11	TIME TO GET DOWN—O'Jays (Gamble-Huff), Gamble-Huff, Philadelphia International 73531 (Columbia)	B-B
★60	72	4	I WAS CHECKIN' OUT SHE WAS CHECKIN' IN—Don Covay (Don Covay for Ragmop Productions), Don Covay, Mercury 73385 (Phonogram)	
61	45	7	GOIN' HOME—Osmonds (Alan Osmond) Alan Osmond, Wayne Osmond, Merrill Osmond, MGM 14562	HAN
62	55	8	PLASTIC MAN—Temptations (Norman Whitfield), Norman Whitfield, Gordy 7129 (Motown)	
63	52	9	NEVER, NEVER, NEVER—Shirley Bassey (Noel Rogers), T. Renis, A. Tosta, N. Newell, United Artists 211	
64	74	4	LOVE, LOVE, LOVE—Donny Hathaway (Arif Mardin), J.R. Bailey, Ken Williams, Atco 6928	SGC
65	61	15	GIVE YOUR BABY A STANDING OVATION—Dells (Don Davis), Marv Johnson, Henry Williams, Cadet 5696 (Chess/Janus)	SGC
66	64	6	TEQUILA SUNRISE—Eagles (Glyn Johns), Don Henley, Glen Frey, Asylum 11017 (Atlantic)	WBM
67	54	16	AND I LOVE YOU SO—Perry Como (Chet Atkins), Don McLean, RCA 74-0906	B-3
68	58	12	SWAMP WITCH—Jim Stafford (Phil Gerphard & Lobo), Jim Stafford, MGM 14496	HAN
69	76	4	SWEET CHARLIE BABE—Jackie Moore (Young Professionals), Phil Hurtt, Bunny Sigler, Atlantic 45-2956	WBM
70	78	4	IT'S FOREVER—The Ebonys (Gamble-Huff), Leon Huff, Philadelphia International 73529 (Columbia)	B-B
71	63	8	FINDER'S KEEPERS—Chairmen of the Board (Jefferson Bowen, General Johnson), General Johnson, Jeffrey Bowen, Invictus 1251 (Columbia)	B-B
★72	88	3	DARLING COME BACK HOME—Eddie Kendricks (Frank Wilson, Leonard Caston) K. Wakefield, F. Wilson, K. Errisson, Tamla 54236 (Motown)	WCP
73	79	7	BLOCKBUSTER—The Sweet (Phil Wainman for New Dawn Productions, Ltd.) Nicky Chinn, Mike Chapman, Bell 45,361	WBM
74	85	2	FUTURE SHOCK—Curtis Mayfield (Curtis Mayfield), Curtis Mayfield, Curtom 1987 (Buddah)	
75	86	4	SWEET HARMONY—Smokey Robinson (Smokey Robinson, Willie Hutch), William Robinson, Tamla 54233 (Motown)	WCP
76	62	10	I'D RATHER BE A COWBOY—John Denver (Milton Okun & Kris O'Connor) John Denver, RCA 74-0955	WBM
77	70	8	SIXTY MINUTE MAN—Clarence Carter (Rick Hall), Allen Toussaint, Fame 250 (United Artists)	SGC
78	89	2	BABY I'VE BEEN MISSING YOU—Independents (Chuck Jackson, Marvin Yancy), Chuck Jackson, Marvin Yancy, Wand 11258 (Scepter)	
79	82	4	LORD, MR. FORD—Jerry Reed (Chet Atkins, Jerry Reed), Jerry Reed, RCA 74-0960	SGC
80	81	2	BONGO ROCK—Incredible Bongo Band (Michael Viner), Epps, Egnoian, MGM 14588	SGC
★81	NEW ENTRY		MY MARIA—B.W. Stevenson (David H. Kershenbaum), Daniel Moore, B.W. Stevenson, RCA 0030	WCP
82	80	5	THERE YOU GO—Edwin Starr (Edwin Starr) Edwin Starr, Soul 35103 (Motown)	WCP
★83	NEW ENTRY		WE'RE AN AMERICAN BAND—Grand Funk (Todd Rundgren), Don Brewer, Capitol 3660	
84	84	2	DIDN'T I—Sylvia (Sylvia Robinson, Michael Burton), Sylvia Robinson, Michael Burton, A. Goodman, B. Brown) Vibration 524 (All Platinum)	
85	75	6	HE DID WITH ME—Vicki Lawrence (Snuff Garrett for Garrett Music Ent.), Gloria Sklerov, Harry Lloyd, Bell 45,362	WCP
★86	NEW ENTRY		THEME FROM "CLEOPATRA JONES"—Joe Simon featuring the Main Streeters (Joe Simon), Joe Simon, Spring 1387 (Polydor)	
87	91	2	SUNSHINE—Mickey Newbury (Buss Miller, Marlin Greene, Dennis Linde), Mickey Newbury, Elektra 45863	
88	95	2	ONE TIN SOLDIER—Coven (Michael Lloyd, Mundell Lowe), Lambert & Potter, MGM 14308	WCP
89	92	5	TOP OF THE WORLD—Lynn Anderson (Glenn Sutton) Richard Carpenter, John Bettis, Columbia 4-45857	
90	NEW ENTRY		THERE IT IS—Tyrone Davis (Willie Henderson), Leo Graham, Dakar 4523 (Brunswick)	SGC
91	83	4	ROLAND THE ROADIE AND GERTRUDE THE GROUPIE—Dr. Hook & the Medicine Show (Ron Haffkine), Shel Silverstein, Columbia 4-45878	
92	93	2	JIMMY LOVES MARY ANNE—Looking Glass (Arif Mardin), E. Lurie, Epic 5-11001 (Columbia)	
93	77	5	MY MERRY-GO-ROUND—Johnny Nash (Johnny Nash) J. Nash, D.D. Brodsky, D. Rogers, Epic 5-11003 (Columbia)	
94	NEW ENTRY		SYLVIA—Focus (Mike Vernor), Thijs Van Leer, Sire 708 (Famous)	
95	NEW ENTRY		SHOW BIZ KIDS—Steely Dan (Gary Katz), W. Becker, D. Fagen, ABC 11382	WCP
96	97	4	SMOKE, SMOKE, SMOKE (That Cigarette)—Commander & His Lost Planet Airmen (An Ozone Production with Stephan Jarvis), Travis, Williams, Paramount 0216 (Famous)	B-3
97	90	4	FRIEND OF MINE—Bill Withers (Bill Withers, Ray Jackson, James Gadson, Melvin Dunlap, Bernorce Blackman), Bill Withers, Sussex 257	WBM
98	NEW ENTRY		L.A. FREEWAY—Jerry Jeff Walker (Free Flow Production), Guy Clark, MCA 40054	
99	99	6	BLACK BYRD—Donald Byrd (Larry Mizell for Sky High) Larry Mizell, Blue Note 212 (United Artists)	SGC
100	100	7	YOU WERE ALWAYS THERE—Donna Fargo (Stan Silver) Donna Fargo, Dot 17460 (Famous)	SG

103

RANK	Title . . . Label & No.	RANK	Title . . . Label & No.

MFSB featuring The Three Degrees
402 TSOP (The Sound Of Philadelphia) .....
....Phil. Int. 3540

BETTE MIDLER
977 The Rose .... Atlantic 3656

MITCH MILLER & The Gang
32 The Yellow Rose Of Texas...............
.... Columbia 40540

STEVE MILLER Band
261 Abracadabra .... Capitol 5126
499 The Joker .... Capitol 3732
638 Rock'n Me .... Capitol 4323
824 Fly Like An Eagle .... Capitol 4372

MINDBENDERS
650 Game Of Love .... Fontana 1509
851 A Groovy Kind Of Love ...... Fontana 1541

MIRACLES
287 The Tears Of A Clown........ Tamla 54199
598 Love Machine .... Tamla 54262
915 Shop Around .... Tamla 54034

MR. MISTER
304 Broken Wings .... RCA 14136
373 Kyrie .... RCA 14258

GUY MITCHELL
2 Singing The Blues .... Columbia 40769
282 Heartaches By The Number ....
.... Columbia 41476

DOMENICO MODUGNO
76 Nel Blu Dipinto Di Blu (Volare) ....
.... Decca 30677

MONKEES
27 I'm A Believer .... Colgems 1002
123 Daydream Believer........... Colgems 1012
493 Last Train To Clarksville .... Colgems 1001
927 A Little Bit Me, A Little Bit You ....
.... Colgems 1004

HUGO MONTENEGRO
889 The Good, The Bad And The Ugly......
.... RCA 9423

MOODY BLUES
801 Nights In White Satin.......... Deram 85023

DORTHY MOORE
955 Misty Blue......................... Malaco 1029

EDDIE MURPHY
713 Party All The Time .... Columbia 05609

WALTER MURPHY
448 A Fifth Of Beethoven....... Private S. 45073

ANNE MURRAY
496 You Needed Me .... Capitol 4574

MUSIC EXPLOSION
772 Little Bit O'Soul................... Laurie 3380

N

JOHNNY NASH
143 I Can See Clearly Now .... Epic 10902

RICKY NELSON
274 Poor Little Fool .... Imperial 5528
343 Travelin' Man.................... Imperial 5741

720 Stood Up .... Imperial 5483
873 A Teenager's Romance .... Verve 10047

NENA
912 99 Luftballons .... Epic 04108

AARON NEVILLE
884 Tell It Like It Is.................... Par-Lo 101

NEWBEATS
819 Bread And Butter .... Hickory 1269

NEW VAUDEVILLE BAND
188 Winchester Cathedral .... Fontana 1562

RANDY NEWMAN
750 Short People .... Warner 8492

JUICE NEWTON
756 Queen Of Hearts .... Capitol 4997

OLIVIA NEWTON-JOHN
3 Physical .... MCA 51182
125 Magic.............................. MCA 41247
424 I Honestly Love You............. MCA 40280
467 You're The One That I Want.... RSO 891
    John Travolta & Olivia Newton-John
583 Have You Never Been
     Mellow .... MCA 40349
959 Heart Attack .... MCA 52100

STEVIE NICKS with TOM PETTY
947 Stop Draggin' My Heart Around ....
.... Modern 7336

MAXINE NIGHTINGALE
776 Right Back Where We Started From ...
.... United Art. 752

NILSSON
130 Without You .... RCA 0604

CLIFF NOBLES & Co.
740 The Horse....................... Phil. L.A. 313

O

OCEAN
898 Put Your Hand In The Hand ....
.... Kama Sutra 519

BILLY OCEAN
368 Caribbean Queen (No More Love On
     The Run) .... Jive 9199
542 There'll Be Sad Songs (To Make You
     Cry) .... Jive 9465
907 Loverboy............................ Jive 9284
930 When The Going Gets Tough, The
     Tough Get Going................. Jive 9432

ALAN O'DAY
528 Undercover Angel................ Pacific 001

OHIO PLAYERS
459 Love Rollercoaster........... Mercury 73734
655 Fire .... Mercury 73643

O'JAYS
617 Love Train....................... Phil. Int. 3524

OLIVER
810 Jean.............................. Crewe 334

ROY ORBISON
211 Oh, Pretty Woman .... Monument 851
654 Running Scared .... Monument 438

RANK	Title . . . Label & No.	RANK	Title . . . Label & No.

PRINCE
- 62 When Doves Cry .... Warner 29286
- 307 Let's Go Crazy................. Warner 29216
- 374 Kiss ....Paisley P. 28751
- 813 Purple Rain .... Warner 29174
- 909 Raspberry Beret............Paisley P. 28972

GARY PUCKETT & THE UNION GAP
- 721 Young Girl..................... Columbia 44450
- 840 Lady Willpower .... Columbia 44547

Q

QUEEN
- 104 Crazy Little Thing Called Love ....
...................................Elektra 46579
- 157 Another One Bites
The Dust.......................Elektra 47031

? (QUESTION MARK) & THE MYSTERIANS
- 492 96 Tears .... Cameo 428

R

EDDIE RABBITT
- 291 I Love A Rainy Night ....Elektra 47066

GERRY RAFFERTY
- 664 Baker Street .... United Art. 1192

RAIDERS
- 476 Indian Reservation (The Lament Of The Cherokee Reservation Indian)....
.... Columbia 45332

RASCALS
- 83 People Got To Be Free....... Atlantic 2537
- 141 Groovin'........................... Atlantic 2401
- 578 Good Lovin'...................... Atlantic 2321

LOU RAWLS
- 781 You'll Never Find Another Love Like Mine ....Phil. Int. 3592

JOHNNIE RAY
- 861 Just Walking In The Rain . Columbia 40729

READY FOR THE WORLD
- 606 Oh Sheila.........................MCA 52636

OTIS REDDING
- 110 (Sittin' On) The Dock Of The Bay ....
.... Volt 157

HELEN REDDY
- 510 I Am Woman.....................Capitol 3350
- 513 Delta Dawn.......................Capitol 3645
- 610 Angie Baby.......................Capitol 3972

DELLA REESE
- 874 Don't You Know .... RCA 7591

JIM REEVES
- 696 He'll Have To Go .... RCA 7643

REO SPEEDWAGON
- 208 Can't Fight This Feeling........ Epic 04713
- 461 Keep On Loving You .... Epic 50953

PAUL REVERE - see RAIDERS

DEBBIE REYNOLDS
- 56 Tammy .... Coral 61851

RHYTHM HERITAGE
- 618 Theme From S.W.A.T. .... ABC 12135

CHARLIE RICH
- 394 The Most Beautiful Girl........ Epic 11040

LIONEL RICHIE
- 9 Endless Love ....Motown 1519
Diana Ross & Lionel Richie
- 97 All Night Long (All Night).....Motown 1698
- 126 Say You, Say Me..............Motown 1819
- 278 Hello ....Motown 1722
- 288 Truly ....Motown 1644

NELSON RIDDLE
- 90 Lisbon Antigua...................Capitol 3287

RIGHTEOUS BROTHERS
- 228 (You're My) Soul And Inspiration........
.... Verve 10383
- 313 You've Lost That Lovin' Feelin' ....
.... Philles 124

JEANNIE C. RILEY
- 494 Harper Valley P.T.A.............Plantation 3

MINNIE RIPERTON
- 517 Lovin' You......................... Epic 50057

JOHNNY RIVERS
- 573 Poor Side Of Town ....Imperial 66205
- 844 Memphis........................Imperial 66032

MARTY ROBBINS
- 301 El Paso......................... Columbia 41511
- 866 A White Sport Coat (And A Pink Carnation) .... Columbia 40864

SMOKEY ROBINSON
- 705 Being With You .... Tamla 54321

ROCKWELL
- 719 Somebody's Watching Me...Motown 1702

JIMMIE RODGERS
- 94 Honeycomb .... Roulette 4015
- 980 Secretly .... Roulette 4070

TOMMY ROE
- 132 Dizzy........................... ABC 11164
- 412 Sheila........................... ABC-Para. 10329

KENNY ROGERS
- 39 Lady................................ Liberty 1380
- 265 Islands In The Stream .... RCA 13615
Kenny Rogers & Dolly Parton
- 956 Coward Of The County.... United Art. 1327

ROLLING STONES
- 111 Honky Tonk Women .... London 910
- 137 (I Can't Get No) Satisfaction London 9766
- 361 Brown Sugar .... Rolling S. 19100
- 393 Paint It, Black .... London 901
- 414 Get Off Of My Cloud ....London 9792
- 471 Miss You .... Rolling S. 19307
- 562 Angie .... Rolling S. 19105
- 596 Ruby Tuesday.................... London 904
- 698 Start Me Up................... Rolling S. 21003
- 747 19th Nervous Breakdown.... London 9823

ROMANTICS
- 992 Talking In Your Sleep......Nemperor 04135

RANK	Title . . . Label & No.	RANK	Title . . . Label & No.

RONETTES
746 Be My Baby .... Philles 116

LINDA RONSTADT
646 You're No Good .... Capitol 3990
806 When Will I Be Loved .... Capitol 4050
954 Blue Bayou .... Asylum 45431

ROOFTOP SINGERS
386 Walk Right In .... Vanguard 35017

ROSE ROYCE
481 Car Wash .... MCA 40615

DAVID ROSE
488 The Stripper .... MGM 13064

DIANA ROSS
9 Endless Love .... Motown 1519
  Diana Ross & Lionel Richie

93 Upside Down .... Motown 1494
201 Ain't No Mountain High Enough ....
.... Motown 1169
310 Love Hangover .... Motown 1392
498 Touch Me In The Morning ... Motown 1239
561 Theme From Mahogany (Do You
    Know Where You're Going To) ....
.... Motown 1377

ROYAL GUARDSMEN
686 Snoopy Vs. The Red Baron ... Laurie 3366

RUBY & THE ROMANTICS
632 Our Day Will Come .... Kapp 501

BOBBY RYDELL
877 Wild One .... Cameo 171

S

SSgt BARRY SADLER
86 The Ballad Of The Green Berets ....
.... RCA 8739

KYU SAKAMOTO
223 Sukiyaki .... Capitol 4945

SAM & DAVE
725 Soul Man .... Stax 231

SAM THE SHAM & The Pharaohs
768 Wooly Bully .... MGM 13322
817 Lil' Red Riding Hood .... MGM 13506

TOMMY SANDS
831 Teen-Age Crush .... Capitol 3639

SANTO & JOHNNY
311 Sleep Walk .... Canadian A. 103

LEO SAYER
529 You Make Me Feel Like Dancing ....
.... Warner 8283
541 When I Need You .... Warner 8332
668 More Than I Can Say .... Warner 49565

JOEY SCARBURY
758 Theme From "Greatest American
    Hero" (Believe It Or Not) ... Elektra 47147

JOHN SEBASTIAN
586 Welcome Back .... Reprise 1349

NEIL SEDAKA
257 Bad Blood .... Rocket 40460
379 Breaking Up Is Hard To Do .... RCA 8046

536 Laughter In The Rain .... Rocket 40313

SEEKERS
788 Georgy Girl .... Capitol 5756

BOB SEGER & THE SILVER BULLET BAND
684 Shame On The Moon .... Capitol 5187

MICHAEL SEMBELLO
300 Maniac .... Casablanca 812516

DAVID SEVILLE
163 Witch Doctor .... Liberty 55132

SHANGRI-LAS
649 Leader Of The Pack .... Red Bird 014

DEL SHANNON
135 Runaway .... Big Top 3067

DEE DEE SHARP
766 Mashed Potato Time .... Cameo 212

SHEP & THE LIMELITES
945 Daddy's Home .... Hull 740

ALLAN SHERMAN
749 Hello Mudduh, Hello Fadduh! (A Letter
    From Camp) .... Warner 5378

SHIRELLES
219 Soldier Boy .... Scepter 1228
370 Will You Love Me
    Tomorrow .... Scepter 1211

SHOCKING BLUE
490 Venus .... Colossus 108

SILHOUETTES
352 Get A Job .... Ember 1029

SILVER CONVENTION
238 Fly, Robin, Fly .... Midland I. 10339
711 Get Up And Boogie (That's Right) ......
.... Midland I. 10571

SIMON & GARFUNKEL
53 Bridge Over Troubled Water ....
.... Columbia 45079
242 Mrs. Robinson .... Columbia 44511
423 The Sounds Of Silence .... Columbia 43396

CARLY SIMON
174 You're So Vain .... Elektra 45824
716 Nobody Does It Better .... Elektra 45413

PAUL SIMON
252 50 Ways To Leave Your Lover ....
.... Columbia 10270
816 Kodachrome .... Columbia 45859
890 Loves Me Like A Rock .... Columbia 45907

SIMPLE MINDS
509 Don't You (Forget About Me) ... A&M 2703

SIMPLY RED
602 Holding Back The Years ..... Elektra 69564

FRANK SINATRA
140 Somethin' Stupid .... Reprise 0561
    Nancy & Frank Sinatra

258 Learnin' The Blues .... Capitol 3102
585 Strangers In The Night .... Reprise 0470
865 All The Way .... Capitol 3793

MARCH 23, 1963

BIG HIT FOR MARCH

(Little Peggy March, That Is)

"I Will Follow Him" #8139
c/w "Wind-Up Doll"
RCA VICTOR

 The most trusted name in sound

POP SPOTLIGHT

LITTLE PEGGY MARCH

WIND-UP DOLL

(Duchess, BMI) (2:27)   RCA Victor 8139

Another attractive ballad about wind-up dolls, is sung with
feeling and sincerity by the young thrush, and the tune, the
arrangement, and her vocal are strong enough to make the
disk happen. Flip is "I Will Follow Him" (Leeds, ASCAP) (2:25).

FOR WEEK ENDING MARCH 12, 1977

Billboard HOT 100®

Copyright 1977, Billboard Publications, Inc. No part of this publication may be reproduced, stored in a retrieval system, or transmitted, in any form or by any means, electronic, mechanical, photocopying, recording, or otherwise, without the prior written permission of the publisher.

*Chart Bound

ON YOUR FACE—Earth, Wind & Fire (Columbia 3-10492)
WHODUNIT—Tavares (Capitol 4398)
TIE YOUR MOTHER DOWN—Queen (Elektra 45385)
SEE TOP SINGLE PICKS REVIEWS, page 118

THIS WEEK	LAST WEEK	WKS. ON CHART	TITLE—Artist (Producer) Writer, Label & Number (Distributing Label)	
★ 1	1	14	LOVE THEME FROM "A STAR IS BORN" (Evergreen)—Barbra Streisand (Barbra Streisand, Phil Ramone), B. Streisand, P. Williams, Columbia 3-10450	WBM
★ 2	3	13	FLY LIKE AN EAGLE—Steve Miller Band (Steve Miller), S. Miller, Capitol 4372	BB
3	4	19	I LIKE DREAMIN'—Kenny Nolan (Kenny Nolan, Charles Calello), K. Nolan, 20th Century 2287	B-3
★ 4	6	14	NIGHT MOVES—Bob Seger (Jack Richardson), B. Seger, Capitol 4369	CPP
5	5	17	BLINDED BY THE LIGHT—Manfred Mann's Earth Band ● (Manfred Mann & The Earth Band), B. Springsteen, Warner Bros. 8252	B-3
★ 6	7	14	DANCING QUEEN—Abba (Benny Andersson, Bjorn Ulvaeus), B. Andersson, S. Anderson, B. Ulvaeus, Atlantic 3372	IMM/B-3
★ 7	9	17	TORN BETWEEN TWO LOVERS—Mary Macgregor ● (Peter Yarrow, Barry Beckett), P. Yarrow, P. Jarrell, Ariola America 7638 (Capitol)	HAN
8	8	14	YEAR OF THE CAT—Al Stewart (Alan Parsons), A. Stewart, P. Wood, Janus 266	WBM
★ 9	12	8	RICH GIRL—Daryl Hall & John Oates (Christopher Bond), D. Hall, RCA 10860	CHA
★ 10	11	10	GO YOUR OWN WAY—Fleetwood Mac (Fleetwood Mac, Richard Dashut, Ken Caylat), L. Buckingham, Warner Bros. 8304	CPP
★ 11	13	13	DON'T LEAVE ME THIS WAY—Thelma Houston (Hal Davis), K. Gamble, L. Huff, C. Gilbert, Tamla 54278 (Motown)	B-3
★ 12	14	9	BOOGIE CHILD—Bee Gees (Albhy Galuten, Karl Richardson), R. Gibb, B. Gibb, M. Gibb, RSO 867 (Polydor)	WBM
★ 13	15	10	THE THINGS WE DO FOR LOVE—10 cc (10 cc), Stewart, Gouldman, Mercury 73875 (Phonogram)	WBM
14	2	13	NEW KID IN TOWN—Eagles (Bill Szymczyk), J.D. Souther, D. Henley, G. Frey, Asylum 45373	ALM/WBM
★ 15	20	5	MAYBE I'M AMAZED—Wings (Paul McCartney), P. McCartney, Capitol 4385	WBM
★ 16	18	12	CARRY ON WAYWARD SON—Kansas (Jeff Glixman), K. Lirgren, Kirshner 4267 (Epic)	WBM
★ 17	23	7	DON'T GIVE UP ON US—David Soul (Tony Macaulay), T. Macaulay, Private Stock 45129	ALM
18	10	16	WEEKEND IN NEW ENGLAND—Barry Manilow (Ron Dante, Barry Manilow), R. Edelman, Arista 0212	B-3
★ 19	24	10	SAY YOU'LL STAY UNTIL TOMORROW—Tom Jones (Gordon Mills), R. Greenaway, B. Mason, Epic 8-50308	WBM
★ 20	27	7	I'VE GOT LOVE ON MY MIND—Natalie Cole (Chuck Jackson, Marvin Yancy), C. Jackson, M. Yancy, Jay's Enterprises, Capitol 4360	CHA
★ 21	29	7	SO IN TO YOU—Atlanta Rhythm Section (Buddy Buie), B. Buie, R. Mix, D. Daughtry, Polydor 14373	CPP
22	22	7	LONG TIME—Boston (John Boylan), T. Scholz, Epic 8-50329	CPP
23	16	18	ENJOY YOURSELF—The Jacksons ● (Kenneth Gamble, Leon Huff), K. Gamble, L. Huff, Epic 8-50289	B-3
★ 24	26	7	CRACKERBOX PALACE—George Harrison (George Harrison, Tom Scott), G. Harrison, Dark Horse 3313 (Warner Bros.)	WBM
25	25	15	LIVING NEXT DOOR TO ALICE—Smokie (Mike Chapman), N. Chinn, M. Chapman, RSO 860 (Polydor)	WBM
★ 26	32	7	SAM—Olivia Newton-John (John Farrar), J. Farrar, H. Marvin, D. Black, MCA 40670	CPP/ALM
★ 27	30	6	HERE COME THOSE TEARS AGAIN—Jackson Browne (Jon Landau), J. Browne, N. Farnsworth, Asylum 45379	WBM
28	28	5	BITE YOUR LIP (Get Up And Dance)—Elton John (Gus Dudgeon), E. John, B. Taupin, MCA/Rocket 40677	MCA
★ 29	35	7	RIGHT TIME OF THE NIGHT—Jennifer Warnes (Jim Ed Norman), P. McCann, Arista 0223	CPP
★ 30	39	5	SOUTHERN NIGHTS—Glen Campbell (Gary Klein), A. Toussaint, Capitol 4376	WBM
★ 31	34	5	THE FIRST CUT IS THE DEEPEST—Rod Stewart (Tom Dowd), C. Stevens, Warner Bros. 8321	MCA
32	17	15	I WISH—Stevie Wonder (Stevie Wonder), S. Wonder, Tamla 54274 (Motown)	CPP
★ 33	38	6	DO YA—Electric Light Orchestra (Jeff Lynne for Jet Records), J. Lynne, United Artists 939	B-3
★ 34	37	14	FREE—Deniece Williams (Maurice White, Charles Stepney), D. Williams, H. Redd, N. Watts, S. Greene, Columbia 3-10429	WBM
★ 35	52	3	HOTEL CALIFORNIA—Eagles (Bill Szymczyk), D. Felder, D. Henley, G. Frey, Asylum 45386	WBM
★ 36	40	7	GLORIA—Enchantment (Michael Stokes), M. Stokes, E. Johnson, United Artists 912	B-3
★ 37	41	10	DISCO LUCY (I Love Lucy Theme)—Wilton Place Street Band (Trevor Lawrence, E. Daniel, H. Adamson), Island 078	ALM
38	19	21	CAR WASH—Rose Royce (Norman Whitfield), N. Whitfield, MCA 40615	MCA
★ 39	45	5	AT MIDNIGHT (My Love Will Lift You Up)—Rufus Featuring Chaka Khan (Rufus), T. Maiden, L. Washburn, ABC 12239	CPP
★ 40	55	4	TRYING TO LOVE TWO—William Bell (William Bell, Paul Mitchell), W. Bell, P. Mitchell, Mercury 73839 (Phonogram)	CPP
41	43	8	SPRING RAIN—Silvetti (Silvetti), Silvetti, Salsoul 2414 (Barnegat, BMI)	B-3
★ 42	49	4	ALL STRUNG OUT ON YOU—John Travolta (Jeff Barry), N. Tempo, J. Riopell, Midland International 10907 (RCA)	HAN
★ 43	47	6	SOMETHIN' 'BOUT 'CHA—Latimore (Steve Alaimo), B. Latimore, Glades 1739 (TK)	CPP
44	31	12	MOODY BLUE/SHE THINKS I STILL CARE—Elvis Presley (Elvis Presley, Felton Jarvis), M. James, RCA 10857	CPP/PLY
45	42	19	WHISPERING/CHERCHEZ LA FEMME/SE SI BON—Dr. Buzzard's Original Savannah Band (Sandy Linzer), Schoenberger, Coburn, Rose, S. Browder Jr., A. Darnell, RCA 10827	CPP/B-3
★ 46	56	5	WINTER MELODY—Donna Summer (Giorgio Moroder, Pete Bellotte), D. Summer, G. Moroder, P. Bellotte, Casablanca 874	CPP
47	33	23	HOT LINE—Sylvers ● (Freddie Perren), K. St. Lewis, F. Perren, Capitol 4336	ALM
48	21	13	HARD LUCK WOMAN—Kiss (Eddie Kramer for Rock Steady Prod.), P. Stanley, Casablanca 873	ALM
49	36	14	SAVE IT FOR A RAINY DAY—Stephen Bishop (Henry Lewis, Stephen Bishop), S. Bishop, ABC 12232	ALM
★ 50	79	3	I WANNA GET NEXT TO YOU—Rose Royce (Norman Whitfield), N. Whitfield, MCA 40662	MCA
51	51	7	REACH—Orleans (Charles Plotkin), J. Hall, J. Hall, Asylum 45375	ALM
52	46	16	LOST WITHOUT YOUR LOVE—Bread (David Gates), D. Gates, Elektra 45365	CPP
53	50	21	YOU MAKE ME FEEL LIKE DANCING—Leo Sayer ● (Richard Perry), L. Sayer, V. Poncia, Warner Bros. 8283	WBM
★ 54	66	4	N.Y., YOU GOT ME DANCING—Andrea True Connection (Gregg Diamond), G. Diamond, Buddah 564	B-3
55	48	6	KONG—Dickie Goodman (Bill Ramal, Dickie Goodman), B. Ramal, D. Goodman, Shock 6 (Janus)	CHA
56	57	10	BE MY GIRL—Dramatics (Michael Henderson), M. Henderson, ABC 12235	
★ 57	69	3	LOVE IN C MINOR—Heart & Soul Orchestra (F. Crocker, M. Simon), Cerrone, Casablanca 876	
58	64	4	YOU + ME = LOVE/LET'S GO DOWN TO THE DISCO—Undisputed Truth (Norman Whitfield), N. Whitfield, Whitfield 8306 (Warner Bros.)	CPP
★ 59	70	3	WHEN I NEED YOU—Leo Sayer (Richard Perry), C.B. Sager, A. Hammond, Warner Bros. 8332	CHA
60	61	12	HA CHA CHA (Funktion)—Brass Construction (Jeff Lane), R. Muller, United Artists 677	B-3
★ 61	72	3	I'M YOUR BOOGIE MAN—K.C. & The Sunshine Band (H.W. Casey, Richard Finch for Sunshine Sound Ent.), H.W. Casey, R. Finch, TK 1022	CPP
62	63	4	I'M SCARED—Burton Cummings (Richard Perry), B. Cummings, Portrait/CBS 70002	ALM
★ 63	73	4	COULDN'T GET IT RIGHT—Climax Blues Band (Mike Vernon), Climax Blues Band, Sire 736 (ABC)	
★ 64	75	3	LOVE IN 'C' MINOR (Pt. 1)—Cerrone (Cerrone), Alec, R. Costandinos, Cerrone, Cotillion 44215 (Atlantic)	
65	67	5	DEDICATION—Bay City Rollers (Jimmy Ienner), G. Fletcher, D. Flett, Arista 0233	ALM
★ 66	78	3	MAGICAL MYSTERY TOUR—Ambrosia (Lou Reizner), J. Lennon, P. McCartney, 20th Century 2327	WBM
67	65	4	RACE AMONG THE RUINS—Gordon Lightfoot (Lenny Waronker, Gordon Lightfoot), G. Lightfoot, Reprise 1380 (Warner Bros.)	WBM
68	71	4	WELCOME TO OUR WORLD OF MERRY MUSIC—Mass Production (Ed. A. Ellerbe), T. Williams, Cotillion 44213 (Atlantic)	CPP
★ 69	81	2	PHANTOM WRITER—Gary Wright (Gary Wright), G. Wright, Warner Bros. 8331	WBM
★ 70	80	4	ANGEL IN YOUR ARMS—Hot (Clayton Ivey, Terry Woodford), T. Woodford, C. Ivey, T. Brasfield, Big Tree 16085 (Atlantic)	CPP
★ 71	82	4	THERE WILL COME A DAY (I'm Gonna Happen To You)—Smokey Robinson (Michael Sutton), K. Wakefield, M. Sutton, B. Sutton, Tamla 54279 (Motown)	CPP
★ 72	NEW ENTRY		LIDO SHUFFLE—Boz Scaggs (Joe Wissert), B. Scaggs, D. Paich, Columbia 3-10491	WBM
73	53	21	DAZZ—Brick (Jim Healy, Johnny Duncan, Robert E. Lee, Brick), R. Ransom, R. Hargis, E. Irons, Bang 727	CPP
74	54	17	WALK THIS WAY—Aerosmith (Jack Douglas for Waterfront Prod. & Contemporary Communications Corp.), S. Tyler, J. Perry, Columbia 3-10449	WBM
★ 75	NEW ENTRY		MY SWEET LADY—John Denver (Milton Okun), J. Denver, RCA 10911	CLM
★ 76	87	2	"ROOTS" MEDLEY: A. MOTHERLAND, B. THEME FROM "ROOTS"—Quincy Jones (Quincy Jones), A: Q. Jones, B: G. Fried, A&M 1909	WBM
★ 77	88	2	SOMETIMES—Facts Of Life (Millie Jackson), B. Anderson, Kayvette 5128 (TK)	
★ 78	NEW ENTRY		HEARD IT IN A LOVE SONG—Marshall Tucker Band (Paul Hornsby), T. Caldwell, Capricorn 0270 (Warner Bros.)	WBM
★ 79	90	2	DISCO INFERNO—Trammps (Ronald Baker, Norman Harris, Earl Young), L. Green, R. "Have Mercy" Kersey, Atlantic 3389	CPP
★ 80	NEW ENTRY		DANCING MAN—Q (Q), R. Peckman, Epic 8-50335	
81	83	6	DREAMIN'—Loleatta Holloway (Norman Harris for Baker Harris Young Prod.), A. Felder, N. Harris, R. Tyson, Gold Mind 4000	CPP
82	84	4	DANCIN'—Crown Heights Affair (Freida Nerangis, Britt Britton), W. Anderson, De-Lite 1588	CPP
83	89	3	SAILING SHIPS—Mesa (Clayton Ivey, Terry Woodford of Wishbone for Bell Bottom Prod.), Pace, Paglia, Notaro, Rekers, Desensants, Ariola America 7654 (Capitol)	CPP
84	86	8	YOU KNOW LIKE I KNOW—Ozark Mountain Daredevils (David Anderle), L. Lee, A&M 1888	WBM
★ 85	NEW ENTRY		YOUR OWN SPECIAL WAY—Genesis (David Hentschel, Genesis), M. Rutherford, Atco 7076	WBM
★ 86	NEW ENTRY		UPTOWN FESTIVAL—Shalamar (Simon Soussan), Holland, Dozier, Holland, Soul Train 10885 (RCA)	CPP
★ 87	NEW ENTRY		DO WHAT YOU WANNA DO—T Connection (Cory Wade, Alex Sadkin), T. Caokley, Dash 5032 (TK)	CPP
88	91	3	BODY HEAT (Part 1)—James Brown (James Brown), D. Brown, D. Brown, Y. Brown, Polydor 14360	CHA
89	93	3	LOVE IS BETTER IN THE A.M.—Johnnie Taylor (Don Davis), H. Scales, M. Griffin, D. Davis, Columbia 3-10478	CPP
★ 90	NEW ENTRY		WAKE UP AND BE SOMEBODY—Brainstorm (Jerry Peters for Music Meca West Prod.), G. Kent, Tabu 10811 (RCA)	ALM
91	94	2	FIRESIGN—Cory Braverman (Hank Medress, Dave Appell for Medress Appell Prod.), C. Braverman, R. Ulfik, Phantom 10856 (RCA)	
92	92	2	ROMEO—Mr. Big (Val Gray), Dicken, E. Carter, Arista 0229	
93	95	2	I THINK WE'RE ALONE NOW—Rubinoos (Matthew King, Kaufman, Gary Phillips, Glen Kolotkin), R. Cordell, B. Gentry, Beserkley 5741 (Playboy)	
94	96	3	THEME FROM ROCKY (Gonna Fly Now)—Rhythm Heritage (Steve Barri, Michael Omartian), B. Conti, C. Conners, A. Robbins, ABC 12243	B-3
95	NEW ENTRY		I WANNA DO IT TO YOU—Jerry Butler (Jerry Butler, Homer Talbert for Fountain Prod.), J. Butler, H. Talbert, P. Henley, Motown 1414	
96	NEW ENTRY		OLD FASHIONED BOY (You're The One)—Stallion (Dik Darnell), W. Damrick, Casablanca 877	CPP
97	97	2	TRY IT ON—Exile (Mike Chapman), M. Chapman, N. Chinn, Atco 7072	WBM
98	NEW ENTRY		TIME IS MOVIN'—Blackbyrds (Donald Byrd), K. Killgo, Fantasy 787	
99	99	2	IT AIN'T EASY COMING DOWN—Charlene Duncan (Ron Miller, Ken Hirsch), R. Miller, Prodigal 0632 (Motown)	CPP
100	NEW ENTRY		FOR ELISE—Philharmonics (Jean Kluger), Beethoven, Capricorn 0268 (Warner Bros.)	CPP

★ **STAR PERFORMERS: Stars are awarded on the Hot 100 chart based on the following upward movement. 1-10 Strong increase in sales / 11-20 Upward movement of 4 positions / 21-30 Upward movement of 6 positions / 31-40 Upward movement of 8 positions / 41-100 Upward movement of 10 positions.** Previous week's starred positions are maintained without a star if the product is in a holding period. This will, in some cases, block out products which would normally move up with a star. In such cases, products will be awarded a star without the required upward movement noted above. ● Recording Industry Assn. Of America seal of certification as "million seller." (Seal indicated by bullet.) ▲ Recording Industry Assn. Of America seal of certification as "two million seller." (Seal indicated by triangle.)

RANK	Title . . . Label & No.

NANCY SINATRA
140 Somethin' Stupid .... Reprise 0561
Nancy & Frank Sinatra
576 These Boots Are Made For Walkin' ....
.... Reprise 0432

SINGING NUN
138 Dominique........................ Philips 40152

SISTER SLEDGE
811 We Are Family ....Cotillion 44251

PERCY SLEDGE
416 When A Man Loves A Woman ....
.... Atlantic 2326

SLY & THE FAMILY STONE
129 Everyday People .... Epic 10407
200 Family Affair .... Epic 10805
380 Thank You (Falettinme Be Mice Elf
Agin).............................. Epic 10555
805 Hot Fun In The Summertime.. Epic 10497

MILLIE SMALL
938 My Boy Lollipop .... Smash 1893

O.C. SMITH
879 Little Green Apples .... Columbia 44616

SONNY & CHER
249 I Got You Babe .... Atco 6359

DAVID SOUL
554 Don't Give Up On Us ...... Private S. 45129

JIMMY SOUL
413 If You Wanna Be Happy .... S.P.Q.R. 3305

SPINNERS
506 Then Came You .... Atlantic 3202
Dionne Warwicke & Spinners
710 The Rubberband Man......... Atlantic 3355
773 Working My Way Back To
You/Forgive Me, Girl........ Atlantic 3637

RICK SPRINGFIELD
264 Jessie's Girl........................ RCA 12201
675 Don't Talk To Strangers .... RCA 13070

BRUCE SPRINGSTEEN
680 Dancing In The Dark .... Columbia 04463

STAPLE SINGERS
515 I'll Take You There .... Stax 0125
572 Let's Do It Again .... Curtom 0109

STARLAND VOCAL BAND
348 Afternoon Delight ....Windsong 10588

EDWIN STARR
217 War.............................Gordy 7101

KAY STARR
31 Rock And Roll Waltz .... RCA 6359

RINGO STARR
571 You're Sixteen .... Apple 1870
623 Photograph .... Apple 1865

STARS ON 45
511 Stars on 45 [Medley]........... Radio 3810

STARSHIP
369 We Built This City............... Grunt 14170
553 Sara............................. Grunt 14253

STEAM
350 Na Na Hey Hey Kiss Him Goodbye.....
.................................Fontana 1667

STEPPENWOLF
741 Born To Be Wild .... Dunhill 4138

RAY STEVENS
220 The Streak ....Barnaby 600
406 Everything Is Beautiful....... Barnaby 2011

AMII STEWART
603 Knock On Wood................. Ariola 7736

ROD STEWART
17 Tonight's The Night (Gonna Be
Alright) ....Warner 8262
67 Maggie May .... Mercury 73224
102 Da Ya Think I'm Sexy? ....Warner 8724

MORRIS STOLOFF
156 Moonglow and Theme From "Picnic"...
.... Decca 29888

STORIES
342 Brother Louie................ Kama Sutra 577

GALE STORM
694 I Hear You Knocking............. Dot 15412

STRAWBERRY ALARM CLOCK
485 Incense And Peppermints ...... Uni 55018

BARBRA STREISAND
159 Love Theme From "A Star Is Born"
(Evergreen) .... Columbia 10450
166 Woman In Love............. Columbia 11364
190 The Way We Were......... Columbia 45944
284 You Don't Bring Me Flowers ....
.... Columbia 10840
Barbra Streisand & Neil Diamond
322 No More Tears (Enough Is Enough)....
.... Columbia 11125
Barbra Streisand/Donna Summer
960 The Main Event/Fight ...... Columbia 11008

STYLISTICS
778 You Make Me Feel
Brand New........................Avco 4634

STYX
275 Babe ....A&M 2188
951 The Best Of Times ....A&M 2300

DONNA SUMMER
71 Bad Girls .... Casablanca 988
158 Hot Stuff...................... Casablanca 978
193 MacArthur Park............. Casablanca 939
322 No More Tears (Enough Is Enough)....
.... Columbia 11125
Barbra Streisand/Donna Summer
767 Dim All The Lights .... Casablanca 2201
798 Love To Love You Baby .... Oasis 401
976 She Works Hard For The Money........
.... Mercury 812370

SUPREMES
149 Baby Love........................Motown 1066
272 Love Child.......................Motown 1135
323 Come See About Me.........Motown 1068
324 Where Did Our Love Go .....Motown 1060

RANK	Title . . . Label & No.
363	You Can't Hurry Love......... Motown 1097
365	Stop! In The Name Of Love. Motown 1074
418	You Keep Me Hangin' On ... Motown 1101
421	I Hear A Symphony........... Motown 1083
478	Someday We'll Be Together Motown 1156
594	Love Is Here And Now You're Gone ... Motown 1103
633	The Happening .... Motown 1107
651	Back In My Arms Again...... Motown 1075
790	I'm Gonna Make You Love Me........... Motown 1137

Supremes & Temptations

| 822 | Reflections .... Motown 1111 |

SURFARIS
| 886 | Wipe Out............................. Dot 16479 |

SURVIVOR
| 36 | Eye Of The Tiger .... Scotti Br. 02912 |
| 823 | Burning Heart .... Scotti Br. 05663 |

BILLY SWAN
| 408 | I Can Help..................... Monument 8621 |

SWEET
| 993 | Little Willy .... Bell 45251 |

SYLVERS
| 535 | Boogie Fever .... Capitol 4179 |

T

TASTE OF HONEY
| 165 | Boogie Oogie Oogie........... Capitol 4565 |
| 978 | Sukiyaki........................... Capitol 4953 |

JAMES TAYLOR
| 522 | You've Got A Friend .... Warner 7498 |
| 984 | Fire And Rain .... Warner 7423 |

JOHNNIE TAYLOR
| 144 | Disco Lady .... Columbia 10281 |

TEARS FOR FEARS
| 237 | Shout .... Mercury 880294 |
| 344 | Everybody Wants To Rule The World.. Mercury 880659 |

TEDDY BEARS
| 168 | To Know Him, Is To Love Him . Dore 503 |

NINO TEMPO & APRIL STEVENS
| 575 | Deep Purple .... Atco 6273 |

TEMPTATIONS
271	I Can't Get Next To You .... Gordy 7093
317	Just My Imagination (Running Away With Me)......................... Gordy 7105
525	My Girl .... Gordy 7038
625	Papa Was A Rollin' Stone ..... Gordy 7121
790	I'm Gonna Make You Love Me........... Motown 1137

Supremes & Temptations

| 974 | Ball Of Confusion (That's What The World Is Today) .... Gordy 7099 |

10cc
| 751 | I'm Not In Love .... Mercury 73678 |

JOE TEX
| 761 | I Gotcha............................. Dial 1010 |

RANK	Title . . . Label & No.

B.J. THOMAS
| 96 | Raindrops Keep Fallin' On My Head ... Scepter 12265 |
| 546 | (Hey Won't You Play) Another Somebody Done Somebody Wrong Song............................... ABC 12054 |

THREE DEGREES
| 402 | TSOP (The Sound Of Philadelphia) ..... Phil. Int. 3540 |

MFSB featuring The Three Degrees

| 913 | When Will I See You Again.. Phil. Int. 3550 |

THREE DOG NIGHT
50	Joy To The World.............. Dunhill 4272
320	Mama Told Me (Not To Come)........... Dunhill 4239
652	Black & White .... Dunhill 4317

JOHNNY TILLOTSON
| 893 | Poetry In Motion............... Cadence 1384 |

TOKENS
| 218 | The Lion Sleeps Tonight........ RCA 7954 |

TORNADOES
| 216 | Telstar............................ London 9561 |

TOTO
| 600 | Africa .... Columbia 03335 |
| 666 | Rosanna .... Columbia 02811 |

TOYS
| 743 | A Lover's Concerto .... DynoVoice 209 |

JOHN TRAVOLTA - see OLIVIA NEWTON–JOHN

TROGGS
| 366 | Wild Thing........................ Fontana 1548 |

TINA TURNER
| 175 | What's Love Got To Do With It .... Capitol 5354 |
| 918 | We Don't Need Another Hero (Thunderdome) .... Capitol 5491 |

TURTLES
| 202 | Happy Together .... White Whale 244 |

CONWAY TWITTY
| 280 | It's Only Make Believe......... MGM 12677 |

BONNIE TYLER
| 106 | Total Eclipse Of The Heart .... Columbia 03906 |

TYMES
| 574 | So Much In Love .... Parkway 871 |

U

UNION GAP - see GARY PUCKETT

USA for AFRICA
| 146 | We Are The World .... Columbia 04839 |

V

RITCHIE VALENS
| 759 | Donna .... Del-Fi 4110 |

FRANKIE VALLI
| 339 | Grease .... RSO 897 |
| 508 | My Eyes Adored You ...... Private S. 45003 |

RANK	Title . . . Label & No.	RANK	Title . . . Label & No.

876 Can't Take My Eyes Off You .... Philips 40446

VAN HALEN
70 Jump.......................... Warner 29384

VANGELIS
475 Chariots Of Fire - Titles ...... Polydor 2189

BOBBY VEE
244 Take Good Care Of My Baby .... Liberty 55354
917 Run To Him...................... Liberty 55388
996 Come Back When You Grow Up .... Liberty 55964

VENTURES
870 Walk--Don't Run.................... Dolton 25

LARRY VERNE
590 Mr. Custer........................... Era 3024

VILLAGE PEOPLE
695 Y.M.C.A. .... Casablanca 945

VILLAGE STOMPERS
899 Washington Square.............. Epic 9617

BOBBY VINTON
121 Roses Are Red (My Love) ...... Epic 9509
139 There! I've Said It Again .... Epic 9638
221 Blue Velvet......................... Epic 9614
486 Mr. Lonely......................... Epic 9730

W

JACK WAGNER
828 All I Need...................... Qwest 29238

JOHN WAITE
468 Missing You .... EMI America 8212

WAR
834 The Cisco Kid .... United Art. 163

ANITA WARD
270 Ring My Bell....................... Juana 3422

JENNIFER WARNES - see JOE COCKER

DIONNE WARWICK
113 That's What Friends Are For . Arista 9422
shown as: Dionne & Friends
506 Then Came You .... Atlantic 3202
Dionne Warwicke & Spinners
688 (Theme From) Valley Of The Dolls ...... Scepter 12203

GROVER WASHINGTON, JR./BILL WITHERS
700 Just The Two Of Us........... Elektra 47103

ERIC WEISSBERG & STEVE MANDELL
690 Dueling Banjos.................. Warner 7659

LAWRENCE WELK
312 Calcutta .... Dot 16161

MARY WELLS
315 My Guy........................... Motown 1056

WHAM!
191 Careless Whisper .... Columbia 04691
207 Wake Me Up Before You Go-Go .... Columbia 04552
399 Everything She Wants ..... Columbia 04840

BARRY WHITE
658 Can't Get Enough Of Your Love, Babe .... 20th Century 2120
808 You're The First, The Last, My Everything................. 20th Century 2133

WILD CHERRY
177 Play That Funky Music .... Epic 50225

ANDY WILLIAMS
186 Butterfly........................... Cadence 1308
687 Can't Get Used To Losing You .... Columbia 42674

BILLY WILLIAMS
952 I'm Gonna Sit Right Down And Write Myself A Letter .... Coral 61830

DENIECE WILLIAMS
306 Let's Hear It For The Boy Columbia 04417
523 Too Much, Too Little, Too Late.......... Columbia 10693
Johnny Mathis/Deniece Williams

MASON WILLIAMS
838 Classical Gas.................... Warner 7190

MAURICE WILLIAMS & The Zodiacs
639 Stay .... Herald 552

ROGER WILLIAMS
89 Autumn Leaves .... Kapp 116

AL WILSON
531 Show And Tell .... Rocky Road 30073

J. FRANK WILSON & The Cavaliers
878 Last Kiss .... Josie 923

WINGS - see PAUL McCARTNEY

EDGAR WINTER GROUP
543 Frankenstein...................... Epic 10967

HUGO WINTERHALTER/EDDIE HEYWOOD
753 Canadian Sunset .... RCA 6537

BILL WITHERS
235 Lean On Me .... Sussex 235
700 Just The Two Of Us........... Elektra 47103
Grover Washington, Jr./Bill Withers
852 Use Me.............................. Sussex 241

STEVIE WONDER
25 Ebony And Ivory............. Columbia 02860
Paul McCartney & Stevie Wonder
182 I Just Called To Say I Love You......... Motown 1745
215 Sir Duke .... Tamla 54281
241 Fingertips - Pt 2 .... Tamla 54080
507 I Wish.............................. Tamla 54274
512 Part-Time Lover .... Tamla 1808
544 You Haven't Done Nothin.... Tamla 54252
559 You Are The Sunshine Of My Life ...... Tamla 54232
613 Superstition .... Tamla 54226
793 For Once In My Life........... Tamla 54174
807 I Was Made To Love Her.... Tamla 54151

SHEB WOOLEY
52 The Purple People Eater ...... MGM 12651

RANK	Title . . . Label & No.	RANK	Title . . . Label & No.

GARY WRIGHT
717 Dream Weaver ....Warner 8167
795 Love Is Alive.....................Warner 8143

PAUL YOUNG
500 Everytime You Go Away .. Columbia 04867

Y

Z

YES
279 Owner Of A Lonely Heart...... Atco 99817

NEIL YOUNG
520 Heart Of Gold .... Reprise 1065

ZAGER & EVANS
55 In The Year 2525................. RCA 0174

ZOMBIES
881 She's Not There.................Parrot 9695

THE SONGS

This section lists, alphabetically, all titles listed in the Top 1000 ranking. The artist's name is listed next to each title along with its Top 1000 ranking.

A song with more than one charted version is listed once, with the artist's names listed below it in rank order. Songs that have the same title, but are different tunes, are listed separately, with the highest ranked song listed first.

RANK	Title ... Artist	RANK	Title ... Artist

A

327	**ABC** ... *Jackson 5*
261	**Abracadabra** ... *Steve Miller Band*
538	**Addicted To Love** ... *Robert Palmer*
600	**Africa** ... *Toto*
771	**After The Love Has Gone** ... *Earth, Wind & Fire*
348	**Afternoon Delight** ... *Starland Vocal Band*
179	**Against All Odds (Take A Look At Me Now)** ... *Phil Collins*
201	**Ain't No Mountain High Enough** ... *Diana Ross*
259	**Ain't That A Shame** ... *Pat Boone*
933	**All American Boy** ... *Bill Parsons*
738	**All By Myself** ... *Eric Carmen*
61	**All I Have To Do Is Dream** ... *Everly Brothers*
828	**All I Need** ... *Jack Wagner*
97	**All Night Long (All Night)** ... *Lionel Richie*
676	**All Out Of Love** ... *Air Supply*
6	**All Shook Up** ... *Elvis Presley*
865	**All The Way** ... *Frank Sinatra*
742	**All Those Years Ago** ... *George Harrison*
597	**All You Need Is Love** ... *Beatles*
754	**Allegheny Moon** ... *Patti Page*
524	**Alley-Oop** ... *Hollywood Argyles*
49	**Alone Again (Naturally)** ... *Gilbert O'Sullivan*
926	**Also Sprach Zarathustra (2001)** ... *Deodato*
108	**American Pie** ... *Don McLean*
212	**American Woman** ... *Guess Who*
901	**And When I Die** ... *Blood, Sweat & Tears*
562	**Angie** ... *Rolling Stones*
610	**Angie Baby** ... *Helen Reddy*
381	**Annie's Song** ... *John Denver*
99	**Another Brick In The Wall** ... *Pink Floyd*
157	**Another One Bites The Dust** ... *Queen*
847	**Apache** ... *Jorgen Ingmann*
38	**April Love** ... *Pat Boone*
47	**Aquarius/Let The Sunshine In** ... *5th Dimension*
51	**Are You Lonesome To-night?** ... *Elvis Presley*
164	**Arthur's Theme (Best That You Can Do)** ... *Christopher Cross*
22	**At The Hop** ... *Danny & The Juniors*
89	**Autumn Leaves** ... *Roger Williams*

B

275	**Babe** ... *Styx*
178	**Baby Come Back** ... *Player*
290	**Baby, Come To Me** ... *Patti Austin & James Ingram*
198	**Baby Don't Get Hooked On Me** ... *Mac Davis*
149	**Baby Love** ... *Supremes*
651	**Back In My Arms Again** ... *Supremes*
335	**Bad, Bad Leroy Brown** ... *Jim Croce*
257	**Bad Blood** ... *Neil Sedaka*
71	**Bad Girls** ... *Donna Summer*
920	**Bad Moon Rising** ... *Creedence Clearwater Revival*
664	**Baker Street** ... *Gerry Rafferty*
974	**Ball Of Confusion** ... *Temptations*
86	**Ballad Of The Green Berets** ... *SSgt Barry Sadler*
557	**Band On The Run** ... *Paul McCartney & Wings*
928	**Bang Bang (My Baby Shot Me Down)** ... *Cher*
859	**Barbara Ann** ... *Beach Boys*
41	**Battle Of New Orleans** ... *Johnny Horton*
746	**Be My Baby** ... *Ronettes*
176	**Beat It** ... *Michael Jackson*
502	**Before The Next Teardrop Falls** ... *Freddy Fender*
705	**Being With You** ... *Smokey Robinson*
	Believe It Or Not...see: Theme From "Greatest American Hero"
582	**Ben** ... *Michael Jackson*
473	**Bennie And The Jets** ... *Elton John*
60	**Best Of My Love** ... *Emotions*
604	**Best Of My Love** ... *Eagles*
951	**Best Of Times** ... *Styx*
	Best That You Can Do...see: Arthur's Theme
7	**Bette Davis Eyes** ... *Kim Carnes*
77	**Big Bad John** ... *Jimmy Dean*
75	**Big Girls Don't Cry** ... *4 Seasons*
389	**Big Hunk O' Love** ... *Elvis Presley*
982	**Biggest Part Of Me** ... *Ambrosia*
28	**Billie Jean** ... *Michael Jackson*
375	**Billy, Don't Be A Hero** ... *Bo Donaldson & The Heywoods*
446	**Bird Dog** ... *Everly Brothers*
652	**Black & White** ... *Three Dog Night*
568	**Black Water** ... *Doobie Brothers*

FOR WEEK ENDING DECEMBER 11, 1982

Billboard HOT 100®

© Copyright 1982 Billboard Publications, Inc. No part of this publication may be reproduced, stored in a retrieval system, or transmitted, in any form or by any means, electronic, mechanical, photocopying, recording, or otherwise, without the prior written permission of the publisher.

This Week	Last Week	Wks. on Chart	TITLE—Artist (Producer) Writer, Label & Number (Distributing Label)	
☆ 1	3	15	MICKEY—Toni Basil (Greg Mathison, Trevor Veitch), N. Chinn, M. Chapman; Radialchoice/Virgin Record/Chrysalis 2638 (WEEKS AT #1: 1)	CPP
2	2	23	GLORIA—Laura Branigan (Jack White), Co-Produced—Greg Mathieson; U. Tozzi, G. Bigazzi, T. Veitch, Atlantic 4048	MCA
☆ 3	4	9	MANEATER—Daryl Hall and John Oates (Daryl Hall and John Oates), D. Hall and J. Oates, S. Allen; RCA 13354	CHA/HL
4	1	10	TRULY—Lionel Richie (Lionel Richie, James Anthony Carmichael), L. Richie; Motown 1644	CLM
☆ 5	8	6	THE GIRL IS MINE—Michael Jackson/Paul McCartney (Quincy Jones), M. Jackson; Epic 34-03288	WBM
☆ 6	7	17	STEPPIN' OUT—Joe Jackson (David Kershenbaum, Joe Jackson), J. Jackson, A&M 2428	CPP/ALM
☆ 7	9	7	DIRTY LAUNDRY—Don Henley (Don Henley, Danny Kortchmar, Greg Ladanyi), D. Henley, D. Kortchmar; Asylum 7-69894 (Elektra)	WBM
☆ 8	12	7	SEXUAL HEALING—Marvin Gaye (Marvin Gaye), M. Gaye; Columbia 38-03302	CLM/APB
☆ 9	11	13	ROCK THIS TOWN—Stray Cats (Dave Edmunds), B. Setzer; EMI-America 8132	CPP
☆ 10	10	11	MUSCLES—Diana Ross (Michael Jackson), M. Jackson; RCA 13348	WBM
☆ 11	13	7	IT'S RAINING AGAIN—Supertramp (Supertramp, Peter Henderson), R. Davies, R. Hodgson; A&M 2502	CPP/ALM
12	6	17	UP WHERE WE BELONG—Joe Cocker And Jennifer Warnes (Stewart Levine), J. Nitzsche, W. Jennings, B. Sainte-Marie, Island 7-99996 (Atco)	CPP
☆ 13	14	9	SHADOWS OF THE NIGHT—Pat Benatar (Neil Geraldo and Peter Coleman), D.L. Byron; Chrysalis CHS 2647	CLM
☆ 14	19	6	DOWN UNDER—Men At Work (Peter Mclan), C. Hay, R. Strykert; Columbia 38-03303	CLM/APB
☆ 15	17	10	HEARTBREAKER—Dionne Warwick (Barry Gibb, Karl Richardson, Albhy Galuten), B. Gibb, R. Gibb, Mr. Gibb; Arista 1015	CHA/HL
16	16	15	HEART ATTACK—Olivia Newton-John (John Farrar), S. Kipner, P. Bliss; MCA 52100	CLM-APB
17	5	14	HEARTLIGHT—Neil Diamond (Bacharach, Sager, Diamond), N. Diamond, B. Bacharach, C.B. Sager; Columbia 38-03219	CLM
☆ 18	27	7	AFRICA—Toto (Toto), D. Paich, J. Porcaro; Columbia 38-03335	WBM
☆ 19	25	11	ROCK THE CASBAH—The Clash (The Clash), The Clash; Epic 34-03245	WBM
☆ 20	21	14	THE LOOK OF LOVE—ABC (T. Horn), ABC; Mercury 76168 (Polygram)	CHA/HL
☆ 21	24	10	YOU AND I—Eddie Rabbitt/Crystal Gayle (David Malloy), F. Myers; Elektra 7-69936	CPP
22	22	12	LOVE ME TOMORROW—Chicago (David Foster), P. Cetera, D. Foster; Full Moon/Warner Bros. 7-29911	CPP
☆ 23	23	10	MISSING YOU—Dan Fogelberg (Dan Fogelberg, Marty Lewis), D. Fogelberg; Full Moon/Epic 34-03289	CLM/APB
☆ 24	28	6	YOU CAN'T HURRY LOVE—Phil Collins (Phil Collins), Holland, Dozier, Holland; Atlantic 7-89933	CPP
☆ 25	31	9	BABY, COME TO ME—Patti Austin (A Duet With James Ingram) (Quincy Jones), R. Temperton; QWest 50036 (Warner Bros.)	CPP/ALM
26	26	10	I.G.Y (What A Beautiful World)—Donald Fagen (Gary Katz), D. Fagen; Warner Bros. 7-29900	CLM
☆ 27	34	4	THE OTHER GUY—Little River Band (Ernie Rose, Little River Band), G. Goble; Capitol 5185	
☆ 28	29	10	BE MY LADY—Jefferson Starship (Kevin Beamish), P. Sears, J. Sears; Grunt 13350 (RCA)	HL
☆ 29	33	6	HAND TO HOLD ON TO—John Cougar (John Cougar Mellencamp, Don Gehman), J. C. Mellencamp; Riva 211 (Polygram)	WBM
☆ 30	32	12	ON THE WINGS OF LOVE—Jeffrey Osborne (G. Duke), P. Schless, J. Osborne; A&M 2434	CPP/ALM
☆ 31	47	3	HEART TO HEART—Kenny Loggins (Bruce Botnick, Kenny Loggins), K. Loggins, M. McDonald, D. Foster; Columbia 38-03377	WBM
☆ 32	38	5	YOU GOT LUCKY—Tom Petty and The Heartbreakers (Jim Iovine), T. Petty, M. Campbell; Backstreet 52144 (MCA)	WBM
☆ 33	35	11	EVERYBODY WANTS YOU—Billy Squier (Mack and Billy), B. Squier; Capitol 5163	CLM
☆ 34	36	13	A PENNY FOR YOUR THOUGHTS—Tavares (J. Senter, K. Nolan), K. Nolan; RCA 13292	HL
☆ 35	45	5	GOODY TWO SHOES—Adam Ant (Adam Ant, Marco Pirroni), A. Ant, M. Pirroni; Epic 34-03367	CPP
☆ 36	37	13	WHAT ABOUT ME—Moving Pictures (Charles Fisher), G. Frost, F. Frost; Network 7-69952 (Elektra)	HL
☆ 37	43	4	I DO—The J. Geils Band (Seth Justman), J. Paden, F. Paden, Smith, Stephenson, Mason; EMI-America 8148	
☆ 38	40	7	LET'S GO DANCIN'—Kool & The Gang (Eumir Deodato, Kool & The Gang), A. Bayyan, J. Taylor, Kool & The Gang; De-Lite 824 (Polygram)	CPP
☆ 39	39	8	SHOCK THE MONKEY—Peter Gabriel (David Lord, Peter Gabriel), P. Gabriel; Geffen 7-29883 (Warner Bros.)	
☆ 40	51	3	LOVE IN STORE—Fleetwood Mac (Lindsey Buckingham, Richard Dashut, Ken Caillat, Fleetwood Mac), C. McVie, J. Recor; Warner Bros. 7-29848	WBM
★ 41	41	8	WHATCHA GONNA DO—Chilliwack (Bill Henderson, Brian MacLeod), B. Henderson and B. MacLeod; Millennium 13110 (RCA)	CLM
42	18	13	SOUTHERN CROSS—Crosby, Stills and Nash (Crosby, Stills and Nash, Stanley Johnston, Steve Gursky), S. Stills, R. Curtis, M. Curtis; Atlantic 7-89969	WBM
☆ 43	48	6	DOES IT MAKE YOU REMEMBER—Kim Carnes (Val Garay), K. Carnes, D. Ellingson; EMI-America 8147	WBM
☆ 44	49	7	1999—Prince (Prince), Prince; Warner Bros. 7-29896	CPP
☆ 45	50	5	TWO LESS LONELY PEOPLE IN THE WORLD—Air Supply (Harry Maslin), H. Greenfield, K. Hirsch; Arista 1004	B-3
★ 46	46	7	USED TO BE—Charlene & Stevie Wonder (Ron Miller), R. Miller, K. Hirsch; Motown 1650	CPP
☆ 47	56	4	(You're So Square) BABY, I DON'T CARE—Joni Mitchell (Joni Mitchell), J. Leiber, M. Stoller; Geffen 7-29849 (Warner Bros.)	CHA/HL
☆ 48	58	5	SPACE AGE LOVE SONG—A Flock Of Seagulls (Mike Howlett), N. Score, A. Score, F. Maudsley, P. Reynolds; Jive/Arista 2003	CPP
☆ 49	54	5	I GOTTA TRY—Michael McDonald (Ted Templeman), M. McDonald, K. Loggins; Warner Bros. 7-29862	WBM
☆ 50	59	3	HEART OF THE NIGHT—Juice Newton (Richard Landis), M. Clark, J. Bettis; Capitol 9864	WBM
☆ 51	63	3	ALLENTOWN—Billy Joel (Phil Ramone), B. Joel; Columbia 38-03413	CLM/APB
★ 52	57	6	THEME FROM DYNASTY—Bill Conti (Bill Conti), B. Conti; Arista 1021	CPP
53	53	4	WAKE UP MY LOVE—George Harrison (George Harrison, Roy Cooper, Phil McDonald), G. Harrison; Dark Horse 7-29864 (Warner Bros.)	WBM
54	20	12	PRESSURE—Billy Joel (Phil Ramone), B. Joel; Columbia 38-03244	CLM/ABP
★ 55	55	7	BAD BOY/HAVING A PARTY—Luther Vandross (Luther Vandross), L. Vandross, M. Miller; Epic 14-03205	CPP
56	15	16	NOBODY—Sylvia (T. Collins), K. Fleming, D. Morgan, RCA 13223	CPP
☆ 57	62	4	MEMORY—Barry Manilow (Barry Manilow), A.L. Webber, T.S. Eliot, T. Nunn; Arista 1025	HL
☆ 58	64	3	RIGHT BEFORE YOUR EYES—America (Bobby Colomby), I. Thomas; Capitol 5177	CPP
☆ 59	70	2	BAD BOY—Ray Parker Jr. (Ray Parker Jr.), R. Parker Jr.; Arista 1030	
60	60	5	FOREVER MINE—The Motels (Val Garay), M. Davis; Capitol 5182	
☆ 61	69	5	PUT IT IN A MAGAZINE—Sonny Charles (B. Paris), S. Charles, B. Paris; Highrise 2001	
★ 62	66	6	I KNOW THERE'S SOMETHING GOING ON—Frida (Phil Collins), R. Ballard; Atlantic 7-89984	ALM/APB
☆ 63	73	3	TWILIGHT ZONE—Golden Earring (Shell Schellekens), G. Kooymans; 21 Records 1-103 (Polygram)	
64	30	13	I'M SO EXCITED—Pointer Sisters (Richard Perry), A. Pointer, J. Pointer, T. Lawrence; Planet 13327 (RCA)	CLM
65	65	5	GOODBYE TO YOU—Scandal (Vin Poncia), Z. Smith; Columbia 38-03234	CPP
★ 66	71	3	PSYCHOBABBLE—The Alan Parsons Project (Alan Parsons), E. Woolfson, A. Parsons; Arista 1029	
★ 67	72	3	NOWHERE TO RUN—Santana (John Ryan), R. Ballard; Columbia 38-03376	CLM/APB
68	68	16	YOU DON'T WANT ME ANYMORE—Steel Breeze (Kim Fowley), K. Goorabian, RCA 13283	
69	42	11	DESTINATION UNKNOWN—Missing Persons (Ken Scott), Bozzio, Bozzio, Cuccurullo; Capitol 5161	
☆ 70	NEW ENTRY		YOUR LOVE IS DRIVING ME CRAZY—Sammy Hagar (Keith Olsen), S. Hagar; Geffen 7-29816 (Warner Bros.)	WBM
★ 71	78	3	THE ELVIS MEDLEY—Elvis Presley J. Leiber, M. Stoller, K. Mann, B. Lowe, O. Blackwell, E. Presley, D. Linde, M. James; RCA 13351	
★ 72	80	2	DO YOU REALLY WANT TO HURT ME—Culture Club (Steve Levine), R. Hay, J. Moss, M. Craig, G. O'Dowd; Virgin/Epic 34-03368	CHA/HL
☆ 73	NEW ENTRY		ALL THOSE LIES—Glenn Frey (Glenn Frey, Allen Blazek, Jim Ed Norman), G. Frey; Asylum 7-69857 (Elektra/Asylum)	WBM
☆ 74	86	2	ON THE LOOSE—Saga (Rupert Hine), M. Sadler, J. Crichton, I. Crichton, J. Gilmour, S. Negus; Portrait 37-03359 (Epic)	
★ 75	84	2	AFTER I CRY TONIGHT—Lanier And Company (G. Bow-Legs Miller), P. Mitchell; Larc 81010 (MCA)	CPP
★ 76	82	2	CROSS MY HEART—Lee Ritenour (Harvey Mason, Lee Ritenour), L. Ritenour, E. Tagg; Elektra 7-69892	
☆ 77	NEW ENTRY		I KNEW YOU WHEN—Linda Ronstadt (Peter Asher), J. South; Asylum 7-69853 (Elektra/Asylum)	CPP
78	44	12	AMERICAN HEARTBEAT—Survivor (Frankie Sullivan, James Peterik), F. Sullivan, J. Peterik; Scotti Bros. 4-03213 (Epic)	CPP/WBM
★ 79	85	2	PAINTED PICTURES—Commodores (James Anthony Carmichael, Commodores), W. Orange, H. Hudson; Motown 1651	
★ 80	NEW ENTRY		PASS THE DUTCHIE—Musical Group (Peter Collins), J. Mittoo; MCA 52149	
81	52	23	WHO CAN IT BE NOW?—Men At Work (Peter Mclan), C. Hay, Columbia 18-02888	CLM/ABP
★ 82	NEW ENTRY		PAPA WAS A ROLLING STONE—Bill Wolfer (Bill Wolfer; Exec Producer-Dick Griffey), N. Whitfield, B. Strong; Constellation 7-69849 (Elektra/Asylum)	CPP
★ 83	NEW ENTRY		GIVE IT UP—The Steve Miller Band (Steve Miller, Gary Mallaber), S. Miller; Capitol 5194	WBM
★ 84	NEW ENTRY		DON'T STOP TRYING—Rodway (Mark Liggett/Steve Rodway), S. Rodway, N. Dolph; Millennium 13111 (RCA)	
85	61	21	JACK AND DIANE—John Cougar ● (John Cougar Mellencamp, Don Gehman), J.C. Mellencamp; Riva/Mercury 210 (Polygram)	WBM
★ 86	NEW ENTRY		FUNNY HOW TIME SLIPS AWAY—The Spinners (Freddie Perren), W. Nelson; Atlantic 7-89922	CPP
87	67	6	YOU'VE GOT ANOTHER THING COMING—Judas Priest (Tom Allom), G. Tipton, F. Halford, K.K. Dowing; Columbia 18-03168	CLM/APB
★ 88	NEW ENTRY		BACK ON THE CHAIN GANG—The Pretenders (Chris Thomas), C. Hynde; Sire 72940 (Warner Bros.)	WBM
89	74	5	PLEDGE PIN—Robert Plant (Robert Plant), Plant, Blunt; Swan Song 7-99952 (Atlantic)	WBM
★ 90	NEW ENTRY		THE CLAPPING SONG—Pia Zadora (Charles Calello), N. Chase; Elektra 7-69889 (Elektra/Asylum)	WBM
91	92	7	STAND OR FALL—The Fixx (Rupert Hine), Curnin, West-Oram, Woods, Greenall, Barrett; MCA 52106	CPP
92	75	20	YOU CAN DO MAGIC—America (Russ Ballard), R. Ballard; Capitol 5142	CLM/APB
93	76	19	I KEEP FORGETTIN' (EVERY TIME YOU'RE NEAR)—Michael McDonald (Ted Templeman, Lenny Waronker), J. Leiber, M. Stoller, M. McDonald, E. Sanford; Warner Bros. 7-29933	CPP
94	77	9	A LOVE SONG—Kenny Rogers (Kenny Rogers), L. Greenwood; Liberty 1485 (EMI-America)	MCA
95	79	24	EYE IN THE SKY—The Alan Parsons Project (Alan Parsons), E. Woolfson, A. Parsons, Arista 0696	CPP
96	81	11	GET CLOSER—Linda Ronstadt (Peter Asher), J. Carroll; Asylum 7-69948 (Elektra)	CLM
97	83	7	I WOULDN'T BEG FOR WATER—Shenna Easton (Christopher Neil), M. Leeson, P. Vale; EMI-American 8142	CHA/HL
98	88	17	THE ONE YOU LOVE—Glenn Frey (Glenn Frey, Allan Blazek, Jim Ed Norman), G. Frey, J. Tempchin, Asylum 7-69974 (Elektra)	WBM
99	90	16	LOVE COME DOWN—Evelyn King (Morrie Brown), Kashif, RCA 13273	MCA
100	91	17	BREAK IT TO ME GENTLY—Juice Newton (Richard Landis), D. Lampert, J. Seneca, Capitol 5148	

☆ Superstars are awarded to those products demonstrating the greatest airplay and sales gains this week (Prime Movers). ★ Stars are awarded to other products demonstrating significant gains. ● Recording Industry Assn. of America seal for sales of 1,000,000 units (seal indicated by dot). ▲ Recording Industry Assn. of America seal for sales of 2,000,000 units (seal indicated by triangle).

Sheet music suppliers are confined to piano/vocal sheet music copies and do not purport to represent mixed publications distribution. ABP = April Blackwo[od] Pub.; ALM = Almo Publications; B-M = Belwin Miss; B-3 = Big Three Pub.; BP = Bradley Pub.; CHA = Chappell Music; CLM = Cherry lane Music Co.; CPI [=] Cimino Pub.; CPP = Columbia Pictures Pub.; HAN = Hansen Pub.; HL = Hal Leonard; IMM = Ivan Mogull Music; MCA = MCA Music; PSP = Peer Southe[rn] Pub.; PLY = Plymouth Music; WBM = Warner Bros. Music.

BILLBOARD, June 6, 1964

Watch the rolling stones crush the beatles!

This space has been given, in the public interest, by an advertiser, who wishes to remain anonymous.

RANK	Title . . . Artist	RANK	Title . . . Artist

Billboard.

HOT 100 SINGLES®

©Copyright 1985, Billboard Publications, Inc.
No part of this publication may be reproduced, stored in any retrieval system, or transmitted, in any form or by any means, electronic, mechanical, photocopying, recording, or otherwise, without the prior written permission of the publisher.

Compiled from a national sample of retail store and one-stop sales reports and radio playlists.

THIS WEEK	LAST WEEK	2 WKS. AGO	WKS. ON CHART	TITLE / PRODUCER (SONGWRITER)	ARTIST / LABEL & NUMBER/DISTRIBUTING LABEL
1	1	3	12	**MONEY FOR NOTHING** (2 weeks at No. One) M.KNOPFLER, N.DORFSMAN (M.KNOPFLER, STING)	◆ DIRE STRAITS WARNER BROS. 7-28950
2	2	4	13	**CHERISH** J.BONNEFOND, R.BELL, KOOL & THE GANG (R.BELL, J.TAYLOR, KOOL & THE GANG)	◆ KOOL & THE GANG DE-LITE 880 869-7/POLYGRAM
3	6	8	10	**FREEDOM** G.MICHAEL (G.MICHAEL)	◆ WHAM! COLUMBIA 38-05409
4	5	6	11	**DON'T LOSE MY NUMBER** P.COLLINS, H.PADGHAM (P.COLLINS)	◆ PHIL COLLINS ATLANTIC 7-89536
5	9	15	9	**OH SHEILA** READY FOR THE WORLD (M.RILEY, G.STROZIER, G.VALENTINE)	◆ READY FOR THE WORLD MCA 52636
6	10	14	7	**DRESS YOU UP** N.RODGERS (P.STANZIALE, A.LARUSSO)	◆ MADONNA SIRE 7-28919/WARNER BROS.
7	13	17	12	**TAKE ON ME** A.TARNEY (P.WAAKTAAR, MAGS, N.HARKET)	◆ A-HA WARNER BROS. 7-29011
8	3	1	15	**ST. ELMO'S FIRE (MAN IN MOTION)** D.FOSTER (D.FOSTER, J.PARR)	◆ JOHN PARR ATLANTIC 7-89541
9	14	18	7	**SAVING ALL MY LOVE FOR YOU** M.MASSER (M.MASSER, G.GOFFIN)	◆ WHITNEY HOUSTON ARISTA 1-9381
10	15	19	6	**LONELY OL' NIGHT** LITTLE BASTARD, D.GEHMAN (J.MELLENCAMP)	◆ JOHN COUGAR MELLENCAMP RIVA 880-984-7/POLYGRAM
11	17	25	5	**DANCING IN THE STREET** C.LANGER, A.WINSTANLEY (I.HUNTER, W.STEVENSON, M.GAYE)	◆ MICK JAGGER & DAVID BOWIE EMI-AMERICA 8288
12	4	2	13	**WE DON'T NEED ANOTHER HERO (THUNDERDOME)** T.BRITTEN (T.BRITTEN, G.LYLE)	◆ TINA TURNER CAPITOL 5491
13	7	9	10	**POP LIFE** PRINCE & REVOLUTION (PRINCE & REVOLUTION)	PRINCE & THE REVOLUTION PAISLEY PARK 7-28998/WARNER BROS.
14	11	13	12	**DARE ME** R.PERRY (S.LORBER, D.INNIS)	◆ THE POINTER SISTERS RCA 14126
15	24	31	4	**PART-TIME LOVER** S.WONDER (S.WONDER)	STEVIE WONDER TAMLA 1808/MOTOWN
16	23	27	6	**FORTRESS AROUND YOUR HEART** STING, P.SMITH (STING)	◆ STING A&M 2767
17	8	5	14	**THE POWER OF LOVE** HUEY LEWIS & NEWS (C.HAYES, H.LEWIS, J.COLLA)	◆ HUEY LEWIS & THE NEWS CHRYSALIS 4-42876
18	19	20	11	**CRY** T.HORN, GODLEY&CREME (GODLEY&CREME)	◆ GODLEY & CREME POLYDOR 881 786-7/POLYGRAM
19	25	28	8	**C-I-T-Y** K.VANCE (J.CAFFERTY)	◆ JOHN CAFFERTY/BEAVER BROWN BAND SCOTTI BROS. 4-05452/EPIC
20	29	36	4	**I'M GOIN' DOWN** B.SPRINGSTEEN, J.LANDAU, C.PLOTKIN, S.VAN ZANDT (B.SPRINGSTEEN)	BRUCE SPRINGSTEEN COLUMBIA 38-05603
21	12	10	13	**INVINCIBLE (THEME FROM THE LEGEND OF BILLIE JEAN)** M.CHAMPMAN (H.KNIGHT, S.CLIMIE)	◆ PAT BENATAR CHRYSALIS 4-42877
22	37	48	4	**MIAMI VICE THEME** J.HAMMER (J.HAMMER)	JAN HAMMER MCA 52666
23	16	7	15	**FREEWAY OF LOVE** N.M.WALDEN (N.M.WALDEN, J.COHEN)	◆ ARETHA FRANKLIN ARISTA 1-9354
24	30	33	6	**LOVIN' EVERY MINUTE OF IT** T.ALLOM, P.DEAN (R.J.LANGE)	◆ LOVERBOY COLUMBIA 38-05569
25	26	29	8	**EVERY STEP OF THE WAY** J.WAITE, S.GALFAS (J.WAITE, KRAL, SIDGWICK)	◆ JOHN WAITE EMI-AMERICA 8282
26	20	16	12	**SMOKIN' IN THE BOYS ROOM** T.WERMAN (M.LUTZ, C.KODA)	◆ MOTLEY CRUE ELEKTRA 7-69625
27	18	12	12	**YOU'RE ONLY HUMAN (SECOND WIND)** P.RAMONE (B.JOEL)	◆ BILLY JOEL COLUMBIA 38-05417
28	39	49	3	**HEAD OVER HEELS** C.HUGHES (ORZABEL, SMITH)	◆ TEARS FOR FEARS MERCURY 880 899-7/POLYGRAM
29	31	35	5	**THE WAY YOU DO THE THINGS YOU DO/MY GIRL** D.HALL, J.OATES, B.CLEARMOUNTAIN (W.ROBINSON,JR., R.ROGERS)	◆ DARYL HALL & JOHN OATES RCA 14178
30	35	41	6	**FOUR IN THE MORNING (I CAN'T TAKE ANYMORE)** P.GLASSER (J.BLADES)	◆ NIGHT RANGER CAMEL/MCA 52661/MCA
31	38	44	4	**I'M GONNA TEAR YOUR PLAYHOUSE DOWN** L.LATHAM (E.RANDALL)	◆ PAUL YOUNG COLUMBIA 38-05577
32	28	32	10	**I GOT YOU BABE** UB40, R.P.FALCONER (S.BONO)	◆ UB40 A&M 2758
33	22	24	9	**THERE MUST BE AN ANGEL** D.A.STEWART (LENNOX, STEWART)	◆ EURYTHMICS RCA 14160
34	40	42	5	**SUNSET GRILL** D.HENLEY, D.KORTCHMAR, G.LADANVI (D.HENLEY, D.KORTCHMAR, TENCH)	DON HENLEY GEFFEN 7-28906/WARNER BROS.
35	21	11	14	**SUMMER OF '69** B.ADAMS, B.CLEARMOUNTAIN (B.ADAMS, J.VALLANCE)	◆ BRYAN ADAMS A&M 2739
36	41	43	6	**BE NEAR ME** M.FRY, M.WHITE (M.FRY, M.WHITE)	◆ ABC MERCURY 880 626-7/POLYGRAM
37	44	56	3	**ONE NIGHT LOVE AFFAIR** B.ADAMS, B.CLEARMOUNTAIN (B.ADAMS, J.VALLANCE)	BRYAN ADAMS A&M 2770
38	43	45	8	**AND WE DANCED** R.CHERTOFF (R.HYMAN, E.BAZILIAN)	◆ THE HOOTERS COLUMBIA 38-05568
39	46	57	3	**YOU BELONG TO THE CITY** G.FREY (G.FREY, J.TEMPCHIN)	GLENN FREY MCA 52651
40	45	51	4	**WE BUILT THIS CITY** P.WOLF, J.SMITH (B.TAUPIN, M.PAGE, D.LAMBERT, P.WOLF)	◆ STARSHIP GRUNT 14170/RCA
41	27	21	11	**SHAME** R.ZITO (M.DAVIS)	◆ THE MOTELS CAPITOL 5497
42	47	52	4	**COMMUNICATION** B.EDWARDS (D.BRAMBLE, R.PALMER, A.TAYLOR, J.TAYLOR)	THE POWER STATION CAPITOL 5511
43	52	64	4	**YOU ARE MY LADY** B.EASTMOND (B.EASTMOND)	◆ FREDDIE JACKSON CAPITOL 5495
44	56	—	2	**LAY YOUR HANDS ON ME** A.SADKIN, N.RODGERS, T.BAILEY (T.BAILEY, A.CURRIE, J.LEEWAY)	THE THOMPSON TWINS ARISTA 1-9396
45	32	22	16	**SHOUT** C.HUGHES (ORZABAL, STANLEY)	◆ TEARS FOR FEARS MERCURY 880 294-7/POLYGRAM
46	57	70	3	**NEVER** R.NEVISON (KNIGHT, BLOCH, CONNIE)	◆ HEART CAPITOL 5512
47	51	69	3	**BOY IN THE BOX** P.CHAPMAN, J.ASTLEY, C.HART (C.HART)	◆ COREY HART EMI-AMERICA 8287
48	50	53	6	**LOVE THEME FROM ST. ELMO'S FIRE (INSTRUMENTAL)** D.FOSTER, H.GATICA (D.FOSTER)	DAVID FOSTER ATLANTIC 7-89528
49	53	60	5	**YOU WEAR IT WELL** E.DEBARGE (C.DEBARGE, E.DEBARGE)	EL DEBARGE WITH DEBARGE GORDY 1804GF/MOTOWN
50	36	34	10	**NO LOOKIN' BACK** M.MCDONALD, T.TEMPLEMAN (M.MCDONALD, K.LOGGINS, E.SANFORD)	◆ MICHAEL MCDONALD WARNER BROS. 7-28960
51	NEW▶			**WHO'S ZOOMIN' WHO** N.M.WALDEN (N.M.WALDEN, P.GLASS, A.FRANKLIN)	ARETHA FRANKLIN ARISTA 9410
52	55	58	10	**TONIGHT IT'S YOU** J.DOUGLAS (R.NIELSEN, R.ZANDER, J.ZANDER, J.BRANDT, M.RADICE)	◆ CHEAP TRICK EPIC 34-05431
53	33	23	17	**NEVER SURRENDER** P.CHAPMAN, J.ASTLEY, C.HART (C.HART)	◆ COREY HART EMI-AMERICA 8268
54	67	76	5	**SO IN LOVE** S.HAGUE (O.M.D., S.HAGUE)	◆ ORCHESTRAL MANOEUVERS IN THE DARK A&M/VIRGIN 2746/A&M
55	34	26	13	**LIFE IN ONE DAY** R.HINE (H.JONES)	◆ HOWARD JONES ELEKTRA 7-69631
56	64	73	5	**WEIRD SCIENCE** D.ELFMAN, S.BARTEK (D.ELFMAN)	◆ OINGO BOINGO MCA 52633
57	63	67	6	**ALL OF ME FOR ALL OF YOU** DIMPLES (DIMPLES, B.WILSON, J.SKLAIR)	◆ 9.9 RCA 14082
58	42	30	18	**WHAT ABOUT LOVE?** R.NEVISON (ALTON, ALLEN, VALLANCE)	◆ HEART CAPITOL 5481
59	73	—	2	**BORN IN EAST L.A.** J.EYRICH (B.SPRINGSTEEN, CHEECH & CHONG)	◆ CHEECH & CHONG MCA 52655
60	48	38	13	**MYSTERY LADY** K.DIAMOND (K.DIAMOND, B.OCEAN, J.WOODLEY)	◆ BILLY OCEAN JIVE 1-9374/ARISTA
61	74	86	3	**I MISS YOU** KLYMAXX, L.MALSBY (L.MALSBY)	KLYMAXX MCA/CONSTELLATION 52606/MCA
62	60	46	17	**I WONDER IF I TAKE YOU HOME** FULL FORCE (FULL FORCE)	◆ LISA-LISA & CULT JAM WITH FULL FORCE COLUMBIA 38-04886
63	70	79	5	**STAND BY ME** M.WHITE (B.E.KING, J.LEIBER, M.STOLLER)	◆ MAURICE WHITE COLUMBIA 38-05571
64	76	82	4	**PERFECT WAY** GREEN, GAMSON, MAHER (GREEN, GAMSON)	◆ SCRITTI POLITTI WARNER BROS. 7-28949
65	61	47	21	**EVERYTIME YOU GO AWAY** L.LATHAM (D.HALL)	◆ PAUL YOUNG COLUMBIA 38-04867
66	84	—	2	**BROKEN WINGS** P.DEVILLIERS, MR.MISTER (R.PAGE, S.GEORGE, J.LANG)	◆ MR. MISTER RCA 14136
67	65	59	7	**FIRST NIGHT** R.NEVISON (F.SULLIVAN, J.PETERIK)	SURVIVOR SCOTTI BROS. 4-05579/EPIC
68	80	95	3	**AFTER THE FIRE** A.SHACKLOCK (P.TOWNSHEND)	◆ ROGER DALTRY ATLANTIC 7-89491
69	49	37	10	**DO YOU WANT CRYING** KATRINA & WAVES, P.COLLIER (V.DELA CRUZ)	◆ KATRINA AND THE WAVES CAPITOL 5450
70	75	83	3	**ALL FALL DOWN** N.MARTINELLI (B.BLUE, R.SMITH)	◆ FIVE STAR RCA 14108
71	66	66	7	**WISE UP** B.BANNISTER (W.KIRKPATRICK, B.SIMON)	AMY GRANT A&M 2762
72	82	90	4	**RUNNING UP THAT HILL** K.BUSH (K.BUSH)	◆ KATE BUSH EMI-AMERICA 8285
73	71	74	5	**TEST OF TIME** P.SOLLEY, G.FORDYCE (PALMAR, CANLER, SKILL)	◆ THE ROMANTICS NEMPEROR ZS4-05587/EPIC
74	62	50	18	**WHO'S HOLDING DONNA NOW** J.GRAYDON (D.FOSTER, J.GRAYDON, R.GOODRUM)	DEBARGE GORDY 1793/MOTOWN
75	NEW▶			**SCREAMS OF PASSION** DAVID Z., THE FAMILY (ST.PAUL, SUSANNAH)	◆ THE FAMILY PAISLEY PARK 7-28953/WARNER BROS.
76	NEW▶			**OBJECT OF MY DESIRE** K.DIAMOND, L.JOB (K.ADEYEMO, E.PHILLIPS, K.DIAMOND)	◆ STARPOINT ELEKTRA 7-69621
77	58	40	10	**SPANISH EDDIE** J.WHITE, H.FALTERMEYER (D.PALMER, C.COCHRAN)	◆ LAURA BRANIGAN ATLANTIC 7-89531
78	83	—	2	**HARD TIMES FOR LOVERS** A.BAKER, R.SCHER, L.GOLDEN (R.SCHER, L.GOLDEN)	JENNIFER HOLLIDAY GEFFEN 7-28958/WARNER BROS.
79	94	—	2	**LOVER COME BACK TO ME** M.STOCK, M.AITKIN (DEAD OR ALIVE)	◆ DEAD OR ALIVE EPIC 34-05607
80	86	89	4	**AND SHE WAS** TALKING HEADS (D.BYRNE)	TALKING HEADS SIRE 7-28917/WARNER BROS.
81	NEW▶			**LIKE TO GET TO KNOW YOU WELL** R.HINE (H.JONES)	HOWARD JONES ELEKTRA 7-69598
82	NEW▶			**I'LL BE GOOD** B.WATSON, B.SWEDIEN, RENE & ANGELA (R.MOORE, A.WINBUSH)	◆ RENE & ANGELA MERCURY 884 009-7/POLYGRAM
83	88	—	2	**EATEN ALIVE** B.GIBB, M.JACKSON, K.RICHARDSON, A.GALUTEN (B.GIBB, M.GIBB, M.JACKSON)	◆ DIANA ROSS RCA 14181
84	NEW▶			**THE OAK TREE** M.DAY (M.DAY)	◆ MORRIS DAY WARNER BROS. 7-28899
85	90	—	2	**ONE IN A MILLION** B.CORONA (S.E.RICE)	◆ EDDIE & THE TIDE ATCO 7-99617/ATLANTIC
86	54	54	7	**DOWN ON LOVE** A.SADKIN, M.JONES (M.JONES, L.GRAMM)	FOREIGNER ATLANTIC 7-89493
87	89	—	2	**JANET** D.LAMBERT (F.GOLDE, P.FOX, B.CALDWELL)	COMMODORES MOTOWN 1802
88	77	77	10	**YOU LOOK MARVELOUS** A.BAKER, B.TISCHLER (B.CRYSTAL, P.SHAFFER)	◆ BILLY CRYSTAL A&M 2764
89	95	—	2	**HURTS TO BE IN LOVE** G.VANNELLI, J.VANNELLI, R.VANNELLI (G.VANNELLI)	◆ GINO VANNELLI CBS ASSOCIATED 4-05586/EPIC
90	NEW▶			**BLUE KISS** G.MASSENBURG, B.PAYNE, R.KUNKEL (KIRSCH, WIEDLIN)	◆ JANE WIEDLIN I.R.S. 52674/MCA
91	NEW▶			**EYE TO EYE** G.STEVENSON, SYSTEM (P.COX, R.DRUMMIE)	GO WEST CHRYSALIS VS4-42903
92	59	39	17	**IF YOU LOVE SOMEBODY SET THEM FREE** STING, P.SMITH (STING)	◆ STING A&M 2738
93	78	63	11	**LOVE AND PRIDE** R.J.BURGESS (P.KING, M.ROBERTS)	◆ KING EPIC 34-04917
94	68	61	18	**YOU SPIN ME ROUND (LIKE A RECORD)** P.WATERMAN (DEAD OR ALIVE)	◆ DEAD OR ALIVE EPIC 34-04894
95	72	55	16	**WHEN YOUR HEART IS WEAK** S.HILLAGE (P.KINGSBERY)	◆ COCK ROBIN COLUMBIA 38-04875
96	91	81	19	**FOREVER** K.LOGGINS, D.FOSTER (K.LOGGINS, D.FOSTER)	◆ KENNY LOGGINS COLUMBIA 38-04931
97	81	85	4	**A LITTLE BIT OF HEAVEN** G.SKARDINA, M.SHARRON (R.KERR, G.LYLE)	NATALIE COLE MODERN 7-99630/ATLANTIC
98	79	75	18	**GLORY DAYS** B.SPRINGSTEEN, J.LANDAU, C.PLOTKIN, S.VAN ZANDT (B.SPRINGSTEEN)	◆ BRUCE SPRINGSTEEN COLUMBIA 38-04924
99	96	78	21	**YOU GIVE GOOD LOVE** KASHIF (LALA)	◆ WHITNEY HOUSTON ARISTA 1-9274
100	93	65	19	**ROCK ME TONIGHT** P.LAWRENCE,III (P.LAWRENCE)	◆ FREDDIE JACKSON CAPITOL 5459

◯ Products with the greatest airplay and sales gains this week. ◆ Video clip availability. ● Recording Industry Assn. Of America (RIAA) seal for sales of one million units. ▲ RIAA seal for sales of two million units.

FONTANA HAS IT!
WILD THING

England's No. 1 Record by
THE TROGGS

F-1548
A Page One Production, England

THE TROGGS—WILD THING (Prod. by Page One
Prod.) (Writer: Chip Taylor) **(Blackwood, BMI)**—
Exciting new group, currently climbing the British
charts, is released by Atco and Fontana in the
U. S. On either label the disk is a surefire smash.
Flip: (on Atco) "With a Girl Like You" (Dick
James, BMI); (on Fontana) "From Home" (Dick
James, BMI).   **Atco 6415 and Fontana 1548**

RANK	Title . . . Artist	RANK	Title . . . Artist
33	**Poor People Of Paris** . . . *Les Baxter*	115	**Reunited** . . . *Peaches & Herb*
573	**Poor Side Of Town** . . . *Johnny Rivers*	293	**Rhinestone Cowboy** . . . *Glen Campbell*
462	**Pop Muzik** . . . *M*	400	**Rich Girl** . . . *Daryl Hall & John Oates*
341	**Power Of Love** . . . *Huey Lewis & The News*	679	**Ride Like The Wind** . . . *Christopher Cross*
295	**Private Eyes** . . . *Daryl Hall & John Oates*	776	**Right Back Where We Started From** . . . *Maxine Nightingale*
903	**Problems** . . . *Everly Brothers*	270	**Ring My Bell** . . . *Anita Ward*
731	**Proud Mary** . . . *Creedence Clearwater Revival*	593	**Ringo** . . . *Lorne Greene*
923	**Puff The Magic Dragon** . . . *Peter, Paul & Mary*	303	**Rise** . . . *Herb Alpert*
815	**Puppy Love** . . . *Paul Anka*		**Rock...also see: R.O.C.K.**
52	**Purple People Eater** . . . *Sheb Wooley*	31	**Rock And Roll Waltz** . . . *Kay Starr*
813	**Purple Rain** . . . *Prince & the Revolution*	11	**Rock Around The Clock** . . . *Bill Haley & His Comets*
898	**Put Your Hand In The Hand** . . . *Ocean*	239	**Rock Me Amadeus** . . . *Falco*
701	**Put Your Head On My Shoulder** . . . *Paul Anka*	608	**Rock Me Gently** . . . *Andy Kim*
		645	**Rock The Boat** . . . *Hues Corporation*

Q

		124	**Rock With You** . . . *Michael Jackson*
358	**Quarter To Three** . . . *U.S. Bonds*	425	**Rock Your Baby** . . . *George McCrae*
756	**Queen Of Hearts** . . . *Juice Newton*	638	**Rock'n Me** . . . *Steve Miller Band*

R

			Rockin' Robin
		757	*Bobby Day*
934	**R.O.C.K. In The U.S.A. (A Salute To 60's Rock)** . . . *John Cougar Mellencamp*	794	*Michael Jackson*
			Romeo & Juliet...see: Love Theme From
387	**Rag Doll** . . . *4 Seasons*	666	**Rosanna** . . . *Toto*
787	**Rain, The Park & Other Things** . . . *Cowsills*	977	**Rose, The** . . . *Bette Midler*
880	**Raindrops** . . . *Dee Clark*	121	**Roses Are Red (My Love)** . . . *Bobby Vinton*
96	**Raindrops Keep Fallin' On My Head** . . . *B.J. Thomas*	260	**Round And Round** . . . *Perry Como*
942	**Rainy Day Women #12 & 35** . . . *Bob Dylan*	710	**Rubberband Man** . . . *Spinners*
818	**Rainy Days And Mondays** . . . *Carpenters*	744	**Ruby Baby** . . . *Dion*
916	**Ramblin Man** . . . *Allman Brothers Band*	596	**Ruby Tuesday** . . . *Rolling Stones*
784	**Ramblin' Rose** . . . *Nat King Cole*	917	**Run To Him** . . . *Bobby Vee*
924	**Rapper, The** . . . *Jaggerz*	326	**Runaround Sue** . . . *Dion*
347	**Rapture** . . . *Blondie*	135	**Runaway** . . . *Del Shannon*
909	**Raspberry Beret** . . . *Prince & the Revolution*	184	**Running Bear** . . . *Johnny Preston*
869	**Raunchy** . . . *Bill Justis*	654	**Running Scared** . . . *Roy Orbison*
410	**Reach Out I'll Be There** . . . *Four Tops*		

S

925	**Red Rubber Ball** . . . *Cyrkle*		**S.W.A.T. ...see: Theme From**
822	**Reflections** . . . *Supremes*	463	**Sad Eyes** . . . *Robert John*
340	**Reflex, The** . . . *Duran Duran*	958	**Safety Dance** . . . *Men Without Hats*
388	**Respect** . . . *Aretha Franklin*	552	**Sailing** . . . *Christopher Cross*
667	**Return To Sender** . . . *Elvis Presley*		**Saint...see: St.**
		845	**Sally, Go 'Round The Roses** . . . *Jaynetts*
		553	**Sara** . . . *Starship*
		621	**Saturday Night** . . . *Bay City Rollers*
		195	**Save The Last Dance For Me** . . . *Drifters*
		941	**Save Your Heart For Me** . . . *Gary Lewis & The Playboys*

RANK	Title ... Artist	RANK	Title ... Artist
534	**Saving All My Love For You** ... *Whitney Houston*	478	**Someday We'll Be Together** ... *Supremes*
678	**Say It Isn't So** ... *Daryl Hall & John Oates*	140	**Somethin' Stupid** ... *Nancy & Frank Sinatra*
40	**Say Say Say** ... *Paul McCartney & Michael Jackson*	474	**Something** ... *Beatles*
126	**Say You, Say Me** ... *Lionel Richie*	627	**Song Sung Blue** ... *Neil Diamond*
973	**School Day** ... *Chuck Berry*	812	**Sorry (I Ran All the Way Home)** ... *Impalas*
825	**Sea Of Love** ... *Phil Phillips*	725	**Soul Man** ... *Sam & Dave*
206	**Seasons In The Sun** ... *Terry Jacks*	423	**Sounds Of Silence** ... *Simon & Garfunkel*
980	**Secretly** ... *Jimmie Rodgers*	503	**Southern Nights** ... *Glen Campbell*
470	**Separate Lives** ... *Phil Collins & Marilyn Martin*	841	**Spanish Harlem** ... *Aretha Franklin*
968	**Sexual Healing** ... *Marvin Gaye*	733	**Spinning Wheel** ... *Blood, Sweat & Tears*
21	**Shadow Dancing** ... *Andy Gibb*	985	**Spirit In The Sky** ... *Norman Greenbaum*
	Shaft...see: Theme From	999	**Spooky** ... *Classics IV*
443	**(Shake, Shake, Shake) Shake Your Booty** ... *KC & The Sunshine Band*	371	**St. Elmo's Fire (Man In Motion)** ... *John Parr*
684	**Shame On The Moon** ... *Bob Seger & The Silver Bullet Band*	116	**Stagger Lee** ... *Lloyd Price*
983	**She Bop** ... *Cyndi Lauper*	964	**Standing On The Corner** ... *Four Lads*
276	**She Loves You** ... *Beatles*	404	**Star Wars Theme/Cantina Band** ... *Meco*
976	**She Works Hard For The Money** ... *Donna Summer*	511	**Stars on 45 [Medley]** ... *Stars on 45*
882	**She's A Lady** ... *Tom Jones*	698	**Start Me Up** ... *Rolling Stones*
963	**She's Just My Style** ... *Gary Lewis & The Playboys*	639	**Stay** ... *Maurice Williams & The Zodiacs*
881	**She's Not There** ... *Zombies*	95	**Stayin' Alive** ... *Bee Gees*
412	**Sheila** ... *Tommy Roe*	435	**Still** ... *Commodores*
87	**Sherry** ... *4 Seasons*	998	**Stoned Soul Picnic** ... *5th Dimension*
637	**Shining Star** ... *Earth, Wind & Fire*	720	**Stood Up** ... *Ricky Nelson*
915	**Shop Around** ... *Miracles*	947	**Stop Draggin' My Heart Around** ... *Stevie Nicks with Tom Petty*
750	**Short People** ... *Randy Newman*	365	**Stop! In The Name Of Love** ... *Supremes*
237	**Shout** ... *Tears For Fears*		
531	**Show And Tell** ... *Al Wilson*	445	**Stranger On The Shore** ... *Mr. Acker Bilk*
66	**Silly Love Songs** ... *Wings*	585	**Strangers In The Night** ... *Frank Sinatra*
2	**Singing The Blues** ... *Guy Mitchell*	220	**Streak, The** ... *Ray Stevens*
215	**Sir Duke** ... *Stevie Wonder*	488	**Stripper, The** ... *David Rose*
656	**Sister Golden Hair** ... *America*	120	**Stuck On You** ... *Elvis Presley*
110	**(Sittin' On) The Dock Of The Bay** ... *Otis Redding*	78	**Sugar Shack** ... *Jimmy Gilmer & The Fireballs*
779	**16 Candles** ... *Crests*	101	**Sugar, Sugar** ... *Archies*
13	**Sixteen Tons** ... *Tennessee Ernie Ford*	100	**Sugartime** ... *McGuire Sisters*
311	**Sleep Walk** ... *Santo & Johnny*		**Sukiyaki**
699	**Slow Hand** ... *Pointer Sisters*	223	*Kyu Sakamoto*
181	**Smoke Gets In Your Eyes** ... *Platters*	978	*Taste Of Honey*
686	**Snoopy Vs. The Red Baron** ... *Royal Guardsmen*	250	**Summer In The City** ... *Lovin' Spoonful*
574	**So Much In Love** ... *Tymes*		**Summer Place...see: Theme From**
670	**So Rare** ... *Jimmy Dorsey Orchestra & Chorus*	581	**Sundown** ... *Gordon Lightfoot*
219	**Soldier Boy** ... *Shirelles*		
719	**Somebody's Watching Me** ... *Rockwell*		

131

The Magnificent

Aretha Franklin
"CHAIN OF FOOLS"

Written by Don Covay
Atlantic #2464
c/w

"PROVE IT"

from the hit album "ARETHA ARRIVES" (8150)

ATLANTIC

 Personal Management: TED WHITE ● Exclusive Representation: QUEEN BOOKING CORP.

ARETHA FRANKLIN— CHAIN OF FOOLS
(Prod. Jerry Wexler) (Writer: Covay) (**14th Hour/Pronto, BMI**)—With the solid beat feel of "Respect," this sure-fire blues mover has all the ingredients of a No. 1 chart topper. Flip: "Prove It" (14th Hour/Pronto/Wellmade, BMI). **Atlantic 2464**

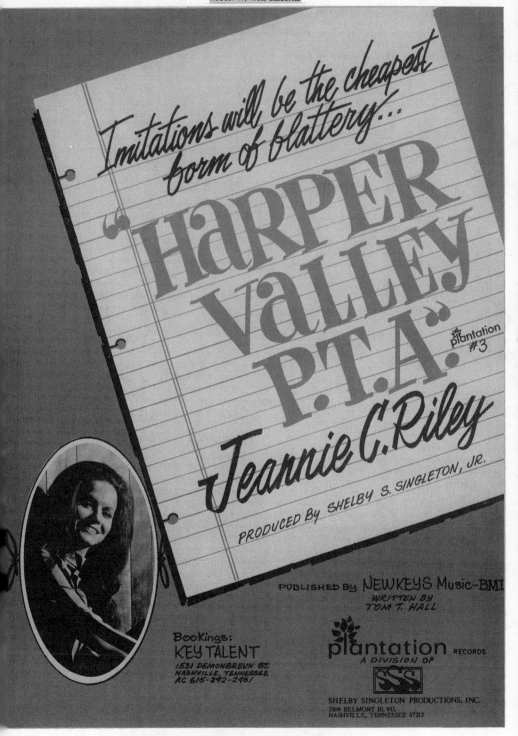

JEANNIE C. RILEY—HARPER VALLEY P.T.A.
(Prod. Shelby S. Singleton Jr.) (Writer: Hall) (Newkeys, BMI)—By far
the most unusual, left field pop-country disk of the week. Has the off beat
sales appeal of an "Ode to Billie Joe." Original lyric, cleverly penned by
Tom T. Hall, is given a strong reading by the newcomer. New label
handled by Shelby Singleton in Nashville. Flip: (No Information Available). **Plantation 3**

RANK	Title . . . Artist	RANK	Title . . . Artist
370	**Will You Love Me Tomorrow** . . . *Shirelles*	939	**You Don't Know Me** . . . *Ray Charles*
188	**Winchester Cathedral** . . . *New Vaudeville Band*	752	**You Don't Own Me** . . . *Lesley Gore*
133	**Windy** . . . *Association*	544	**You Haven't Done Nothin** . . . *Stevie Wonder*
886	**Wipe Out** . . . *Surfaris*	418	**You Keep Me Hangin' On** . . . *Supremes*
163	**Witch Doctor** . . . *David Seville*	4	**You Light Up My Life** . . . *Debby Boone*
353	**With A Little Luck** . . . *Wings*	778	**You Make Me Feel Brand New** . . . *Stylistics*
130	**Without You** . . . *Nilsson*	529	**You Make Me Feel Like Dancing** . . . *Leo Sayer*
697	**Woman** . . . *John Lennon*	496	**You Needed Me** . . . *Anne Murray*
166	**Woman In Love** . . . *Barbra Streisand*	161	**You Send Me** . . . *Sam Cooke*
183	**Wonderland By Night** . . . *Bert Kaempfert*	979	**You Sexy Thing** . . . *Hot Chocolate*
570	**Wooden Heart** . . . *Joe Dowell*	565	**You Should Be Dancing** . . . *Bee Gees*
768	**Wooly Bully** . . . *Sam The Sham & The Pharaohs*	781	**You'll Never Find Another Love Like Mine** . . . *Lou Rawls*
773	**Working My Way Back To You/Forgive Me, Girl** . . . *Spinners*	255	**(You're) Having My Baby** . . . *Paul Anka*
526	**World Without Love** . . . *Peter & Gordon*	228	**(You're My) Soul And Inspiration** . . . *Righteous Brothers*
826	**Wreck Of The Edmund Fitzgerald** . . . *Gordon Lightfoot*	646	**You're No Good** . . . *Linda Ronstadt*
		571	**You're Sixteen** . . . *Ringo Starr*

Y

RANK	Title . . . Artist	RANK	Title . . . Artist
695	**Y.M.C.A.** . . . *Village People*	174	**You're So Vain** . . . *Carly Simon*
480	**Yakety Yak** . . . *Coasters*	808	**You're The First, The Last, My Everything** . . . *Barry White*
32	**Yellow Rose Of Texas** . . . *Mitch Miller*	467	**You're The One That I Want** . . . *John Travolta & Olivia Newton-John*
929	**Yellow Submarine** . . . *Beatles*	522	**You've Got A Friend** . . . *James Taylor*
797	**Yes, I'm Ready** . . . *Teri DeSario with K.C.*	313	**You've Lost That Lovin' Feelin'** . . . *Righteous Brothers*
152	**Yesterday** . . . *Beatles*	745	**You've Made Me So Very Happy** . . . *Blood, Sweat & Tears*
922	**Yesterday Once More** . . . *Carpenters*	721	**Young Girl** . . . *Gary Puckett & The Union Gap*
990	**Yo-Yo** . . . *Osmonds*		**Young Love**
642	**You Ain't Seen Nothing Yet** . . . *Bachman-Turner Overdrive*	42	*Tab Hunter*
559	**You Are The Sunshine Of My Life** . . . *Stevie Wonder*	434	*Sonny James*
804	**You Belong To The City** . . . *Glenn Frey*	887	**(Your Love Has Lifted Me) Higher And Higher** . . . *Rita Coolidge*
363	**You Can't Hurry Love** . . . *Supremes*		
284	**You Don't Bring Me Flowers** . . . *Barbra Streisand & Neil Diamond*		
495	**You Don't Have To Be A Star (To Be In My Show)** . . . *Marilyn McCoo & Billy Davis, Jr.*		

MISCELLANEOUS

THE TOP 50 ARTISTS OF THE TOP 1000

RANK	TOP 1000		RANK	TOP 1000	
1)	24	Elvis Presley	26)	5	Marvin Gaye
2)	24	The Beatles	27)	5	Prince
3)	14	The Supremes	28)	5	John Denver
4)	12	Paul McCartney	29)	5	Creedence Clearwater Revival
5)	11	Stevie Wonder			
6)	10	Bee Gees	30)	4	The Platters
7)	10	The Rolling Stones	31)	4	Bobby Vinton
8)	10	Elton John	32)	4	Blondie
9)	8	Michael Jackson	33)	4	Sly & The Family Stone
10)	8	Carpenters	34)	4	Roberta Flack
11)	7	Daryl Hall & John Oates	35)	4	The Monkees
			36)	4	Frank Sinatra
12)	7	Donna Summer	37)	4	Connie Francis
13)	7	The Jackson 5	38)	4	Madonna
14)	7	KC & The Sunshine Band	39)	4	Ray Charles
			40)	4	The 5th Dimension
15)	6	Pat Boone	41)	4	The Beach Boys
16)	6	Diana Ross	42)	4	Neil Diamond
17)	6	Barbra Streisand	43)	4	Cher
18)	6	The Everly Brothers	44)	4	Ricky Nelson
19)	6	Olivia Newton-John	45)	4	Steve Miller
20)	6	The Eagles	46)	4	Duran Duran
21)	6	The Temptations	47)	4	John Lennon
22)	5	Lionel Richie	48)	4	Roy Orbison
23)	5	The Four Seasons	49)	4	Barry Manilow
24)	5	Paul Anka	50)	4	Billy Joel
25)	5	Phil Collins			

Top 1000: Artist's total records making the Top 1000.

For artists with the same number of Top 1000 hits, ties are broken by totaling the final ranking of each record by these artists, and the artist with the lowest total ranks first, and so on.

SONGS WITH MORE THAN ONE HIT VERSION
Peak Position/Year (Top 1000 Rank)

1. **Young Love**
   Tab Hunter   1/'57 (42)
   Sonny James   1/'57 (434)

2. **Butterfly**
   Andy Williams   1/'57 (186)
   Charlie Gracie   1/'57 (349)

3. **Go Away Little Girl**
   Donny Osmond   1/'71 (199)
   Steve Lawrence   1/'63 (325)

4. **The Loco-Motion**
   Grand Funk   1/'74 (398)
   Little Eva   1/'62 (569)

5. **Please Mr. Postman**
   The Marvelettes   1/'61 (533)
   Carpenters   1/'75 (643)

6. **I Heard It Through The Grapevine**
   Marvin Gaye   1/'68 (29)
   Gladys Knight & The Pips   2/'67 (714)

7. **MacArthur Park**
   Donna Summer   1/'78 (193)
   Richard Harris   2/'68 (936)

8. **Sukiyaki**
   Kyu Sakamoto   1/'63 (223)
   A Taste Of Honey   3/'81 (978)

9. **The Lion Sleeps Tonight**
   The Tokens   1/'61 (218)
   Robert John   3/'72 (987)

10. **Rockin' Robin**
    Bobby Day   2/'58 (757)
    Michael Jackson   2/'72 (794)

SAME TITLES — DIFFERENT SONGS

The following Top 1000 songs have the same titles, but are not by the same composer(s). The artist with the highest ranked version is listed first, along with the year the record peaked.

Best Of My Love
Emotions ('77)
The Eagles ('75)

Fire
Ohio Players ('75)
Pointer Sisters ('79)
The Crazy World Of
 Arthur Brown ('68)

I'm Sorry
Brenda Lee ('60)
John Denver ('75)

My Love
Paul McCartney & Wings ('73)
Petula Clark ('66)

Venus
Frankie Avalon ('59)
The Shocking Blue ('70)

RE-CHARTED SINGLES

The Top 1000 singles which hit the charts more than once.

RANK   **Peak Position/Year(Weeks Charted)**

11)   **Rock Around The Clock** . . . Bill Haley & His Comets
1/'55(24); 39/'74(14)

12)   **The Wayward Wind** . . . Gogi Grant
1/'56(28); 50/'61(9)

61)   **All I Have To Do Is Dream** . . . The Everly Brothers
1/'58(17); 96/'61(2)

151)   **The Chipmunk Song** . . . The Chipmunks
1/'58(13); 41/'59(5); 45/'60(3); 39/'61(3); 40/'62(4)

134)   **Ode To Billie Joe** . . . Bobbie Gentry
1/'67(14); 54/'76(6)

153)   **The Twist** . . . Chubby Checker
1/'60(18); 1/'62(21)

194)   **Light My Fire** . . . The Doors
1/'67(17); 87/'68(6)

334)   **Monster Mash** . . . Bobby "Boris" Pickett & The Crypt-Kickers
1/'62(14); 91/'70(3); 10/'73(20)

424)   **I Honestly Love You** . . . Olivia Newton-John
1/'74(15); 48/'77(8)

665)   **Louie Louie** . . . The Kingsmen
2/'63(16); 97/'66(2)

691)   **Honky Tonk** . . . Bill Doggett
2/'56(29); 57/'61(10)

886)   **Wipe Out** . . . The Surfaris
2/'63(16); 16/'66(14)

878)   **Last Kiss** . . . J. Frank Wilson & The Cavaliers
2/'64(15); 92/'74(5)

THE TWIST

"The Twist" is the only record of the rock era to peak at position #1, drop off the charts, and then return to the charts and again peak at position #1. #1-'60(1 week); #1-'62(2 weeks)

2-SIDED HITS

Don't Be Cruel/Hound Dog ... Elvis Presley
Come Together/Something ... Beatles

The above two records are rare instances of a #1 record in which Billboard had a hard time determining the side that deserved to be listed first. Both sides received heavy airplay, and both sides were equally requested at record shops, therefore, in both cases the records flip-flopped during their peak weeks on the charts - in other words, one week Elvis Presley's hit was listed as "Don't Be Cruel/Hound Dog", and another week it was listed as "Hound Dog/Don't Be Cruel".

BREAKDOWN BY YEAR

Total records making the Top 1000 year-by-year

YR	TOP 1000		YR	TOP 1000	
55	10		70	33	
56	25		71	29	
57	32		72	33	
58	34		73	40	
59	29		74	42	
			75	39	
Total	130	(13%)	76	42	
			77	37	
			78	26	
			79	30	
60	30				
61	32		Total	351	(35.1%)
62	30				
63	31		80	27	
64	32		81	30	
65	33		82	23	
66	41		83	30	
67	32		84	30	
68	31		85	36	
69	33		86	18	
Total	325	(32.5%)	Total	194	(19.4%)

JOEL WHITBURN:
THE COLLECTOR'S COLLECTOR

What started as a casual hobby for Joel Whitburn back before the birth of rock and roll has flourished into the most successful business of its kind anywhere in the world.

Record Research Inc. had its real roots in the 45 r.p.m. records Whitburn began collecting in the early 1950's. By the mid-1960's, this ever-expanding collection had grown considerably in size and scope, prompting Whitburn to begin keeping tabs on his records by categorizing each one according to the highest position it had reached on Billboard's "Hot 100."

In 1970, at the urging of a disc jockey friend who realized both the importance and the usefulness of this research, Whitburn published the basic chart information he had gathered in a slim volume titled simply *Record Research.*

Today, Whitburn's Record Research books and supplements can be found on record collectors' bookshelves, radio station reference racks and in many artists' private libraries the world over, providing essential statistics and data on Billboard's pop singles, pop albums, country, black, adult contemporary and other major charts.

Widely recognized as the foremost authority on charted music, Whitburn assisted by his staff of fulltime researchers, supplies chart information to Casey Kasem, Dick Clark, Don Imus, Dr. Demento, and other prominent disc jockeys and music show hosts nationwide.

Whitburn's personal pop record collection - perhaps the largest in the world - currently includes all of the 18,000 pop singles to ever appear on the "Hot 100", as well as the more than 14,000 LPs that made it to Billboard's pop album charts. These, along with the balance of Whitburn's collection - *over 100,000 albums and singles in all* - are housed in an environmentally controlled, underground vault adjacent to the Record Research offices in Whitburn's Menomonee Falls, Wisconsin home.

THE RECORD RESEARCH LIBRARY OF BOOKS

Joel Whitburn's
TOP POP SINGLES 1955-1986

ⁿNew revised edition of our all-time runaway best seller! Featuring hundreds of new and expanded artist biographies. A complete up-to-date listing, by artist and by title, of each of the over 17,000 singles to appear on Billboard's "Hot 100" charts. Over 700 pages. Hardcover $60.00 Softcover $50.00 (anticipated publication date: December, 1986)

Joel Whitburn's
POP ANNUAL 1955-1986

Every pop programmers dream — a book that lists all "Hot 100" charted singles in rank order, year by year. And now, for the first time, lists the playing time of each record! Includes a complete A-Z song title section.
Over 700 pages. Hardcover $60.00 Softcover $50.00 (anticipated publication date: December, 1986)

Joel Whitburn's
TOP POP ALBUMS 1955-1985

The only book of its kind to list complete chart data for every album to ever appear on Billboard's weekly "Top Pop Albums" charts. Arranged by artist, it lists over 14,000 titles and 3,000 artists.
516 pages. Softcover $40.00

Joel Whitburn's
POP MEMORIES 1890-1954

From Edison to Elvis — the first book to document the history of America's recorded popular music from its very beginning. Find out who had the hit versions of those popular standards you've heard for generations. Arranged by artist and by title, it lists over 12,000 titles and 1,600 artists.
660 pages. Hardcover $50.00 Softcover $40.00

MUSIC YEARBOOK 1985

The complete story of 1985's charted music in one concise volume. Covers 11 major Billboard charts. Updates all previous Record Research books and includes data on the exciting new "Top Pop Compact Disks" chart.
240 pages. Softcover $25.00

Billboard's
MUSIC YEARBOOK 1983
MUSIC YEARBOOK 1984

Two comprehensive books listing complete chart data on each of the records to appear on the 14 major Billboard charts in 1983 and 1984. Updates all previous Record Research books, plus complete data on 6 additional charts.
Softcover — $25.00 each (1983 edition: 276 pages/1984 edition: 264 pages.)

Joel Whitburn's
BUBBLING UNDER THE HOT 100 1959-1981

Lists over 4,000 hits that never made the "Hot 100". The only reference book of its kind. 240 pages. Softcover $25.00

UP AND COMING!

BILLBOARD'S TOP VIDEOCASSETTES 1979-1986

Our first venture into the movie industry. The over one thousand hottest videos from the past 8 years, researched and ranked for the first time.

TOP BLACK 1942-1986

We've gone back further than ever before! Our research has been expanded to not only include every single to hit Billboard's Top 100 "Hot R&B (Black) Singles" chart, but also their "Best Selling," "Disc Jockey," and "Juke Box" R&B charts. The book will include well over a thousand artist biographies, and for the very first time, the complete history of every album to ever hit Billboard's "Top R&B (Black) Albums" chart.

TOP COUNTRY 1944-1986

Here's the revision you've been waiting for — featuring numerous artist biographies, title trivia and greatly expanded research. This book will begin with the first "Most Played Juke Box Folk Records" chart in 1944 and will list every single to ever hit Billboard's "Best Selling," "Disc Jockey," "Juke Box," and Top 100 "Hot Country Singles" charts. Also, for the very first time, the complete history of every album to ever hit Billboard's "Top Country Albums" chart.

Record Research Inc.
P.O. Box 200
Menomonee Falls, Wisconsin 53051